D0216308

HISTORY IN OVID

HISTORY IN LOVE

HISTORY IN
OVID

RONALD SYME

OXFORD
AT THE CLARENDON PRESS
1978

937.07
S986h

Oxford University Press, Walton Street, Oxford OX2 6DP

OXFORD LONDON GLASGOW
NEW YORK TORONTO MELBOURNE WELLINGTON
KUALA LUMPUR SINGAPORE JAKARTA HONG KONG TOKYO
DELHI BOMBAY CALCUTTA MADRAS KARACHI
NAIROBI DAR ES SALAAM CAPE TOWN

© *Sir Ronald Syme, 1978*

All rights reserved. No part of this publication may be reproduced, stored in a retrieval system, or transmitted, in any form or by any means, electronic, mechanical, photocopying, recording, or otherwise, without the prior permission of Oxford University Press

British Library Cataloguing in Publication Data
Syme, *Sir* Ronald, b. 1903
    History in Ovid.
    1. Ovid.   2. Rome – History – Augustus,
    30 B.C.–14 A.D. – Sources
    I. Title
    937'.07   DG279   77–30645
    ISBN 0–19–814825–9

PA   Syme, Ronald
6537
.S9   History in Ovid

937.07 S98

*Printed in Great Britain
at the University Press, Oxford
by Eric Buckley
Printer to the University*

DABNEY LANCASTER LIBRARY
LONGWOOD COLLEGE
FARMVILLE, VIRGINIA 23901

PREFACE

MORE history than Ovid, some will say. Anxious apologia is not in place. Better, brief statement about the origin of this opuscule. It goes back to an ancient predilection for the *Epistulae ex Ponto*, reinforced by that faithful companion, portable on long peregrinations.

Two chapters began as lectures, while others were at first intended for inclusion in a larger work (*The Augustan Aristocracy*). The appeal of the poet becoming ever more seductive, scope and direction changed. No commentary happens to exist on Ovid's latest poems, their use and value tend to be ignored. The outcome is therefore a kind of manual, albeit not altogether predictable, designed to cover life and letters in the obscure decade that concludes the long reign of Caesar Augustus.

Each of the twelve chapters was composed to be read and understood by itself. Coherence and structure has been accorded proper attention, so I trust. The time and order of composition may (or may not) engage the curious and the erudite.

I am happy to acknowledge manifold debts. A grant from the Leverhulme Trust facilitated the preparation of the manuscript. But nothing can equal what could never be repaid, a personal gratitude that belongs to institutions and to many friends across the water, notably in Cambridge and at the Institute for Advanced Study (Princeton).

The example of Ovid was inspiriting, who put to good employ the years of exile on less friendly shores—as the last chapter will demonstrate, as the poet himself declared: 'mors nobis tempus habetur iners'.

The book came to completion in the burning summer of 1976, within the walls and battlements of a college newly established on the northern outskirts of Oxford: a community whose indulgence abates the distempers that encroach upon the evening of life.

R. S.

Wolfson College
March 11, 1977

'79– 4994

The *Amores* carry only two items for dating, not of special importance. But the projected Parthian War to be waged by the prince Gaius Caesar (in *AA* I) is in another case, permitting narrow limits of time. Elsewhere negative instances can sometimes be of value: no reference, so it appears, to Tiberius in the first edition of the *Fasti*.[1]

Second, the rhythm of writing. Ovid, born in 43 B.C., was a fluent composer in youth, with a distinctive manner early shaped. At one late stage in his writing rapid composition can be proved, with no loss of force and elegance.[2] Given the long period antecedent to I B.C. (he was forty-two in the spring of that year), an abatement or some intervals may have to be postulated. When, and for how long, not so easy.

The case of the historian Livy is instructive. This steady citizen operated without respite or fatigue (so some have fancied), turning out on an average three volumes each year (the total production was 142) until death took the pen from his hand.[3] On the contrary, at least one interval can be surmised. For Livy the culmination of Roman history was the end of the Civil Wars and the triple triumph celebrated in 29 B.C. (in Book CXXXIII). What follows is an epilogue, and perhaps an afterthought: namely the Republic of Caesar Augustus in nine books from 28 to 9 B.C., terminating with the death of Drusus in warfare beyond the Rhine.[4] Livy did not set about writing his epilogue (it may be conjectured) until the change of dynastic politics in A.D. 4 (Claudius Nero becoming Tiberius Caesar) showed the safe path and proper emphasis.

Third, simultaneous composition. Ovid was mobile and versatile. His temperament might encourage him to compose in different genres at the same time. That cannot be denied or confirmed. Yet, for a parallel in artistic prose, observe Cornelius Tacitus writing the tranquil *Dialogus* when he was already immersed in the murderous history of the year 69.

Fourth, revisions or additions. An insertion may often be betrayed by inconsistency with the context. But a new sentence or a whole

---

[1] Below, p. 34. [2] Viz. *Ex Ponto* I-III (below, p. 42).

[3] Schanz–Hosius, o.c. 300, and other scholars cited in *Harvard Studies* LXIV (1959), 38 = *Roman Papers* (1978), 412.

[4] For this thesis, ibid. (1959), 62 ff. = (1978), 438 ff. It would still allow Livy a long stretch of years for the first 133 books.

I

THE CHRONOLOGY

THE poems of Ovid offer the historian much more than he might expect. First of all, it is necessary to discover the chronology. The general position can be defined without undue hesitations. In the poet's productivity, prolonged over a good forty years, a turning-point is discerned about the year A.D. 1. An item in Book I of the *Ars Amatoria* (it comes as a surprise) permits a close dating, by a precise event in 1 B.C.[1] There was a period of intense activity, terminated before the early months of A.D. 2. Ovid now revised and supplemented a whole corpus of elegiac verse, to be put on show as his mature achievement. Then follow *Fasti* and *Metamorphoses*. The poems from exile present no problems. Indeed, the latest instalment, his *Epistulae ex Ponto*, offers unexpected precisions.

By contrast, the earlier products: *Amores*, *Heroides* (and the lost *Medea*). At first sight, and on second thoughts, the problems appear insuperable.[2] The field is open to conjectures of wide range, in competition often uninhibited.[3] Brief prolegomena are expedient to a summary statement.

.   .   .   .

I. First, references in poets to contemporary transactions. In general, scholars have a propensity to assume that these echoes are heard and reported as soon as possible after the event in question.[4] For love poetry, the question hardly ever arises. Which is natural.

---

[1] A war against the Parthians, to be conducted by the prince Gaius Caesar (*AA* I. 177 ff.).

[2] Thus the judicious and sceptical L. P. Wilkinson, *Ovid Recalled* (1955), 83.

[3] For earlier work, E. Martini, *Einleitung zu Ovid* (Prague, 1933); Schanz–Hosius, *Gesch. der r. Literatur* II⁴ (1935); W. Kraus, *RE* XVIII (1943), 1910 ff. Among recent studies may be noted S. d'Elia in *Ovidiana* (ed. N. I. Herescu, 1958), 210 ff.; G. Luck, *Die r. Liebeselegie* (1961), 161 f.; A. D. E. Cameron, *CQ* XVIII (1968), 320 ff.; E. J. K(enney) in *OCD²* (1970), 763 ff.; and, especially, H. Jacobson, *Ovid's Heroides* (1974), 300 ff.

[4] Below, p. 37.

passage might be inserted either almost at once or after a lapse of years. That concerns a passage in the *Ars* and another in *Remedia Amoris*.[1]

Fifth. Second editions. That is acknowledged by the author for *Amores*, it is patent in Book I of the *Fasti*, and it ought to be assumed (and it can be rendered highly plausible) for *Ars Amatoria*. As concerns the *Heroides*, they began (it appears) as fifteen epistles from ladies of ancient legend. At some stage, not ascertainable, three pairs of antiphonal products (male and female responding) were added.

. . . . .

II. The *Amores*. Two references to external events never fail to be registered, little though they tell. First, the elegy on Tibullus (III. 9), who passed away in 19 B.C. An attempt to prolong his life by two years adds nothing.[2]

Second, in deprecation of wigs for women, the poet rebukes the lady for wearing alien hair,

> nunc tibi captivos mittet Germania crines;
> tuta triumphatae munere gentis eris.   (I. 14. 45 f.)

He goes on to specify the tribe,

> nescioquam pro me laudat nunc iste Sygambram.   (14. 49)

That name evokes an episode notorious in the standard histories, the 'clades Lolliana'. The Sugambri in a foray across the Rhine inflicted a defeat on Marcus Lollius, the consular legate. But when they learned that Lollius was preparing a counterstroke, and Augustus was taking the field, they desisted, agreed to a treaty, and gave hostages. Thus Cassius Dio, under the year 16 B.C.[3] He had already assigned other reasons for the ruler's decision to leave the capital.[4]

---

[1] Below, p. 13 and p. 14. And there is what looks like an insertion in *Met.* I. 200–5, from 'sic' to 'Iovi', referring to the assassination of Caesar: presumably added on completion of Book XV.

[2] Thus E. Bickel, *Rh. Mus.* CIII (1960), 97 ff. He was misled by a false assumption about the age of Messallinus (Tibullus II. 5. 115); cf. below, p. 118. Bickel's notion was approved by G. Luck, o.c. 215 f.: 'mit guten Gründen'. That Tibullus in II. 5 refers to the published *Aeneid* is maintained and used as an argument for decease later than 19 by V. Buchheit, *Philol.* CIX (1965), 104 ff.

[3] Dio LIV. 20. 6.

[4] LIV. 19. 1 ff.

The account obtruded in a digression of Velleius Paterculus is more vivid and alarming. Disaster and the loss of the eagle of Legio V, summoning Caesar Augustus to Gaul: disaster caused by the totally unsatisfactory Lollius, 'homine in omnia pecuniae quam recte faciendi cupidiore et inter summam vitiorum dissimulationem vitiosissimo'.[1] The first on record, but not the last and best dereliction of Marcus Lollius.

It is normal in any age for a government to exalt and embellish trivial successes in the field; and the epoch of Caesar Augustus can show imperatorial salutations taken and registered for next to nothing. Paradox therefore to admit, let alone magnify, a defeat. The reason is no mystery: the role and vicissitudes of Marcus Lollius in the sequel. It is unfortunate that the author of the *Annales* was taken in. At the funeral of Caesar Augustus the 'prudentes' holding discourse are made to bring up 'Lollianas Varianasque clades'.[2] He might have given a thought to the great rebellion of Pannonians and Dalmatians that broke out in A.D. 6.

It was not in fact a disaster incurred by Lollius that brought Augustus to Gaul in 16 B.C. That episode belongs to the previous year, as recorded by Julius Obsequens in his catalogue of prodigies and portents drawn from Livy.[3] Commentators on more texts than one tend to retain 16 B.C.: allusions to the event have been discovered both in a passage of Propertius and in two poems of Crinagoras.[4]

However that may be, there was sharp repercussion at the time. At least, the Sugambri pass on at once into Roman poetry. The first trace is in Propertius Book IV,

ille paludosos memoret servire Sygambros.   (6. 77)

No poem of Propertius can be put later than 16 B.C. Then Horace in

---

[1] Velleius II. 97. 1.   [2] *Ann.* I. 10. 4.

[3] Obsequens 71, cf. Jerome, *Chron.* p. 166 H. For a devaluation of the incident, *JRS* XXIII (1933), 17 ff. In fact Suetonius called it 'maioris infamiae quam detrimenti' (*Divus Aug.* 23. 1). The year 16 B.C. was preferred by Groag, *RE* XIII, 1381 ff.

[4] Propertius relates the fate of the sons of Arria, Lupercus (an officer), and Gallus (a centurion protecting the eagle of a legion): cf. Barber and Butler in their commentary (1933) on IV. 1. 89 ff. Cichorius adduced in Crinagoras (*Anth. Pal.* VII. 741) a centurion: by Nile or by Rhine, it is not clear (*Römische Studien* (1922), 312 f.). See the exhaustive commentary by Gow and Page, *The Garland of Philip* II (1968), 228 f. Further, for Cichorius *Anth. Pal.* IX. 291 is an expression of confidence in the power of Rome, despite the disaster of Lollius (o.c. 309 ff.); and so, more about M. Lollius and 16 B.C. in Gow–Page, o.c. 237.

Book IV of the *Odes* expects a triumph (2. 34 f.); and he concludes another poem (in 13) with the submission of this people,

> te caede gaudentes Sygambri
> compositis venerantur armis.   (14. 51 f.)

The Sugambri could still come in handy for Horace. When Caesar Augustus returned to Rome after three years spent in Gaul and Spain he could not bring with him any pretext for holding a triumph.

Ovid's reference might therefore be regarded likewise as a fairly prompt response.[1] Caution is in place. As some scholars have pointed out, the Sugambri recur as a factor of some moment (or rather of greater moment) in history. In 8 B.C. Tiberius dealt with them: massacre and the transportation of the forty thousand survivors to the left bank of the Rhine. That was the end of the Sugambri, and the principal exploit justifying the German triumph which Tiberius celebrated in January of 7 B.C.[2]

In the poem of Ovid in question, the girl's wig is a trophy 'triumphatae . . . gentis' (I. 14. 46). The word recurs in the next poem,

> Roma triumphati dum caput orbis erit.   (15. 26)

There is a chance that 'triumphatus' in Ovid carries a proper and precise meaning. The only other places where he employs it confirm: for the Pannonian triumph of Tiberius Caesar, and for his earlier German triumph.[3] Like Tacitus, he knew that it was a strong and solid word. Of the Germans the historian proclaimed 'triumphati magis quam victi'.[4]

On that showing, *Am.* I. 14 might be shifted. Subsequent to 7 B.C., not just later than 16 B.C. Hence belonging to the second edition, as can be argued for the following poem, which opens with the protest against envy and detraction (15. 1).[5] It matters little, save for scholastic or literary disquisitions—whereas there is still something of

---

[1] Like that of Propertius and of Horace (IV. 2. 34 f.). Horace's poem, to the address of Iullus Antonius, is generally dated to 16, or very soon after. See further below, p. 171.

[2] Suetonius, *Tib.* 9. 2; Dio LV. 6. 1 ff.

[3] *Ex P.* II. 2. 75; *Fasti* I. 647.

[4] Tacitus, *Germ.* 37. 5.

[5] However that may be, it is easier (in view of the use of Sugambri in Propertius and in Horace) to take Ovid's reference as literary, rather than as allusion to a historical event.

value for history to be got out of the *Ars Amatoria* and the *Epistulae ex Ponto*.

.   .   .

III. Ovid issued the books of *Amores* separately, compare II. I. I: 'hoc quoque'. Five in number to begin with, they were reduced to three in a second edition, as the quotation prefixed to Book I states, and a later passage confirms (*AA* III. 343 f.). When was the first of the original five given to the world, when the last? There is an extreme variance in opinions.

Ovid's recitals of poems about Corinna began when he was very young. As he says,

> barba resecta mihi bisve semelve fuit.   (*Tr.* IV. 10. 58)

Perhaps as early as eighteen.[1] Hence some scholars incline to put the first book *c.* 25 B.C., with completion of the series over the next ten years or so.[2] Others carry it all the way from 25 to 9 B.C.[3] By contrast, however, termination of this first edition has recently been assigned *c.* 20 B.C.[4] On that view a long interval ensues, with not much writing until the vicinity of 2 B.C.

The second edition imports complications. Not many perhaps, because changes are not easy to verify. The epigraph to Book I clearly implies a number of excisions,

> ut iam nulla tibi nos sit legisse voluptas,
> at levior demptis poena duobus erit.[5]

On the other hand, nothing precludes the addition of several poems. Notably II. 18, which provokes continual debate.

Ovid there refers to his transit to another genre, to tragedy,

> sceptra tamen sumpsi curaque tragoedia nostra
> crevit, et huic operi quamlibet aptus eram.   (18. 13 f.)

He then avows his profession as an instructor in erotic science,

> quod licet, aut artes teneri profitemur Amoris
> (ei mihi, praeceptis urgeor ipse meis),

---

[1] The 'barbae depositio' of his close coeval Claudius Marcellus (born in 42, or perhaps late in 43) is celebrated by Crinagoras (*Anth. Pal.* VI. 161): perhaps just before his marriage to Julia in 25.   [2] A. D. E. Cameron, o.c. 326, cf. 333.

[3] S. d'Elia, o.c. 210 ff.   [4] E. J. Kenney, o.c. 763.

[5] Cf. *Tr.* IV. 10. 67 f. (the burning of 'quae vitiosa putavi').

and the poem passes on at once to describe the *Heroides*,

> aut quod Penelopes verbis reddatur Vlixi
>   scribimus et lacrimas, Phylli relicta, tuas.   (18. 19–22)

The allusion, it can hardly be doubted, is to the *Ars Amatoria* ('artes' and 'praecepta'). That is the natural and easy assumption, any prepossessions apart.[1] The poem therefore belongs to the second edition, which edition (along with *Heroides*) is also referred to in *AA* III. 343 ff.

Other poems have been solicited, with less cogency.[2] Because of the Sugambri, one might wonder about I. 14 (discussed above). Again, the protest against envy and detraction in the last poem of Book I: 'Livor edax' (15. 1) later recurs in the long digression which interrupts the argument in *Remedia Amoris*,

> rumpere, Livor edax: magnum iam nomen habemus.   (389)

The protest suits, not a beginner terminating his first book, but a poet of long-established performance and notoriety, as was Ovid after he had reached the age of forty.[3]

But enough. The dating of the *Amores*, and the additions, are not the main concern of the present brief enquiry.

With the *Heroides* confusion reigns. Why not? A recent subtle and thorough investigation records in catalogue form the opinions of twenty-two scholars.[4] To abridge, therefore: the author of that study suggests in due moderation that the *Heroides* were not begun much before 10 B.C., bringing them towards *AA* I and II (the latter work itself perhaps begun as early as 6 B.C.).[5] In comment on which, it

---

[1] Thus G. Luck, o.c. 169 f. and notably H. Jacobson, arguing against d'Elia and Cameron (o.c. 307 ff.; 315). Further, A. S. Hollis in his edition of Book I (Oxford, 1977), xii; 150 f.

[2] A number by R. P. Oliver, *TAPA* LXXVI (1945), 191 ff.

[3] Below, p. 20. G. Luck also assumes the second edition (o.c. 169). For an argument that the poems addressed to Atticus, Graecinus, and Macer (I. 9; II. 10; 18) belong to the second edition, see below, p. 75 (on the friends of Ovid).

[4] Jacobson, o.c. 312 f.

[5] Jacobson, o.c. 316. Cameron, who puts the *Amores* c. 25–15, suggests an early date for the *Heroides*: 'before the last book or books, some or all of the *Heroides*' (o.c. 333). D'Elia placed them shortly after the *Medea*, which, he assumed, was published before 15 (o.c. 216; 219). At the other extreme, Kenney notes that 'certain metrical features may suggest that they were composed contemporaneously with the' *Fasti* (o.c. 764). If that were so, and if the first edition of *Amores* is put c. 20 B.C., the poet had little to show but the *Medea* for some twenty years of his life, before *AA* I–II.

might be added that nothing precludes for *Heroides* a date closer to *Amores*.

There remains a lost masterpiece, the *Medea*, alluded to in *Am.* II. 18 (of the second edition, as assumed). Ovid bids farewell to elegy, emphatically, in the first poem of Book III, and in the last (III. 1. 67 ff.; 15. 18 ff.). The *Medea* may be lodged without discomfort somewhere between 15 and 8 B.C.[1]

The easy order therefore is to have *Amores*, then *Medea*, then a reversion to elegy in the shape of *Heroides* (that is, the fifteen epistles). Were the *Amores* (the original five books) to be placed at a very early stage in the poet's progression, there is not much left for the long years elapsing before the renewed activity on show between 2 B.C. and A.D. 1.

That epoch evokes *AA*, and with it certain engaging perspectives that hitherto have failed to entice the investigators.

.   .   .

IV. Sheer felicity for the enquiry, baffled so long by the dearth of firm dates, the *Ars* offers comfort and certitude. The first book exhibits six lines that bring on a conspicuous episode in the pageantry put on show in the late summer of 2 B.C., namely the naval battle staged between Athenians and Persians (I. 171–6).[2] On which suitably follows the long excursus on a Parthian War in imminent prospect (177–278).

Caesar Augustus has decided to conquer the Eastern world,

> ecce, parat Caesar, domito quod defuit orbi
>   addere: nunc, Oriens ultime, noster eris.   (177 f.)

Now therefore, revenge for Crassus,

> ultor adest primisque ducem profitetur in annis.   (181)

It is the young Gaius Caesar, the destined heir to the power,

> nunc iuvenum princeps, deinde future senum.   (194)

The poet can even adduce a noble pretext for hostilities. Gaius has brothers, he can avenge an injury to brothers. 'fratres ulciscere

---

[1] Jacobson suggests the period 12–8, with *Heroides* following (o.c. 316 f.).
[2] *RG* 23 (full and emphatic); Dio LV. 10. 7.

laesos'. That is an allusion to the recent usurpation of the Parthian monarch, who

> hostis ab invito regna parente rapit.   (198)

Hence 'pietas' will be vindicated, 'tu pia tela feres' against criminal arrows, 'sceleratas . . . sagittas' (199).[1] And the prince goes forth to war under the best of auspices,

> Marsque pater Caesarque pater, date numen cunti.   (203)

Flight will not avail to save the Parthian, and a triumph can be predicted, with all the pomp,

> ergo erit illa dies, qua tu, pulcherrime rerum, etc.   (213 ff.)

The second book brings in briefly the foreign enemy,

> proelia cum Parthis, cum culta pax sit amica.   (II. 175)

There is likewise an allusion in the third, deprecating untidy coiffure in women,

> hostibus eveniat tam foedi causa pudoris
> inque nurus Parthas dedecus illud eat!   (III. 247 f.)

Finally, *Remedia Amoris*. The Parthian is still likely to be the victim of a Roman triumph,

> ecce fugax Parthus, magni nova causa triumphi,
> iam videt in campis Caesaris arma suis.   (155 f.)

Further, as the poet is careful to point out when urging the lover to make an escape, the Parthian is a good example for he is still elusive,

> sed fuge: tutus adhuc Parthus ab hoste fuga est.   (224)

The interval was still short before these vaticinations became obsolete. It was a war intended to be advertised rather than waged. And the truth came out very soon. Hence, for dating, a terminus in both directions, such as is rarely vouchsafed.

It is expedient to establish, so far as possible, the movements of C. Caesar. As for other events in the obscure decade 6 B.C.–A.D. 4,

---

[1] Phraates had recently been murdered by his young son Phraataces (Josephus, *AJ* XVIII 39; 42). The 'laesi fratres' are the four princes who had been surrendered to M. Titius, the governor of Syria (Strabo XVI, p. 748), *c.* 10 B.C. For the situation in Parthia see the full commentary of A. S. Hollis in his edition (Oxford, 1977), 65 ff.

during which Tiberius was absent from public life, the record is defective. There are three gaps in the text of Cassius Dio. The second extends from late 2 B.C. to a point in A.D. 1.[1]

The prince set forth early in 1 B.C., it may be surmised: the disaster incurred by his mother Julia in the previous autumn would counsel departure, to some destination or other, even if war against the Parthians (or rather the threat of war) had not already been intended or predictable. He first visited the camps of the Danubian armies—but did not there fight in any campaign.[2] Whether or no Gaius now returned to Rome for a space is uncertain. He is next found on islands of the Aegean, in Asia, and he had been as far as the coasts of the Pontus, so a member of his staff reports, in happy memory of the tour.[3]

Next the consulate, his colleague being L. Aemilius Paullus (the husband of his sister Julia). He entered on office in Syria, and subsequently went to Egypt and to Arabia. Here begins perplexity. That there should be no trace of this journey in Velleius Paterculus, that was only to be expected. Velleius suppresses anything that might redound to the credit of the prince (save alleged deference paid to the exile at Rhodes), covering himself by a double generalization about Gaius' conduct in the East: 'tam varie se ibi gessit ut nec laudaturum magna nec vituperaturum mediocris materia deficiat.'[4]

Isolated notices in the elder Pliny indicate the prospect of a war in Arabia, and perhaps something more.[5] Further, the mortuary decree of the loyal town council of Pisa has the defunct prince waging distant warfare in that year precisely: 'consulatum quem ultra finis extremas populi Romani bellum gerens feliciter peregerat'.[6]

A recent epigraphic discovery turns up conveniently. On receipt of good news a quaestor in the province Achaea ordains thanksgivings, 'having learned that Gaius the son of Augustus, who was fighting against the barbarians for the safety of all mankind was well and had

---

[1] Between LV. 10. 15 and 10a. 1.   [2] Dio LV. 10. 7 (*Exc. Val.* 180).
[3] Velleius II. 101. 3.
[4] Velleius II. 101. 1. For more amicable estimates of Velleius all through, see G. V. Sumner, *Harvard Studies* LXXIV (1970), 257 ff.; A. J. Woodman, *CQ* XXV (1975), 272 ff.
[5] Pliny, *NH* VI. 141; 160. Cf. G. W. Bowersock, *JRS* LXI (1971), 227 f.
[6] *ILS* 140.

avenged himself on the barbarians, having escaped dangers'.[1] The reference, it is argued, is to a campaign in A.D. 1, not to the later occasion when C. Caesar, besieging a place in Armenia called Artagira, suffered a wound, with a nasty and lingering illness in consequence, which (among other things) impelled him to despondency and the desire to renounce public life.[2]

A further step has been taken. Augustus was 'imp. XIV' as the result of Tiberius' German campaign in 8 B.C. The next salutation, certainly not taken before 2 B.C., has escaped documentation. It baffles conjecture. Perhaps the Danubian campaign of a legate of Illyricum in 1 B.C. or A.D. 1.[3] However, 'imp. XV' for Augustus may derive from some action of C. Caesar in Arabia, however trivial and lapsing from the historical record.[4] Not long after, when the fortress Artagira fell, a salutation was recorded.[5] That is to say, Augustus is now 'imp. XVI', which seems clear and acceptable. The next three acclamations (XVII–XIX) are assigned without doubt to the wars in Germany and Illyricum from 4 to 9.

The exotic theme of Arabia, with the crimson ocean and the aromatic lands, might have conveyed a strong appeal to vivid and pictorial talent. No sign. Which may (or may not) support the hypothesis (reasonable enough) that the excursus in *AA* I belongs (as it purports) before C. Caesar set out on his expedition. That is, quite early in 1 B.C.

.   .   .

V. To revert to Parthia. In the winter of A.D. 1/2, and hardly later than the spring of 2, the king came to the Euphrates and on an island in the river encountered C. Caesar. In perfect amity. They parted after an agreement satisfactory to both (and the prince could deal as he chose with Armenia).[6]

---

[1] *AE* 1967, 458, cf. the full commentary by G. J. E. Zetzel, *Greek, Roman and Byzantine Studies*, XI (1970), 259 ff. The quaestor who ordained the celebrations was P. Cornelius Scipio, not elsewhere on record. Probably a son of the consul of 16 B.C.

[2] Gaius suffered the wound on September 9, so the *Fasti Cuprenses* record. The year appears to be A.D. 3.

[3] As proposed in *Danubian Papers* (1971), 39.

[4] Thus T. D. Barnes, *JRS* LXIV (1974), 23.   [5] Dio LV. 10a. 7.

[6] The matter had been arranged by correspondence between Augustus and Phraataces, as may be inferred from Dio LV. 10a. 4 (under A.D. 1).

The colloquy had an unexpected result. The Parthian king revealed sinister activities of Marcus Lollius, who had been the guide and counsellor of the young prince: 'perfida ac plena subdoli ac versuti animi consilia'. And Lollius died a few days later, perhaps by his own hand.

Thus Velleius Paterculus.[1] The truth evades enquiry. Discord between a prince of the dynasty and the senior consular, juxtaposed to counsel or to curb, duly emerged on the next occasion: Germanicus Caesar and Cn. Piso the legate of Syria. Lollius is styled 'velut moderator' by Velleius.[2] That is, function, not status. Title and competence might be something else. That is, Caesar's legate in charge of Syria and its army.[3] Lollius was replaced in A.D. 2 by P. Sulpicius Quirinius (cos. 12 B.C.).[4]

Lollius was a bitter enemy of Tiberius, which explains Velleius both here and in another place.[5] And Tiberius did not relent: rancorous language about Lollius twenty years later when he requested the Senate to accord Quirinius a public funeral.[6]

Augustus had left to C. Caesar all decision concerning the recluse at Rhodes. The youth graciously consented to his repatriation, being then, so Suetonius says, 'M. Lollio offensior'.[7] So Claudius Nero came back, but to no honour or occupation, in the summer of 2.

Ovid's references to Parthia thus circumscribe narrowly the *Ars* and the *Remedia*: between 1 B.C. and, at the latest, quite early in A.D. 2. That is not all. The first two books of *AA* are a unit, as the author declares: 'finis adest operi' (II. 733). But he there goes on to announce the third book (745 f.), which was an afterthought.[8] On the augmented *AA* follows very soon the ostensible palinode, the *Remedia*.

Next, in the close context of those years, the second edition of

---

[1] Velleius II. 102. 1. By poison, so Pliny states, after the prince renounced 'amicitia' (*NH* IX. 118).

[2] Velleius II. 102. 1. In Suetonius, 'comes et rector' (*Tib.* 12. 2), in Tacitus 'rector' (*Ann.* III. 48. 1).

[3] As briefly suggested in *Akten des VI. Internat. Cong. für gr. u. lat. Epigraphik* (Munich, 1973), 601 (on the Titulus Tiburtinus, *ILS* 918).

[4] Tacitus, *Ann.* III. 48. 1.   [5] Above, p. 4.

[6] *Ann.* III. 48. 2: 'incusato M. Lollio quem auctorem C. Caesari pravitatis et discordiarum arguebat'.

[7] Suetonius, *Tib.* 13. 2.   [8] The two lines are a patent addition.

Amores, five books reduced to three. A passage in *AA* III alludes to the three books (343 ff.). Hence the assumption, generally conceded, that the second edition came out during the interval, brief indeed, between *AA* I–II and *AA* III.

Furthermore, the same passage, with the word 'epistula' (345) gives the sign of the *Heroides*. Perhaps also a second edition. That is to say, to the fifteen letters written by ladies of ancient legend were now added the three pairs of 'double letters', authenticity of which has sometimes been contested. The *Heroides* were referred to in *Am.* II. 18 (discussed above and assigned to the second edition of *Amores*). Ovid was very active in the vicinity of 1 B.C.

.   .   .

VI. A question subsists concerning the *Ars Amatoria*. The two passages in Book I, viz. the Naumachia and the digression on the Parthian War of C. Caesar, indicate 1 B.C. patently, or, at the least and lowest, no point later than the spring of A.D. 2. Was that the date of the first and only edition of Books I and II of the *Ars*? In the recent age it stands as the general and conventional assumption.[1]

Inspection insinuates a grave doubt. The poet's initial theme is the hunt for women,

> ante frequens quo sit disce puella loco.   (I. 50)

Opportunity abounds. Various places offer in Rome: porticoes, temples, the theatre, horse races (67–162). Also, the gladiatorial shows will permit amorous approaches,

> hos aditus Circusque novo praebebit amori.   (163 ff.)

Then there is the recent Naumachia,

> quid, modo cum belli navalis imagine Caesar
> Persidas induxit Cecropiasque rates?   (171 f.)

The four lines following expatiate on the abundance of accessible females. Then, with 'ecce parat Caesar' (177) comes the Parthian War of C. Caesar and the triumph to ensue (177–228). After which

---

[1] No point therefore in cataloguing opinions. For slight divergences note Cameron, o.c. 327: 'the *Ars* was written when Ovid was 40.' That is to say, 3/2 B.C. And A. S. Hollis puts *AA* I–II towards the end of 2 B.C. (in *Ovid*, ed. J. W. Binns (1973), 115); also in his edition of Book I (Oxford, 1977), xiii.

the main topic resumes, with another method of approach to women:
banquets, and not for the sake of the wine,

> dant etiam positis aditum convivia mensis;
> est aliquid praeter vina, quod inde petas.   (229 f.)[1]

Along with the Naumachia, the digression about C. Caesar patently
interrupts the sequence of operations in the chase for women. Not
merely a digression, but an addition. That was pointed out long ago,
in 1913.[2] Not much attention was paid in the sequel. The thing may
have appeared obvious to many scholars, but it has not been noticed
in the recent time, still less taken to its consequences.[3]

Before proceeding, caution is prescribed. In itself an insertion
(even if patent and palpable) does not prove a long interval ensuing
after the original text has been indited. Days or weeks perhaps rather
than a long space of years. There is a parallel for warning in *Remedia
Amoris.*

The author there proposes to furnish instruction in devices (not at
all delicate) for repulsing a woman's affection,

> multa quidem ex illis pudor est mihi dicere, sed tu
> ingenio verbis concipe plura meis.   (359 f.)

And he in fact embarks on the lesson,

> ergo, ubi concubitus et opus iuvenale petetur.   (399)

Between the announcement and the exposition, forty lines intervene:
a diatribe against detractors, beginning with

> nuper enim nostros quidam carpsere libellos,
> quorum censura Musa proterva mea est.   (361 f.)

No call, however, to postulate a second edition of *Remedia Amoris.*
Enough that the outburst may have a casual origin in some attack
from personal malice, or in the poet's sudden realization that it was

---

[1] Observe 'aditum', continuing and echoing 'hos aditus' in line 163.

[2] 'Wohl eine nachträgliche Einlage', according to M. Pohlenz, *Hermes* XLVIII (1913), 3.

[3] Otherwise inadvertence might be the reason, or the intensity of erudition at the expense
of the reading of classical texts. It is not easy to discover sponsors for the view that the
passage is an insertion. Observe, however, the brief statement of H. Bardon, *Les Empereurs et
les lettres latines* (1940), 90 f.: 'le passage (du v. 171 au v. 228) est gauchement rattaché à ce
qui précède, et semble avoir été composé après coup.' See now the brief statement in
Bayerische S-B, 1974, Heft 7, 16 f. However, a later insertion is deprecated by A. S. Hollis in
his edition of Book I (1977), xiii.

high time to put out some defence for his issuing *AA* when he did, so soon after the unfortunate transactions of autumn, 2 B.C.

In spite of that warning, it can be maintained that both the digression and the preceding six lines (the Naumachia) belong to a second edition. If so, when was the original *Ars* (in two books) presented to the polite world? If a year or two previous to 1 B.C., it hardly matters. Yet it might be something like a decade earlier. Which touches not only the chronology and the rhythm of Ovid's writing but the rancour of Caesar Augustus.

. . .

VII. Ovid's own language furnishes a clue, and what looks like a proof. In the long apologia which he composed in the year after his banishment to the shore of Pontus he undertakes to vindicate the poetry of love. Ovid appeals from Caesar to the classic glory of Augustan Rome. What passage enjoys more fame and favour than the illicit amours of Aeneas and Dido? The same poet when a 'iuvenis' had descanted upon light loves, upon Phyllis and Amaryllis: 'luserat' (*Tr.* II. 538).

Now Ovid's poem, so he argues, was comparable to the *Eclogues* of Virgil. His transgression fell long ago,

> nos quoque iam pridem scripto peccavimus isto:
> supplicium patitur non nova culpa novum.   (539 f.)

Ovid wrote when a 'iuvenis', he now suffers as a 'senex'. Most unjustly, after so long a lapse of time. As he says,

> ergo quae iuvenis mihi non nocitura putavi
> scripta parum prudens, nunc nocuere seni.
> sera redundavit veteris vindicta libelli,
> distat et a meriti tempore poena sui.   (543 ff.)

Thus far *Tristia* II, in firm discourse to the address of Caesar Augustus. The *Ars* was a 'vetus libellus', Ovid had been a young man when he wrote it, like the author of the *Eclogues*.

A similar plea is urged in three other places. Addressing an anonymous friend at an early stage Ovid states,

> scis vetus hoc iuveni lusum mihi carmen, et istos,
> ut non laudandos, sic tamen esse iocos.   (*Tr.* I. 9. 61 f.)

Again,

> id quoque, quod viridi quondam male lusit in aevo,
> heu nimium sero damnat et odit opus.   (III. 1. 7 f.)

And finally,

> integer et laetus laeta et iuvenalia lusi:
> illa tamen nunc me composuisse piget.   (V. 1. 7 f.)

The learned tradition in antiquity assigned the writing of the *Eclogues* to a period of three years. Modern scholarship generally acquiesces in a quinquennium (42–37 B.C.). The *Fourth Eclogue*, celebrating the consulship of Asinius Pollio, was a natural, easy, and inevitable point of reference; and Virgil himself attained the age of thirty in 40 B.C.[1] Though lacking the benefit of Arabic numerals, adepts of polite letters some forty or fifty years later would not go far astray: no need for anxious recourse to consular *fasti*.

In Book II of the *Tristia* (A.D. 9) Ovid asserts that the *Ars* was a 'vetus libellus', written at the season of life when Virgil composed the *Eclogues*. When the catastrophe occurred, Ovid was fifty. Peculiar therefore, if the *AA* had been published for the first time only eight or nine years earlier. That is, on the standard dating less than a decade from 'iuvenis' to 'senex': is Ovid extending poetic licence to cover arrant deception?[2]

Ovid is all too often under suspicion of exaggeration, or worse. For example, the *Ars* referring to Augustus 'mille locis' (II. 62). Further, statements about the climate of Dobrogea (the ice lasting from one winter to the next), or the quality of life in Tomis, an ancient colony of Miletus. Greek cities, who would believe it? (*Tr.* III. 9. 1). Armed barbarians parade the streets (V. 7. 13 f.), they dwell within the walls (10. 27 f.). As for the ostensible Greeks, they prefer to use the native language, and they wear trousers (10. 33 ff.). There is no civil existence, only violence and murder in the forum (10. 43 f.).[3]

Another specimen may afford entertainment. Ovid had been able to acquire a fluency in speaking foreign languages beyond parallel

---

[1] The argument is not affected if the publication of the *Eclogues* is put as late as 35 B.C., as by G. W. Bowersock, *Harvard Studies* LXXV (1971), 73 ff.

[2] Referring to 'iuveni' (in *Tr.* I. 9. 61), J. André observes that, since Ovid was 42, 'la formule est quelque peu inexacte' (in his edition, Budé 1968, viii).

[3] For the population of Tomis and of its territorium, below, p. 164.

among the Romans in any age. His progress can be documented. At a quite early stage, in the year 10, he fancies that he might learn to compose 'Geticis . . . modis' (III. 14. 48). Next, he has had to do a lot of talking 'Sarmatico . . . more', hence barbarisms will no doubt creep into his writings (V. 7. 59 f.). Almost at once, however, he has the mastery of both tongues,

nam didici Getice Sarmaticeque loqui. (12. 58)

The useful line recurs a year or so later in a missive sent to Cotta Maximus (*Ex P.* III. 2. 40). Ovid had been telling a group of Sarmatians and Getae about the virtues of his loyal and illustrious friend. Upon which, an aged native, coming (so he affirmed) from the Tauric Chersonese, proceeded to narrate a local legend: in fact the story of Orestes and Pylades, fraternally active in that cruel land.

After that incident it was a short step to a poem in Getic. Not long after the decease of Augustus,

a, pudet, et Getico scripsi sermone libellum. (*Ex P.* IV. 13. 19)

It conveyed eager homage to Tiberius Caesar, to Livia, to Germanicus and Drusus. Corroborative evidence is subjoined: the native audience shook their quivers in applause (13. 35).

Scholars can be found who give credence to the 'Getic poem'.[1] They do not offer estimates of Ovid's proficiency in spoken Getic and spoken Sarmatian (the latter tongue would not be of much use at Tomis or in the vicinity).[2] It is only a piece of fantasy, such as convention accorded to orators as well as poets—and especially to panegyrists.[3]

Graver charges should not be suppressed. Ovid asserts that when leaving Rome he consigned to the flames the manuscript of the *Metamorphoses* (*Tr.* I. 7. 13 ff.), that he had already completed his *Fasti*, in twelve books (II. 549 f.): assertions on the lowest count hardly verifiable. In his apologia to Caesar Augustus, he has the face

---

[1] Thus in three papers in the volume *Ovidiana* (1958): O. Adamasteanu, 391 ff.; E. Lozovan, 396 ff.; N. I. Herescu, 404 f.

[2] Spoken Sarmatian is claimed by N. Lascu, *Maia* X (1958), 312.

[3] Observe two visions reported in the *Pan. Lat.*, namely what Constantine saw in a temple in Gaul (VI. 21. 4) and armies seen in the sky, led by Constantius (IV. 14). Both panegyrists use the revealing and damaging word 'credo'.

to allege that the *Ars* was designed only for 'meretrices' (303), that
the name of the Princeps stands in his poems 'mille locis' (62).

Flagrant untruths. The advocate's trained talent has run away with
him—and by overstatement it impairs and subverts a legitimate plea,
a sound case.

That being so, does this man command credit when he affirms,
more than once, that the *Ars* is a youthful peccadillo? The terms
'iuvenis' and 'senex' are elastic, according to context and atmosphere.
Thus the historian Tacitus will bring 'iuvenes ad senectutem' in the
fifteen long years of tyranny.[1] But the device could hardly be made
plausible when applied to the interval between A.D. 1 and A.D. 8.

.   .   .

VIII. The case for a first edition has been put, viz. the structure of
Book I and the author's statement about his own age. The question
remains, how far should the original *Ars* be taken back before 1 B.C.
Not indeed as far as 13 B.C., his thirtieth year: a margin of latitude
may be conceded.[2] Perhaps five years, or even eight years anterior to
1 B.C. To have *AA* I–II follow fairly close on *Heroides* will not excite
disquiet everywhere.[3]

An item from Book I now comes in. The instructor tells the lover
where to seek his prey. Should his predilections go, not to youth, but
to 'sera et sapientior aetas' (65), he has only to frequent public halls
and ambulatories. For example, the Portico of Octavia (constructed
in memory of her son Marcellus),

> aut ubi muneribus nati sua munera mater
> addidit, externo marmore dives opus.   (69 f.)

Next, the Portico of Livia,

> nec tibi vitetur quae priscis sparsa tabellis
> porticus auctoris Livia nomen habet.   (71 f.)

The notice is valuable. The Porticus Liviae was built on the site of
the mansion of Vedius Pollio, demolished on the decease of that

---

[1] Tacitus, *Agr.* 3. 2.

[2] The period 13–10 B.C. was proposed in *Bayerische S-B*, 1974, Heft 7, 17: too early.

[3] *AA* I–II were perhaps begun as early as 6 B.C., completed in 1 B.C.–A.D. 1 in the view of
H. Jacobson (o.c. 317): without argument, however, or any hint that I. 171–228 is an
insertion.

person in 15 B.C.[1] It was dedicated in the first months of 7 B.C., about the time when Tiberius, entering on his second consulship, celebrated his German triumph.[2]

Hence a terminus is fixed for a first edition of the *Ars*. Which is welcome. A slight doubt might supervene. This portico may have been finished and open to the strolling public several years before it was officially inaugurated.

Strong reasons advocated a postponement of that ceremony, namely the death of Drusus and his brother's absence in Germany in 8 B.C. Drusus died on September 14, 9 B.C. Long and lavish manifestations of mourning ensued, in public and in the family circle.[3] January of 7 B.C. became highly suitable: a concentration of ceremonies embracing the dynasty. A shrine to Concordia was announced, to carry the conjoined names of Tiberius and his brother.[4] The Porticus Liviae fits very well.

There is therefore a chance that the first edition of the *Ars* belongs a year or two earlier than 7 B.C. Not that it matters much: 9 B.C. or 6 B.C.

What stands in contradiction? Only the modern 'tradition', based on the uncritical acceptance of two linked passages in Book I which, it can be maintained, are a subsequent insertion. As Symmachus said, 'consuetudinis magnus amor est.'[5]

The first two books are a unit, and as such complete, so the author affirms: 'finis adest operi' (II. 733). The third, conveying advice to 'puellae', is a supplement (745 f.). The concluding couplet of Book III commands attention,

> ut quondam iuvenes, ita nunc, mea turba, puellae
> inscribant spoliis NASO MAGISTER ERAT.   (811 f.)

Mark the word 'quondam'. It is revealing. In the mind of the author *AA* I–II was not a recent work, written some months before, or a year before. A longer interval had elapsed. Hence added support for the thesis of a first edition.

·   ·   ·

[1] Dio LIV. 23. 6, cf. *Fasti* VI. 639 ff.   [2] Dio LV. 28. 2.
[3] Dio LV. 2. 2 ff.; Suetonius, *Divus Claudius* 1. 3; *Cons. ad Liviam* 67 ff.; 161 ff.; 216 ff.
[4] Dio LV. 8. 1 f. It was not dedicated until A.D. 10 (LVI. 25. 1): on January 16, cf. below, p. 29.
[5] Symmachus, *Rel.* III. 4.

IX. On March 20, 1 B.C., Ovid was forty-two, the standard age at which a *novus homo* can accede to the consulship. He had forsworn the occupations prescribed, 'more patrum', for the career of honours and the energetic season of life. Namely warfare, the law, or public eloquence (*Am.* I. 15. 2 ff.). Instead, literary excellence. Such is the proud pronouncement in the last poem of *Amores* I, emphatic by its placing. Ovid could now put out a substantial claim to glory in the present as well as beyond the grave. The years had not been consumed in idleness,

> quid mihi, Livor edax, ignavos obicis annos
> ingeniique vocas carmen inertis opus? (15. 1 f.)

This looks like a poem added to the second edition.[1] It is not youth but maturity that regrets or defends the wasted years.

. . .

A reconstruction can therefore be hazarded. Ovid was now revising and supplementing his elegiac corpus. As follows:

AA I–II. The second edition, probably in 1 B.C.
Amores I–III. The second edition, registered in *AA* III. 343.
Heroides. The final edition, with the addition of XVI–XXI.
AA III.
Remedia Amoris.

[1] Cf., for others, above, p. 7.

II

EVIDENCE IN THE *FASTI*

AFTER A.D. 1 Ovid's production takes a new direction. No more love poems. The assumption would be hasty that this fluent and innovatory performer was at a loss for congenial themes. However, his *Ars* had run into criticism, as is shown by the digression in *Remedia Amoris*; and that poem may be regarded as a farewell to erotic elegy, although no kind of recantation. Ovid again defies 'Livor edax', he asserts that elegy owes as much to him as epic to Virgil.[1] He might continue to affirm that he had not spent 'ignavos . . . annos'.[2]

By contrast now, *Fasti* and *Metamorphoses*. The two works, it has often been supposed, were written during the same period of time.[3] No proof is to hand. Priority can be claimed for the *Fasti* on various grounds, putting the six extant books between the years 1 and 4.

Book I originally carried a dedication to Caesar Augustus. It has been transferred to the exordium of the next book (II. 3–18).[4] The invocation of Germanicus Caesar took its place (I. 1–26, with 63 f.); and a number of other additions were inserted. None subsequent to Book I can be detected, save the isolated allusion to Sulmo, the exiled poet's 'patria', evoked by Solymus, a companion of Aeneas (IV. 81 f.). The facts have long been clear and are nowhere in dispute.[5]

* * *

[1] Ovid, *Rem.* 389; 395 f.

[2] *Am.* I. 15. 1 (an emphatic poem), cf. above, p. 20.

[3] Thus L. P. Wilkinson, *Ovid Recalled* (1955), 241; B. Otis, *Ovid as an Epic Poet* (1966), 21 f.; E. J. Kenney, *OCD*² (1970), 764, who has the *Heroides* into the bargain. Decision is suspended by F. Bömer in his edition of the *Fasti*, vol. I (1957), 15. Advocates of the priority of the *Fasti* are not easy to find: one is F. Stoessel, *Ovid, Dichter und Mensch* (1959), 23. According to H. Fränkel, 'in most of its execution it dates from A.D. 7 and 8' (*Ovid, a Poet between Two Worlds* (1945), 143).

[4] However, the last two lines (17 f.) may refer to Germanicus: for 'placido . . . vultu' cf. I. 3 'pacato . . . vultu'.

[5] As established by R. Merkel in the Prolegomena to his edition (1841): still worth consulting. See further Schanz–Hosius, o.c. 236 f.; W. Kraus, *RE* XVIII, 1951 f.; F. Bömer,

I. The six books register a number of Augustan festivals and anniversaries, the dates also being given by contemporary calendars, notably the *Fasti* of Praeneste.[1] A summary catalogue will be convenient for various purposes:

January 13, 27 B.C.	I. 589–616. The memorable day when the Princeps announced the return of 'normal government'. Ovid conflates the conferment of the *cognomen* 'Augustus' (590), which occurred on January 16.
January 30, 9 B.C.	I. 709–22. The Ara Pacis.
February 5, 2 B.C.	II. 127–44. The title 'pater patriae'.
March 10, 12 B.C.	III. 419–28. Augustus becomes 'pontifex maximus'.
March 30, 11 B.C.	III. 881 f. Altars of Concordia, Salus, and Pax, cf. Dio LIV. 35. 2.
April 14, 43 B.C.	IV. 627 f. The first victory (at Mutina).
April 16, 43 B.C.	IV. 673–6. The first imperatorial salutation.
May 12, 2 B.C.	V. 550–78. Forum Augusti and Mars Ultor. Really on August 1, cf. below.

Not a large total, and there are some omissions. Augustus is duly acclaimed as

templorum positor, templorum sancte repostor.   (II. 63)[2]

This follows the notice that the temple of Juno Sospita was restored. But Ovid does not furnish many other instances of the 'sacrati provida cura ducis' (II. 60). A brief hint indicates the Templum Divi Iulii (III. 703 f.), which was vowed at Philippi and dedicated on August 18, 29 B.C.; and there is the shrine and altar of Vesta established on the Palatine, on April 28 (IV. 949–54), in 12 B.C.[3]

o.c. 18. For the additions, ibid. 18 f. He strongly questions other passages that scholars have adduced, e.g. VI. 219 ff.; 666 f.; 763 ff.

[1] For the full testimonia see the appendix, 'Le Calendrier d'Auguste', in J. Gagé's edition of the *Res Gestae* (1935), 163 ff. For the *Fasti* in relation to the Augustan programme, K. Allen, *AJP* XLIII (1922), 250 ff.

[2] Cf. Livy IV. 20. 7. For the detail, *RG* 19 ff., with the commentary of Gagé.

[3] Dio LIV. 27. 3, cf. *Met.* XV. 864. For the restoration of the temple of Cybele (IV. 347), see below, p. 30.

Two January dedications by Tiberius Caesar (Castor and Pollux; Concordia) belong to another context. They were added to the second edition of Book I.[1]

Ovid did not neglect the beneficent activities of the august consort. Livia reconstructed the temple of Bona Dea (V. 157). Further, she erected a 'magnifica aedes' to Concordia (VI. 637 f.), not elsewhere on record, except for the allusion to an altar of Concordia set up by her (I. 649 f.). Also the portico bearing her name. It occupied the site of the huge mansion of Vedius Pollio, which Augustus demolished when inheriting the possessions of his ill-famed friend and favourite (VI. 639 ff.).[2]

·　　·　　·

II. Several omissions can be discovered. They may (or may not) prove instructive for some purpose or other. Though Ovid refers to the young Caesar at Mutina (April 14 and April 16), nothing is said about his assumption of *imperium* on January 7, 43 B.C.[3] Not very grave, perhaps. Again, no sign of Dea Dia, the goddess to whom sacrifice was made by the Arvales, a confraternity revived by Augustus from ancient desuetude and intended to convey high prestige.[4] No extant antiquarian writer knows of Dea Dia, and she might well baffle the ingenious fancy of Ovid.[5]

More serious, no *Ludi Saeculares*. This unique festival was celebrated with great pomp, to inaugurate a new age. It began with sacrifices on the first day of June of 17 B.C. The college of *quindecimviri* presided (in their ranks the first men in the state) and the ceremony gave scope for a poet to write about Apollo and the Sibyl.

---

[1] Below, p. 29.

[2] The solitary Ovidian reference in the lengthy rubric of *PIR*², L 301 (six pages). Livia is named also in V. 157; and in I. 536 she appears as 'Iulia Augusta'. Again as 'Livia' no fewer than six times in the poems of exile: apart from the consort of Augustus or the mother of Tiberius.

[3] At Spoletum (Pliny, *NH* XI. 190), a fact of some interest: the *patria* of his adherent C. Calvisius Sabinus (*cos.* 39 B.C.), cf. *ILS* 925, as interpreted in *Rom. Rev.* (1939), 221; *CP* L (1955), 134.

[4] The annual sacrifices to Dea Dia took place at the end of May, as shown by the *Acta Fratrum Arvalium*. For this goddess see R. Schilling, *Hommages Renard* II (1969), 675 ff.

[5] It is significant that the Fratres Arvales find mention only once before the time of Augustus (in Varro, *De lingua latina* V. 85). They were not known to the sources of Livy and Dionysius of Halicarnassus.

The hymn composed by Q. Horatius Flaccus might not have been forgotten by a fellow bard.[1]

Finally, and most peculiar, the treatment of the Gates of War. Under the opening day of the year Ovid at once plunges into a disquisition on Janus, erudite, fanciful, and frivolous (I. 65–284), in the course of which the god proffers variegated information. At the end Janus proclaims the rule of peace,

> pace fores obdo, ne qua discedere possit,
> Caesareoque diu nomine clusus ero.   (I. 281 f.)

The pronouncement seems to imply that the Janus Geminus is closed at the time, or about to be closed. Which could hardly apply to the years A.D. 1–4.

The god now casts his glance over the whole world (283 f.), and,

> pax erat, et vestri, Germanice, causa triumphi,
> tradiderat famulas iam tibi Rhenus aquas.   (285 f.)

Then follows a prayer to Janus,

> Iane, fac aeternos pacem pacisque ministros
> neve suum, praesta, deserat auctor opus.   (287 f.)

The historical reference is to the triumph which Germanicus Caesar celebrated on May 26, A.D. 17. An insertion in the revised edition, as is perhaps also the first of the couplets quoted above (281 f.). One may not be so sure about the third (287 f.). In any event, the passage has been remodelled: the transition to the next item, the temple of Aesculapius on the Insula Tiberina (dedicated on January 1), is obscure (289 ff.).

The god makes an affirmation and a prophecy,

> Caesareoque diu nomine clusus ero.   (282)

But the god neglects certain facts. It was the proud boast of the ruler that Janus had been closed three times, 'me principe', as a sign that warfare had ceased by land and sea 'per totum imperium populi Romani'.[2] By the same token, Janus must also have been opened

---

[1] *Carm. saec.*, cf. *ILS* 5050, l. 149. Ovid might not have found them in his sources. The earlier celebrations are obscure and controversial, cf. K. Latte, *R. Religionsgeschichte* (1970), 298 f.; P. Weiss, *R. Mitt.* LXXX (1973), 205 ff.

[2] *Res Gestae*, 13, cf. Suetonius, *Divus Aug.* 22. Velleius has only one closing (II. 38.3): not in the Augustan context.

three times in the course of the reign: the dates are not anywhere on record.

.   .   .

III. Let the facts therefore be set out in brief statement. The first ceremony was enacted in 29 B.C., on January 11, inaugurating a year of multiple pageantry. Cassius Dio also has the second closing, under 25.[1] Better, perhaps, January of 24. It advertises the official view that north-western Spain had been subjugated by Caesar Augustus in two campaigns (in 26 and 25 B.C.). In truth, a ten years' war, from 29 or 28 to 19.[2]

The third closing is a problem.[3] It must be squarely faced, for there are various repercussions. According to Dio, the Senate towards the end of 11 decreed that Janus be shut, but the ceremony had to be postponed: an incursion of Dacians across the frozen Danube into Pannonia.[4] Senators, or the Princeps himself, had perhaps been impelled to premature optimism by the campaigns of 12 and 11, conducted by Tiberius and Drusus in Illyricum and in Germany; and L. Piso won a great victory over the rebel peoples in Thrace.[5] Hence a ceremony in prospect for January of 10.[6]

The closure happens not to be registered by Dio in the sequel. It can be assigned without discomfort to 8 or 7. For 7 speaks the German triumph of Tiberius on January 1. A mention might indeed have come later in Dio: there is a gap in the text, from the summer of 6 until August of 2. Various arguments converge.[7]

There is a linked question: when were the Gates of War opened again? A ready response offers—when Gaius Caesar set out in 1 B.C. to wage war and earn a triumph in the East.[8] There is a providential gap in the text of Cassius Dio. Resuming with the pageantry of August, 2 B.C., the narrative breaks off in the autumn towards the conclusion of the scandal of Julia.[9]

---

[1] Dio LIII. 26. 5.   [2] Below, p. 66.   [3] Below, p. 170.

[4] Dio LIV. 36. 2.

[5] Velleius II. 98. 1 f.; Dio LIV. 34. 6 f. (under 11 B.C.).

[6] Bömer (on I. 287) has closings of Janus in 31, 25, and 10.

[7] The absence of warfare between 8 and 1 B.C. was emphasized by Mommsen, *Res Gestae Divi Augusti*[2] (1883), 50. No suggestion from Gagé in his commentary. For 7 B.C. see now *Bayerische S-B*, 1974, Heft 7. 1.

[8] Above, p. 10.   [9] Dio LIV. 10. 15, to resume in A.D. 1 (with 10a. 1).

Conjecture, but there is nothing else to go by. To be sure, a passage in Orosius might still perplex the unwary or the retarded. Augustus, he says, closed the Gates for the third time in 2 B.C., and they remained firmly shut for about twelve years, in peace unbroken, until close on the end of the reign in the 'extrema senectus' of the ruler.[1]

The design of Orosius is patent and flagrant. He puts the Nativity in 2 B.C. Hence the necessary consequence of peace among all the nations; and in another place he invents boldly: 'facta pace cum Parthis'.[2] The facts refute. A sequence of wars ensued, throughout the world. Since the allegation of Orosius is compounded of error and fraud, no more need be said.[3]

Another passage in Orosius is relevant, and even useful. He quotes from a lost book of the *Historiae* of Cornelius Tacitus: 'sene Augusto Ianus patefactus'.[4] Caesar Augustus became a 'senex' at sixty, shortly before 1 B.C. That year thus becomes highly attractive. Janus had remained closed for half a dozen years. The ruler's titulature shows no acclamation after 8 B.C. ('imp. xiv') or earlier than A.D. 1.[5]

.   .   .

IV. To revert to Ovid. He has failed to notice all or any one of the three closures of Janus, conspicuous titles to the glory of a ruler who assiduously advertised both conquest and peace. Which at first sight baffles explanation. If the original passage in the *Fasti* was changed at the revision in A.D. 17, Ovid would hardly expunge a triple closure— had it been there. On the other hand, if he was composing Book I before the Parthian War of C. Caesar failed to occur (that is, early in A.D. 2 at the latest),[6] the emphasis would have gone to war, not to peace. Hence the chance, but only the chance, that at some stage or other in the composition, some lines were excised. If so, they were eventually replaced by the exaltation of peace in the context of the triumph of Germanicus: 'pax erat' (I. 285).

---

[1] Orosius VI. 22. 1.   [2] Orosius I. 1. 6.

[3] As Mommsen concluded, 'fraus tam pia quam absurda' (o.c. 51). For fuller comments, especially on the 'Dacorum commotio' said by Orosius to have caused the opening of Janus, see *Danubian Papers* (1971), 38 f.

[4] Orosius VII. 3. 7.

[5] For the fifteenth salutation see *Danubian Papers* (1971), 39; T. D. Barnes, *JRS* LXIV (1974), 23. Also above, p. 11.

[6] Above, p. 12.

There are apparent paradoxes in the evocation of Janus by Augustan writers. 'Sunt geminae Belli portae', and their opening is a solemn and archaic ceremony.[1] Thus Virgil, with auspicious thoughts for imperial Rome on the path of conquest in the Orient,

> seu tendere ad Indos
> Auroramque sequi Parthosque reposcere signa.[2]

Now Janus was opened when C. Caesar went forth to war in 1 B.C., so it may be conjectured: or when, if not then?

But the main emphasis rests upon Janus closed and peace prevailing even when there was evidence to the contrary. The first closing in January of 29 B.C. tends to be accorded permanent validity. It overshadows and eclipses the second and the third. Ovid passed them by, and so did Velleius Paterculus. Furthermore, it was convenient (though quite illicit) to bring Janus into association with another symbol of peace throughout the world, namely the submission of the Parthians, so largely advertised in 20 B.C. and in the sequel. Thus Horace in the last of his Odes, in 13, on the eve of the great wars of conquest in the North: Augustus has recaptured the 'signa' from the Parthians and closed Janus.[3]

Finally, two other brief statements about 'pax' in Book I. They look like insertions. Concluding remarks about Ceres and her gifts, the author adds

> gratia dis domuique tuae; religata catenis
> iam pridem vestro sub pede bella iacent.   (I. 701 f.)

Then, a little lower down, subjoined to the Ara Pacis,

> utque domus, quae praestat eam, cum pace perennet,
> ad pia propensos vota rogate deos!   (721 f.)

These passages hardly suit A.D. 1 and the following years.[4]

The poet at distant Tomis perhaps expected another ceremony to wind up the long chapter of the German Wars and corroborate by

---

[1] Although an authentic precedent for the Augustan ceremony is highly dubious, cf. K. Latte, o.c. 132.

[2] *Aen.* VII. 605 f.

[3] *Odes* IV. 15. 6 ff., cf. *Epp.* II. 1. 255 f. See further below, p. 171. Later writers also conflate, e.g. Florus II. 34. It may be noted in passing that Horace had neglected in *Odes* I–III to register the first and second closures.

[4] Cf. R. Merkel, o.c. cclxv.

public show the sagacious policy of Tiberius Caesar. If he was still writing (and still alive) when the news arrived later in the year 17 that Germanicus was on a mission to the eastern lands, that was no impediment. No fighting of any kind was intended, and none ensued except for the clash between the prince and Cn. Piso, Caesar's legate in Syria, which led to armed violence.

.   .   .

V. So far Janus. Another curious phenomenon in the *Fasti* may turn out to be not a problem but a clue. It concerns Tiberius Caesar. The references are confined to Book I, they are all clear additions, and they tend to name him in the context of other members of the 'domus regnatrix', or he is subsumed in it.

1. Tiberius is referred to as 'pater' in the invocation of Germanicus (I. 10).

2. Evander utters a prophecy about the 'patriae tutela' abiding with the dynasty of the Augusti,

> hanc fas imperii frena tenere domum.   (532)

The venerable Arcadian hero even predicts that, like himself, Livia will end as a divinity,

> sic Augusta novum Iulia numen erit.   (536)

In between comes the son (and grandson) of a god, the inheritor,

> inde nepos natusque dei, licet ipse recuset,
> pondera caelesti mente paterna feret.   (533 f.)

The language recalls closely that used by Ovid in a letter written in the winter of 14,

> esse parem virtute patri: qui frena rogatus
> saepe recusati ceperit imperii.   (*Ex P.* IV. 13. 27 f.)

It reflects the 'recusatio imperii' in the Senate on September 17, a necessary part of the ceremonial, after which there came at last an end of entreaties, and an end of denials.[1] The form of deprecation should not be confused with doubts in the mind of Tiberius Caesar, or hesitations in his demeanour.

---

[1] *Ann.* I. 13. 5.

3. In epilogue on the transactions of January 13 (and 16) of 27 B.C., after an excursus on *cognomina*, not neglecting 'Maximus' of the Fabii (605 f.), the author inserts a reference to the heir of Augustus. It implies (wrongly) that he bore the *cognomen*,

> auspicibusque deis tanti cognominis heres
> omine suscipiat, quo pater, orbis onus!   (615 f.)

4. The temple of Concordia Augusta (639 ff.). After a proper allusion to Furius Camillus, the poet proceeds,

> causa recens melior: passos Germania crines
> porrigit auspiciis, dux venerande, tuis;
> inde triumphatae libasti munera gentis
> templaque fecisti, quam colis ipse, deae.   (645 ff.)

The temple, symbolizing the happy relations that had obtained between Tiberius and his deceased brother was vowed, in their joint name after Tiberius' German triumph, in 7 B.C.[1] It was dedicated on January 16, A.D. 10, by Tiberius before setting out for the Rhine.

5. Castor and Pollux, likewise in the joint name,

> hac sunt Ledaeis templa dicata deis:
> fratribus illa deis fratres de gente deorum
> circa Iuturnae composuere lacus.   (706 ff.)

The date was January 27, A.D. 6.[2]

These two temples, it may be observed in passing, were sadly misdated by Suetonius. He lumps them together and, in his compressed account of the years 12 and 13, puts them subsequent to the Pannonian triumph celebrated in October of 12.[3] Finally, two small omissions in the revision. Ovid neglected the 'ara numinis Augusti', dedicated on January 17 in a year that cannot be ascertained. Some argue for A.D. 9.[4] Next, the 'ara iustitiae Aug.' of January 8, A.D. 13. Ovid had mentioned it in an epistle from the Pontus.[5]

. . .

VI. The rest of the work carries no word or hint of Tiberius Caesar. The fact deserves to be exploited, being relevant to the season of writing.

---

[1] Dio LV. 8. 2, cf. LVI. 25. 1.   [2] Dio furnishes the year (LV. 27. 4).
[3] Suetonius, *Tib.* 20. 2.
[4] Thus Gagé, o.c. 166. For this cult, D. Fishwick, *Harv. Th. Rev.* LXII (1969), 357.
[5] Ovid, *Ex P.* III. 6. 25 f. (below, p. 41).

A point of time has been detected in Book IV. Ovid recounts the bringing of the statue of Cybele to Rome and narrates in full the story of Claudia Quinta: the virgin of Vesta, 'casta quidem, sed non et credita' (IV. 307). A Metellus established the temple, but his name lapsed,

> templi non perstitit auctor.
> Augustus nunc est, ante Metellus erat.   (347 f.)

A valuable item has been transmitted by a compiler. According to Valerius Maximus, the shrine was destroyed by fire, but not the statue of Claudia: 'in sua basi flammis intacta stetit.' Maximus subjoins the consular date, A.D. 3.[1] That is unique in his references to events in his own time. Maximus was writing *c.* 28–32. Hence relevant at first sight to the *Fasti*.[2]

Strong doubt is in place. If Ovid had that conflagration in mind, with a rebuilding to bear the name of Augustus, he might have said so, with powerful and pointed epilogue on Claudia Quinta, her name and image preserved intact through the ages. On the other hand, given the dangers of an argument from silence, it may not be safe to assume that Ovid must have completed the passage about Claudia Quinta in Book IV before the fire in A.D. 3. Yet that might be the case.

Augustus in the *Res Gestae* registers the temple, not as repaired, but as his own construction. It comes at the end of the list: 'aedem Matris Magnae in Palatio feci.'[3] His edifice may go back many years, well before 2 B.C., that memorable year when (so it is conjectured) the Princeps drew up the text, the changes and additions in the sequel not being numerous. The clear climax of the document is the conferment of 'pater patriae', on the motion of Messalla Corvinus (February 5, 2 B.C.).[4]

.   .   .

VII. To render plausible the hypothesis that Ovid wrote the *Fasti* in the period 1–4, a venturesome and vulnerable approach may be

---

[1] Valerius Maximus I. 8. 11. For this fire, which ravaged a part of the Palatine, see Suetonius, *Divus Aug.* 57. 2; Dio LV. 12. 4 (supplied by Zonaras and Xiphilinus).

[2] Bömer, however (ad loc.), denies that it is evidence for the date of Book IV, or even of a large part of it. The contrary was assumed by W. Kraus, *RE* XVIII, 1955.

[3] *RG* 19.   [4] *RG* 35; Suetonius, *Divus Aug.* 58. 1 f.

essayed, adducing the political situation and the vicissitudes of the dynasty during those years. As follows.

Instead of waiting until the calendar brought him to the month of August, when the Forum and the temple of Mars Ultor were dedicated, Ovid described the ceremony prematurely, under May 12 (V. 550 ff.). Now the May festival, the *Ludi Martiales*, celebrated the surrender of Roman standards by the Parthians in 20 B.C., it will be recalled. Until Mars Ultor should be ready the 'signa' were lodged in a small shrine on the Capitol.[1]

Augustus went to Syria in 20 and there received the submissive envoys of the Parthian monarch.[2] He insisted on parading an inordinate commemoration of this diplomatic triumph: it was even linked on coins with his ninth imperatorial salutation.[3] The transaction kept on being acclaimed; and the original significance of Mars Ultor was astutely modified to advertise, not vengeance for the divine parent, but atonement exacted from the foreign enemy. Thus Augustus, in Ovid's phrase,

persequitur Parthi signa retenta manu.[4]

About the same time (or perhaps shortly after) the young Ti. Claudius Nero entered Armenia with an army and installed a king, without effort or danger. Velleius is up to form, with a double artifice. Tiberius, he states, was sent 'ad visendas ordinandasque, quae sub Oriente sunt, provincias'.[5] And, in a later passage, the actions of Tiberius are held worthy of an ovation, for his bestowing a diadem on a king and for something else: 'ordinatisque rebus Orientis'.[6] The language implies a mission with proconsular *imperium*, such as later for the princes C. Caesar and Germanicus Caesar. Indeed it describes the activities of the ruler himself.[7]

Velleius also states that the Parthian monarch surrendered his sons as hostages, such was the fear that the name of Tiberius inspired:

[1] Dio LIV. 8. 3, cf. Horace, *Odes* IV. 15. 6: 'et signa nostro restituit Iovi.'

[2] For this transaction see the lucid and succinct account of J. G. C. Anderson, *CAH* X (1934), 263.

[3] *BMC, R. Emp.* I. 108 ff. There was an additional justification, namely Agrippa's subjugation of the Cantabrians, reported by Dio under 19 B.C., but perhaps belonging to the previous year, cf. Horace, *Epp.* I. 12. 26.

[4] *Fasti* V. 580.   [5] Velleius II. 94. 4.   [6] Velleius II. 122. 1.

[7] Velleius II. 92. 1.

'tanti nominis fama territus liberos suos ad Caesarem misit obsides.'[1]
That is false.[2]

The recovery of the Roman 'signa' is registered by Velleius, but in another place: out of chronology and without marked emphasis.[3] Which indicates and proves that Tiberius had no active share. However, Suetonius assumed it, and the error is easily made.[4]

Without recourse to mendacity, the artful Ovid might have been able to introduce the name of Tiberius somewhere on the margin of the martial ceremony of May 5. That is, if Ovid was writing Book V subsequent to the adoption of Ti. Claudius Nero on June 26, A.D. 4. Which on various grounds may be doubted.

Transferring from August to May the dedication of the Forum and Mars Ultor, Ovid expatiated on the vengeance exacted from the Parthians (V. 579 ff.). By the time when he was finishing Book V the poet may have wondered whether he would have the heart to go on and deal with the second half of the Roman year.[5]

Along with Mars Ultor a conspicuous and symbolic action in the pageantry of 2 B.C. was the naval battle between fleets of Athenians and Persians. The Naumachia (it has been argued above) was inserted not long after in the second edition of the *Ars Amatoria* (I. 171–6), as was the linked digression predicting war on Parthia and a triumph for C. Caesar.[6]

That panegyric, however, was rendered obsolete by transactions of A.D. 2. And it soon became inexpedient to say anything about the princes on whom Caesar Augustus had set his dearest hopes. Lucius died at Massilia (August 20, A.D. 2), Gaius in his turn at a small coastal port of Lycia (February 21, 4). Gaius had proved a failure, incompetent for the power and refusing to share the 'tanta moles' with the ruler of the world.

[1] Velleius II. 94. 4.

[2] The four sons of Phraates were handed over to M. Titius (*suff.* 31 B.C.), the governor of Syria (Strabo XVI, p. 748). Probably in 10 B.C. For the circumstances, N. C. Debevoise, *A Political History of Parthia* (1938), 143 f.

[3] Velleius II. 91. 1.

[4] Suetonius, *Tib.* 9. 1. Also J. Gagé (on *RG* 19); N. C. Debevoise, o.c. 40.

[5] To be sure, Ovid, coming to mention 'mille Lares geniumque ducis', rebuked himself: 'quo feror? Augustus mensis mihi carminis huius/ius habet' (V. 147 f.). The reference is to the cult of the Lares Augusti (*ILS* 3612 ff.), instituted on August 1 of 7 B.C. (*Inscr. It.* XIII. 1, p. 285).

[6] Above, p. 14.

If Ovid was composing the fifth book of the *Fasti* in 3 or 4, normal awareness precluded any mention of the young Caesars. Silence was 'sanctius ac reverentius'.[1]

On the decease of C. Caesar, the Princeps had to turn for support to the son of Livia, without public honour since he was permitted to return from Rhodes two years earlier: he had been living in seclusion in the Gardens of Maecenas.[2] Augustus proceeded to adopt Tiberius, after a decent interval had elapsed (and there may have been some hesitations, or a chance for other aristocrats in the dynastic nexus).

The ceremony took place at mid-summer, on June 26.[3] The date conveys no small significance: the day of the *tribunicia potestas*, not only now for Tiberius but for the ruler himself, so it is inferred.[4] And there is something else. On June 24 occurred the festival of Fors Fortuna. Her temple across the Tiber had been founded by good king Servius, the son of a slave woman—and the friend of the Roman plebs.

Ovid describes the merrymaking (the like of which is still kept up in Trastevere). It included a carnival on the river, with much potation,

> ferte coronatae iuvenum convivia lintres,
> multaque per medias vina bibantur aquas.   (VI. 779 f.)[5]

The effects would enjoin rest and recuperation for citizens the day after, as Ovid implies (under June 25),

> ecce, suburbana rediens male sobrius aede.   (785)

The date selected for adopting a Claudius was therefore doubly congenial and auspicious. In the false reports emanating from rivals and enemies, the patrician Claudii have a sinister repute: arrogant and intolerable, they hated and despised the Roman plebs. There was another side. The modest truth can be recovered.[6] In the contest for power the Claudii had recourse to extraneous alliances and the promotion of *novi homines*. They were also eager and active in attaching the urban plebs to their *clientela*. P. Clodius embodies the tradition,

---

[1] To borrow a useful phrase from Tacitus (*Germ.* 34. 2)—or from Florus (II. 34).

[2] Suetonius, *Tib.* 15. 1.

[3] The day is given by the *Fasti Amiternini*. Velleius has the next day (II. 103. 3).

[4] A. Degrassi, *Inscr. It.* XIII. 1. 218, cf. 157.

[5] The festival is referred to by Cicero, *De finibus* V. 70: 'Tiberina descensio festo illo die'.

[6] Mommsen, *Römische Forschungen* I (1864), 287 ff.; G. C. Fiske, *Harvard Studies* XIII (1902), 1 ff.

and Tiberius Caesar was not alien to it. Without many constructions to his credit, this ruler built or restored a temple to Fors Fortuna in 16, 'Tiberim iuxta in hortis quos Caesar dictator populo Romano legaverat'.[1]

As has been shown, Ovid's references to Tiberius Caesar do not go beyond the additions in Book I; and no excisions have so far been detected in subsequent books (it would not be easy to establish them). If Book VI never carried a reference to Tiberius' adoption in the entry for June 26, that would have a bearing on the date of the *Fasti*—and perhaps on the reasons for Ovid's renunciation.

The political situation had changed abruptly. If by A.D. 4 Ovid had got as far as the month of June, discretion and the desire to avoid a delicate topic might encourage him to stop: for a time, perhaps for a long time. Having paid handsome tribute already to Augustan festivals, he may, for all his fluent versatility and skilful adulation, have acquired a distaste for laudations of the dynasty—which must now include the rehabilitated Claudian who became Tiberius Caesar.

More of it was in the offing. That month loomed ahead which bore the *cognomen* of the ruler, and the three paramount anniversaries in his career, as the Senate's decree of 8 B.C. proclaimed: the first consulate, the fall of Alexandria, the triple triumph after the end of all the wars, in 29 B.C.[2] That year was further signalized by the dedication of the temple of Divus Julius on August 18, of the Ara Victoriae in the Curia on August 28.[3]

Tiberius Caesar himself, well before his accession, had ample reason to grow weary of dynastic celebrations. He had even been constrained to pay public honour to the 'Numen Augusti' and to 'Iustitia Augusta'.[4]

In the course of the year 4 Ovid decided to stop, that is the conjecture here presented. Whether before or after the month of June, it need not matter. He had had enough for the present.[5]

---

[1] *Ann.* II. 41. 1.   [2] Quoted by Macrobius I. 12. 34: 'huic imperio felicissimus'.
[3] For the evidence, Gagé, o.c. 176 ff. Ovid was aware of another August ceremony, concerning 'Lares geniumque ducis' (V. 145), which he must postpone: cf. above, p. 32, n. 5.
[4] Below, p. 41.
[5] Other and differing reasons were adduced for a firm decision to terminate with June by R. Heinze and H. Magnus: cited by Ehwald and Levy in their edition (Teubner, 1924), praef. iii.

The last day of June offered an innocuous point of termination: the monument of Philippus (VI. 801 ff.). That is, the temple of Hercules and the Muses, built by L. Marcius Philippus (*suff.* 38 B.C.) from the war booty after his triumph in 33 B.C. One of the Muses, Clio, expounds the lineage of the family and pays a graceful compliment to his daughter Marcia,

> in qua par facies nobilitate sua. (804)

Nor does Clio pass over the lady whom Philippus married,

> nupta fuit quondam matertera Caesaris illi. (809)

She was an Atia, Marcia thus being in fact the first cousin of the Princeps. Marcia is also the wife of the eminent Paullus Fabius Maximus (*cos.* 11 B.C.).[1] No other person in contemporary Rome save members of the dynasty gains entrance to the *Fasti*. Not even Messalla Corvinus.

.   .   .

Apart from hazards inherent in dynastic politics, sheer fatigue may have supervened to discourage. The versified calendar of the state religion was designed to deprecate censure and atone for the impropriety of the *Ars*, so some opine. However that may be, the theme, despite enlivenment through quaint legends or frivolous mythology, proved uncongenial. A man needs to have the passion for antiquarian erudition as well as a certain sympathy with superstition or entrancement with mystery. Parts of the work are hasty or superficial (observe for example the failure to exploit the three closings of Janus). Ovid was on the wrong track, and he ran into impediments.

In his apologia to Caesar Augustus the poet asserted that he had in fact digested the calendar of the whole year:

> sex ego Fastorum scripsi totidemque libellos
> cumque suo finem mense volumen habet. (*Tr.* II. 549 f.)

Most unlikely: to defend the assertion, the positive word 'scripsi' has

---

[1] Some have supposed that this passage (and also the reference to 'Maximus' as the *cognomen* of the Fabii in I. 605 f.) are later insertions by the author. Not a necessary hypothesis, cf. Bömer, o.c. 19.

to be interpreted so as to cover a 'rough draft' of the second six books.[1]

The *Fasti* have been judged by scholars and critics the least satisfactory of his writings.[2] The author himself might concur.[3]

[1] A 'satis magna pars', according to Ehwald and Levy (Teubner, 1924), praef. iii. Cf. also W. Kraus, *RE* XVIII, 1950. Authors (and scholars) in other ages have been known to put out optimistic statements about unpublished works.

[2] For some of the defects, Schanz–Hosius, o.c. 232.

[3] For a friendly appraisal, R. Schilling, *Mélanges Carcopino* (1966), 863 ff. According to H. Fränkel, 'to be read as if it were a book for children' (o.c. 149).

III

THE LATEST POEMS

THE epistles from exile stand apart. No serious problems. The author discloses from time to time the interval elapsing since he reached the shore of Pontus.[1] The *Tristia* may engender tedium, but the second instalment is superior on all counts. Along with precision of detail the *Epistulae ex Ponto* carry precious pieces of information about events and persons, not all discerned and exploited by historians in the recent age.

The last decade in the reign of Caesar Augustus, marked by the return of Tiberius and by the wars in Germany and in Illyricum (where the great rebellion took three years to suppress), remains obscure and baffling, for more reasons than one. Velleius perverted history, bias infected the sources of Cassius Dio, that author was himself inadvertent—and gaps occur in his text.[2] That being so, the witness of Ovid proves variously instructive.

Loyal friends at Rome responded. One of them (not named) sent a vivid account of the Pannonian triumph celebrated by Tiberius Caesar, not omitting the serene skies after days of heavy rain from the south (*Ex P.* II. 1. 25 f.). Also a notable item, the preliminary act of homage paid by Tiberius to 'Iustitia', one of the four cardinal virtues of the Princeps.[3]

.   .   .

I. *Tristia*. The first book purports to be written during the journey, which lasted for some time. The Adriatic was crossed in December (11. 3), and after delay at various places Ovid reached his prescribed

---

[1] For chronology, Schanz–Hosius, *Gesch. der r. Lit.* II⁴ (1935), 244 f.; 247; A. L. Wheeler in his edition of *Tristia* (Loeb, 1924); G. Luck, *Tristia*, vol. II (1968), 7 f. Also, for the *Epp. ex Ponto*, D. M. Pippidi, *Recherches sur le culte impérial* (1941), 179 ff.: reprinted from *Atheneum* II (Iaşi, 1936), 3 ff.

[2] Viz. four folia absent for the year 8, one each for 9, 10, and 13/14. Cf. below, pp. 55 ff.

[3] Cf. below, p. 41.

destination in spring or early summer of the year 9. No sooner established at Tomis than he composed the long apologia to the address of the despot (*Tristia* II). What he says about Pannonia and Dalmatia (225 ff.), about Victoria ever abiding in the camps of Caesar (169 ff.), about the 'Ausonius dux' still on campaign (171 ff.), is anterior to the disaster of Quinctilius Varus which occurred in the autumn of 9.

The next book indicates spring and summer of 10. The spring is registered (III. 12. 1), also the poet's birthday (13. 2), on March 20. In this year he anticipates a triumph from warfare in Germany,

> teque, rebellatrix, tandem, Germania, magni
> triste caput pedibus supposuisse ducis.　(12. 47 f.)

Now Tiberius Caesar, 'perpetuus patronus Romani imperii', went to the Rhine and crossed it, with rapid actions ensuing and great glory. Thus the enthusiastic and mendacious Velleius.[1] The facts refute. The 'magnus dux' did not venture beyond the river during that year.[2]

Tristia IV notes the passage of two summers since Ovid reached the Pontic shore (6. 19), and the sun returning twice after the chill of winter (7. 1). Further, a long poem consecrated to the dynasty expounds a coming triumph lavishly, Germania being humbled by the 'dux invictus'.[3] It opens in fine style,

> iam fera Caesaribus Germania, totus ut orbis,
> victa potest flexo succubuisse genu.　(2. 1 f.)

There will be a grand parade, with captive kings, and so on (2. 19 ff.); and there is a hint of Arminius himself on show,

> perfidus hic nostros inclusit fraude locorum.　(2. 33)

In fact, Tiberius had now invaded Germany, with the same 'virtus et fortuna' as before, according to Velleius.[4] With him he had

---

[1] Velleius II. 120. 1 f. Velleius could know the facts since he served under Tiberius as a legate (II. 104. 3).

[2] Dio LVI. 24. 5a (from Zonaras). That is also the impression conveyed by Suetonius (*Tib.* 18 f.), who conflates the activities of the two years 10 and 11. Cf. M. Gelzer, *RE* X, 494; C. M. Wells, *The German Policy of Augustus* (1972), 240.

[3] For the epithet, cf. Suetonius, *Tib.* 17. 2: 'censuerunt etiam quidam ut Pannonicus, alii ut Invictus, nonnulli ut Pius cognominaretur' (in A.D. 9).

[4] Velleius II. 121. 1.

Germanicus Caesar (observe 'Caesar uterque' in Ovid), a fact duly suppressed by Velleius. Not much was achieved or attempted in 11.[1] A signal victory was advertised by an imperatorial salutation (the twentieth for Caesar Augustus, the sixth for Tiberius); and Velleius in another place asserts that Tiberius deserved a triumph for what he had achieved in Germany in the aftermath of the Varian disaster.[2]

The last poem in *Tristia* IV rounds off the series most elegantly with a full and detailed autobiography (IV. 10). But Ovid went on to compose another book,

> Hunc quoque de Getico, nostri studiose, libellum
> litore praemissis quattuor adde meis.   (V. 1. 1 f.)

A third winter on the Pontus had now passed (10. 1), the winter of 11/12. Therefore the summer of 12. The book discloses no sign of the triumph celebrated on October 23 of that year. Not Germany, which would have been justified by the recent acclamation. It was the postponed triumph of Tiberius Caesar over Pannonians and Dalmatians.

.   .   .

II. The *Tristia* carry no names, save one poem to an accomplished lady called Perilla (III. 7). Some of Ovid's friends were timid, fearing the 'ira Iovis' and not wishing to be compromised by open commerce with a delinquent—or so he professed to believe, enhancing his own misfortune and the odium of Caesar Augustus.

With the *Epistulae Ex Ponto* comes not so much an alleviation of his lot as an innovation. Highly welcome: named correspondents, no fewer than twenty-one. The order of their emergence is worth noting.[3] And there are a number of close datings, even consulates.

The first three books comprise a unit, clearly marked. The first poem carries the address of a friend called Brutus, and so does the last; and no fresh correspondents turn up in Book III. In the last poem Ovid states that he did not want to make up a book, only to let each friend have his due and personal epistle. They are just a random collection,

> postmodo collectas utcumque sine ordine iunxi.   (9. 53)

---

[1] Dio denies any victory or any subjugation of a German tribe (LVI. 25. 2 f.). His account of these years, however, is unfriendly to Tiberius.
[2] Velleius II. 122. 2: 'excisa Germania'.   [3] Ch. V.

That profession finds a parallel in what Pliny said when introducing his own collection.[1] As with Pliny, it does not exclude artistic arrangement, eschewing however any violent (or detectable) transgression of chronology. The order chosen by Ovid often serves to put emphasis on eminent personages. Next after the introductory epistle of Book I comes Fabius Maximus; and the sons of Corvinus (Messallinus and Cotta Maximus) are honoured in II. 2 and 3.

Books I–III were published in the course of the year 13. A new patron leads on the next book, namely Sex. Pompeius, and it hails his coming consulship (IV. 4). He was *ordinarius* with Sex. Appuleius in 14.

As for the individual books, a letter to Fabius Maximus has Ovid's fourth winter on the Pontus, 'quarta fatigat hiems' (I. 2. 26). That is, the winter of 12. Next, to a certain Severus,

> ut careo vobis, Stygias detrusus in oras,
> quattuor autumnos Pleias orta facit. (8. 27 f.)

The Pleiades rise towards the end of October. This missive was therefore composed a little earlier than I. 2.

Still no sign in Book I of the Pannonian triumph of Tiberius Caesar. He departed from the Rhine in the course of the year 12, and it was celebrated on October 23, the date being certified by a piece of the *Fasti Praenestini* discovered in 1921.[2] Which modified a number of previous discussions (not always by much: January 16 of 13 had been favoured).

·   ·   ·

III. The first poem of *Ex Ponto* II describes the ceremony (1. 21–46). It passes quickly into an invocation of Germanicus,

> pertulit hic idem nobis, Germanice, rumor,
> oppida sub titulo nominis isse tui.
> atque ea te contra nec muri mole nec armis
> nec satis ingenio tuta fuisse loci. (1. 49–52)

---

[1] Pliny, *Epp.* I. 1. 1: 'collegi non servato temporis ordine (neque enim historiam componebam), sed ut quaeque in manus venerat.'

[2] *AE* 1922, 96. The consequences were drawn by G. Wissowa, *Hermes* LVIII (1923), 169 ff.

Further, Ovid continues with a long prediction (1. 53–62). Germanicus too shall triumph,

> te quoque victorem Tarpeias scandere in arces
> laeta coronatis Roma videbit equis. (1. 57 f.)

Germanicus had his part in the war. He received *ornamenta triumphalia*, as did the generals of consular rank.[1] Velleius confined his exploits to the last stage, the Bellum Delmaticum of 9, with brief but honorific mention.[2] The prince had also seen action in the previous year. Cassius Dio, using a full and panegyrical source, has the operations of both campaigns, with the names of several native strongholds, the 'oppida' alluded to by Ovid.[3]

The second poem, to Messallinus, also includes the triumph (2. 75 ff.), with praise for Germanicus (81 ff., cf. 71), while the third is addressed to Cotta. An elegant sequence, and well designed.

The opening poem of *Ex Ponto* II may be one of the latest to be composed in this book.[4] The exordium suggests a lapse of time since the pageantry, and it mentions the wind that brings warm weather,

> Huc quoque Caesarei pervenit fama triumphi,
> languida quo fessi vix venit aura Noti. (1. 1 f.)

There is something else to be noted. On that occasion Tiberius, before donning the triumphant robe, performed an especial act of veneration.

> tura prius sanctis imposuisse focis
> iustitiamque sui caste placasse parentis,
> illo quae templum pectore semper habet. (32 ff.)

The 'Iustitia' of Caesar Augustus, a virtue of long practice, finds an explicit habitation in the next book,

> Iustitia vires temperat ille suas.
> nuper eam Caesar facto de marmore templo,
> iampridem posuit mentis in aede suae. (III. 6. 24 ff.)

---

[1] Dio LVI. 17. 2. Ovid alludes to honours and decorations for the generals (*Ex P.* II. 1. 30; 2. 89 f.). Velleius registers Valerius Messallinus (II. 112. 2), M. Lepidus (115. 3), C. Vibius Postumus (116. 2). But not M. Plautius Silvanus (*cos.* 2 B.C.): attested by *ILS* 921.

[2] Velleius II. 116. 1: 'magna in bello Delmatico experimenta virtutis in incultos ac difficilis locos praemissus Germanicus dedit.'

[3] Dio LV. 32. 4; LVI. 11. 1–12. 1. For the detail, J. Wilkes, *Dalmatia* (1969), 74.

[4] *Ex P.* II. 5 (to Salanus) looks later.

The reference in Book III is clear and welcome. A 'signum Iustitiae Aug(ustae)' was consecrated on January 8 of the year 13, as the *Fasti Praenestini* record.[1]

The poem describing the Pannonian triumph (it is sometimes assumed) was elicited at once, as soon as the glad tidings reached Tomis. That is, presumably in the last weeks of 12.[2] Now Ovid was capable of conjuring up a vivid triumph, more than once, as has been seen (in 10 and 11, from Germany); and he had done it long ago for Gaius Caesar.[3] This time he waited for (or solicited) a friend's letter to furnish the precise and novel details of that memorable day. He soon went on to compose a whole poetical piece on the exciting theme. Two friends were told about his *Triumphus*.[4]

One poem in Book III can be made to yield a reference to military operations in the summer of 13. The matter is important, it demands separate treatment.[5] As has been shown, the triumph held in October of 12 was first registered in the second volume.

· · ·

IV. Issued before the end of 13, the three books attest skill and variety no less than rapid production. Not much more than one year, whereas the last three of the *Tristia* (III–V) covered about three years.

The fourth and last book extends over a much wider space of time, from 13 (with the prospect of Sex. Pompeius as consul for the next year) as far as the late summer of 16.[6] Cotta Maximus and others vanish, and eight fresh characters make their entrance.

The sixth year has begun since Ovid came to Pontus (IV. 6. 5 f.), and the sixth summer passes (10. 1). It is now the autumn of 14, not long after the death of Augustus. In the letter to the faithful Brutus, Ovid hopes for some abatement, 'sacrae mitior ira domus' (6. 20), for he has composed a poem about the new denizen of the celestial region: 'de caelite, Brute, recenti' (6. 17). The poet had been unfortunate for death forestalled the intercession of an eminent patron,

---

[1] Cf. J. Gagé in his edition of the *Res Gestae* (1935), 163.
[2] Thus D. M. Pippidi, o.c. 185.   [3] *AA* I. 213 ff.
[4] *Ex P.* II. 5. 27 ff. (Salanus); III. 4. 3 f. (Rufinus).
[5] III. 4 (Rufinus), cf. Ch. IV.
[6] Or perhaps autumn, since the poem to Graecinus has a reference to Ovid's celebrating the birthday of Augustus (IV. 9. 115 f.).

certus eras pro me, Fabiae laus, Maxime, gentis,
   numen ad Augustum supplice voce loqui.
occidis ante preces, causamque ego, Maxime, mortis
   (nec fuero tanti) me reor esse tuae. (6. 9 ff.)

Ovid feels in a way responsible for the death of Paullus Fabius
Maximus. So did his wife Marcia, according to the rumour reported
by Tacitus. Her loud self-reproach was heard at his obsequies 'quod
causa exitii marito fuisset'.[1] She had revealed to Livia a fateful secret,
namely the visit paid by the Princeps to the exiled Agrippa Postumus
on the island Planasia, Fabius Maximus being his sole companion on
the journey.[2]

Next, the poem addressed to Suillius Rufus also alludes to the
recent divinization (8. 63). It can be assigned to 15 or 16.[3] Then in
spring or early summer of 16 Graecinus is greeted,

sine me tanges Capitolia consul. (9. 5)

C. Pomponius Graecinus became suffect consul on July 1 with
C. Vibius Rufus for colleague. The poem also alludes to his brother
Flaccus, who will take over the *fasces* and inaugurate the following
year (9. 59 ff.).

The next poem, however, belongs to 14 (the sixth summer, 10. 1);
and the thirteenth, describing how Ovid celebrated in the Getic
tongue the deified ruler, his successor, and the imperial family, points
to the winter of that year ('sexta bruma', 13. 40). The arrangement
of Book IV was not dictated by chronology.

Ovid took care to end a volume sharply and neatly. Book IV
terminates with a long chronicle of poets in his time. In climax stands
a tribute to the younger son of Messalla Corvinus,

Pieridum lumen praesidiumque fori. (16. 42)

The last letter to Cotta (III. 8) had been written well before the end
of 13. There is no sign that Cotta deserved this honour. There follows
an apostrophe denouncing 'Livor'. One recalls 'Livor edax' in the
last poem of the *Amores* I (15. 1), in the last of *Tristia* IV (10. 123)—

---

[1] *Ann.* I. 5. 2.
[2] Some believe in the fable. See below, p. 150.
[3] Below, p. 89.

and in the sharp rebuke to critics inserted in the *Remedia* (389). Then the note was confidence rather than defiance. This time despair,

omnia perdidimus: tantummodo vita relicta est. (16. 49)

. . .

V. Bare life was left, but not to endure for long. The latest poems betray no loss of vigour or ingenuity. And the citizens of Tomis, condoning those earlier aspersions of barbarism, now accorded honour and privileges (14. 53 f.). Their gentility showed them true children of Greece (47 f.); Sulmo and the Paeligni could not have done better (49 f.).

None the less, Ovid grew weary. So many entreaties sent to Rome, so much supplication of eminent personages, and all in vain. He writes no more epistles after the summer of 16: the latest went to Pomponius Graecinus, suffect in July (9. 5).

Ovid still cherished some hopes. Not from Tiberius Caesar. Even did the ruler not profess himself bound by the actions of his parent and sanctified predecessor, he was inaccessible to the most discreet and indirect of solicitations; and his umbrageous nature might well take offence when finding a long laudation of Germanicus obtruded on his Pannonian triumph (*Ex Ponto* II. 1).

Ovid had not been afraid to invoke Livia. Apart from other honorific references, her name occurs twice in *Tristia*, four times in *Ex Ponto*.[1] A firm advance was attempted through the agency of Ovid's wife (III. 1). Ovid extols in Caesar's consort 'Veneris formam, mores Iunonis' (1. 117); and he tells his wife what demeanour to adopt when she approaches 'vultum Iunonis' (1. 145).[2] The frequent obtrusion of Livia cannot have been to the liking of the Princeps (or of her son). Horace, the personal friend of the ruler, had shown the proper tact and reserve. He nowhere names Livia.

A remote austere matron and wayward princesses, the 'domus regnatrix' exhibits sharp contrast. Between those extremes lay a wide area infested by friction and frustrations that had been imported by the dynastic plans of Caesar Augustus. The decision he announced in

[1] *Tr.* II. 161; IV. 2. 11; *Ex P.* II. 8. 4; III. 3. 87; 4. 96; IV. 13. 29. Not one of these passages is registered in *PIR²*, L 301. For Livia in the *Fasti*, above, p. 23.

[2] Compare the dedication 'Iunoni Liviae' set up in Africa (*ILS* 120), or her honours at Assos (*IGR* IV. 249). Similarly, 'Cereri Iuliae Augustae' (*ILS* 121: Gaulus).

the summer of the year 4 was not welcome to Aemilius Paullus, the husband of Julia; and Tiberius himself missed entire satisfaction since as a preliminary Augustus constrained him to take Germanicus in adoption.

His own son Drusus was only a year younger than Germanicus, yet he was to reach the quaestorship four years later (in 11).[1] Nor was Drusus allowed a share, however modest, in the efforts and glory of the northern wars.

The evidence of Ovid is instructive. The two grandsons enter together in his apologia to the ruler as 'tui, sidus iuvenale, nepotes' (*Tr.* II. 167). But it is not easy to discover precise and individual mention of Drusus in the sequel.

In the poem which celebrates the campaign of 11, with the prospect of a triumph, the pair appears as

> et qui Caesareo iuvenes sub nomine crescunt   (*Tr.* IV. 2. 9)

with an allusion to their wives in the company of Livia, 'cumque bonis nuribus' (2. 11). That is, Agrippina and Livia Julia, the sister of Germanicus (and once the wife of Gaius Caesar). Those 'bonae nurus' appear later in an invocation of Livia with the prayer 'sic sint cum prole nepotes' (*Ex P.* II. 8. 45).

On a strict computation, the inconspicuous Claudius, the younger brother of Germanicus should belong with her 'nepotes'. After having forfeited his betrothed in 8, the daughter of Aemilius Paullus, because of the grave dereliction of her parents, Claudius may by now have acquired a wife, namely Plautia Urgulanilla.[2] But Claudius was denied public honour.

Drusus happens to be named, but only once. It is in a poem early in 13: after Germanicus, as was natural,

> nec vigor est Drusi nobilitate minor.   (*Ex P.* II. 2. 72)

And the poet goes on to acclaim the 'pia proles' of Tiberius as resembling Castor and Pollux (2. 81 ff.).

Next, the reader could detect Drusus in Ovid's Getic poem composed, in honour of Tiberius and the dynasty, in the winter of 14/15,

> esse duos iuvenes, firma adiumenta parentis.   (*Ex P.* IV. 13. 31)

---

[1] For the age of Drusus, born in 14 B.C., see G. V. Sumner, *Latomus* XXVI (1967), 413 ff.

[2] Suetonius, *Divus Claudius* 26. 1 f.: the daughter of the 'vir triumphalis' M. Plautius Silvanus (*cos.* 2 B.C.).

Finally, in a similar and imprecise context Drusus occurs in the epistle to Graecinus, written in late summer or in the autumn of 16 (IV. 9. 109 f.)

That is all. Ovid had reflected faithfully the policy of Augustus. By the same token, however, he would not be conciliating Tiberius Caesar. A father's feelings were now getting some satisfaction. In 14 (before the month of August) Drusus was designated consul for the next year.

Germanicus, therefore. The first advance was indirect, an invocation inserted in a poem addressed to somebody else—or rather to the reading public.[1] Ovid went on with that technique when writing to friends of the young prince.[2] After an interval, he took a further step. Was not Germanicus himself a master of verse, the author of the *Aratea*? Ovid reverted to his *Fasti* (which included a number of references to constellations) and equipped the work with a new preface (I. 1–26).[3] A poet shall be guide to a poet,

> si licet et fas est, vates rege vatis habenas.   (I. 25)

Ovid's revision was cursory and half-hearted. Apart from a single sporadic allusion (IV. 81 ff.), he went no further than Book I. Death is not the only explanation, or the best. He had abandoned the *Fasti* once already, a dozen years ago.[4]

. . .

VI. The latest date furnished by the *Fasti* is the German triumph of Germanicus Caesar (I. 285 f.). Voted already by the Senate at the beginning of 15, it was celebrated at last on May 26 of 17. To be sure, the obtuse ingenuity of scholars can go one better.

In the course of that year Tiberius repaired and dedicated several edifices, among them 'Iano templum quod apud forum holitorium C. Duilius struxerat'.[5] Calendars record October 18 as the day of dedication of that temple of Janus.[6] Now a passage in the *Fasti* (I. 223 f.) carries a direct allusion, so it is asserted. Therefore, given

---

[1] *Ex P.* II. 1.   [2] Ch. V.   [3] Above, p. 21.
[4] As suggested above, p. 34.   [5] *Ann.* II. 59. 1.
[6] For the detail, Platner–Ashby, *A Topographical Dictionary of Ancient Rome* (1929), 277; W. F. Otto in *RE*, Supp. III, 1183. This was the only temple of Janus at the time. It had a golden statue brought by Augustus from Egypt (Pliny, *NH* XXXVI. 28).

time for the information to percolate to Tomis, Ovid was still alive at the end of 17. He died in the course of the next year.[1]

As often, inspection of a text demolishes tralatician scholarship. The god Janus, in amicable colloquy with the poet, adverts severely on wealth and luxury,

creverunt et opes et opum furiosa cupido.   (I. 211)

The standards of the present age are plutocratic,

in pretio pretium nunc est. dat census honores,
    census amicitias. pauper ubique iacet.   (217 f.)

However, one makes concessions to the times,

nos quoque templa iuvant, quamvis antiqua probemus,
    aurea. maiestas convenit ista deo.
laudamus veteres, sed nostris utimur annis.   (223 ff.)

A delightful passage. The god corroborates the poet's modernity and dismisses, by implication, the archaic fancies and fraudulence on high show in Augustan Rome. That the 'aurea templa' approved by Janus denotes a construction of October 18, A.D. 17, precisely, what could be less plausible? The item belongs to a coherent line of discourse: it is patently not something added to the abortive second edition of the *Fasti*. Nor, for that matter, was it likely that a poet who ignored the second consulship of Germanicus (in 18) would care (or know) about a temple of Janus.

Jerome registers Ovid's death under the year 17.[2] He may be accurate, and even correct. There is no sign that Ovid reached his sixtieth birthday in the spring of the next year. Ovid died, but his close coeval, the unrelenting Tiberius, lived on for two decades.

.   .   .

Not being a senator and a consular, Ovid had no prospect of a decease (and a funeral) that might secure an entry in Roman annals. None the less, Tacitus may have been aware of Ovid and his ill fortune when coming upon a notable piece of senatorial business in the year 20. On entreaty from his brother, a nobleman (D. Silanus) was permitted to return to Rome. The paramour of the younger Julia: but, as Tiberius Caesar stated, 'not exiled under any law or by decree of the Senate'.[3]

[1] Schanz–Hosius, o.c. 41; H. J. Rose, *A Handbook of Latin Literature* (1936), 236; W. Kraus, *RE* XVIII, 1920.   [2] Jerome, *Chron.* p. 171 H.   [3] *Ann.* III. 24. 4.

IV

FORGOTTEN CAMPAIGNS

I. THE dearth of contemporary historians is a grievous impediment to the study of the wars. Further, though Cassius Dio furnishes a copious narration, with a number of campaigns not elsewhere on record, there are gaps that swallow up several vital years, and he is guilty of strange omissions. That being so, evidence from the Augustan poets acquires an abnormal value, both for detail and for context and atmosphere.

Caution is requisite in the interpretation. First (concerning the dates of individual poems), there is the danger of assuming that a poet must be eager to document an event as soon as it occurs.[1] None the less, a close date sometimes emerges if the outcome quickly contradicts expectations, as when Horace anticipated victory over the Sugambri in 16 B.C., and a triumph for Caesar Augustus.[2]

Second, disproportion resulting from the time of writing. Most of the historical references that are commonly cited belong to the first epoch of a long reign, to the two decades subsequent to the Battle of Actium. Horace finished the last book of his *Odes* in 13 B.C. The concluding poem enlarges on peace throughout the world—just before the grand scheme of conquest in central Europe unfolded.[3] To the later and abundant warfare there is next to nothing in the way of allusions anywhere, since of the extant poets only Ovid and Manilius lived on.

Third, distortion for political reasons. Members of the dynastic group engrossed attention and publicity. Tibullus, it is true, did not neglect the deeds of his patron Messalla Corvinus. But, although

---

[1] Specimens may be culled from R. G. M. Nisbet and M. Hubbard, *A Commentary on Horace: Odes Book I* (1970), xxviii ff. And doubt might be felt about *Odes* III. 2–5 being put at precise dates in 29–26 B.C., as by P. Grimal, *Rev. ét. lat.* LIII (1975), 135 ff.

[2] *Odes* IV. 2 (to Iullus Antonius), cf. below, p. 171.

[3] *Odes* IV. 15 (below, p. 171).

Marcus Lollius gets an ode,[1] no military action conducted by a general of Augustus receives commemoration from Horace.

Finally, adulation or sheer fantasy. As though the victory at Actium were not enough, Virgil at once has the young Caesar thundering in war beside the Euphrates or parading as a conqueror in furthest Asia, for the protection of Rome against a non-belligerent adversary,

> et te, maxime Caesar,
> qui nunc extremis Asiae iam victor in oris
> imbellem avertis Romanis arcibus Indum.[2]

Later, in the prophecy of Anchises, Augustus Caesar will extend the dominion of Rome 'super et Garamantas et Indos'; and when an opening of Janus is described, the ceremony portends a campaign to the ends of the world: India and the lands of dawn and the recapture of Roman standards from the Parthians.[3]

Despite the Roman and contemporary relevance of Janus, motives and language owe much to panegyrics of the world conqueror, Alexander the Macedonian.[4] And another phenomenon comes in. Far lands and the names of exotic nations became a potent appeal during the years of warfare and despotism. The escape from harsh reality sought remoteness in place or time: romantic ethnography, bucolic poetry, the legends of ancient Rome.[5]

The new dispensation soon added substance. Two Prefects of Egypt conducted distant expeditions. Aelius Gallus, crossing the Red Sea, invaded Arabia Felix, that land fabulous for wealth, but got no profit from an arduous march. In Ethiopia C. Petronius reached Napata. A remarkable feat, which was advertised by the ruler: 'usque ad oppidum Nabata perventum est, cui proxima est Meroe.' He artfully slips in Meroe, a portentous name.[6] Meroe, however, had next to no repercussion in the poetry of the time.[7]

However that may be, interest was kept up by embassies from remote peoples (including Indians) that paid homage to Augustus at

---

[1] *Odes* IV. 9 (below, p. 69).   [2] *Georg.* IV. 560 f.; II. 170 ff.

[3] *Aen.* VI. 794; VII. 605 ff.

[4] E. Norden, *Rh. Mus.* LIV (1899), 466 ff. = *Kleine Schriften* (1966), 422 ff.; and in his commentary (ed. 4, 1934) on *Aen.* VI. 791 ff.   [5] *Sallust* (1964), 193 ff.; 232 ff.

[6] *RG* 26. Meroe was 430 miles beyond Napata (Pliny, *NH* VI. 184 f.).

[7] Only in Propertius IV. 6. 77 (of 16 B.C.). The name of Meroe stands conspicuous in a splendid quatrain on death (*Anth. Pal.* x. 3).

Tarraco (in 25) and at Samos (in the winter of 21/20). Indians thus became suitably linked to Parthians in grandiose effusions foretelling conquest in the Orient.[1] Horace not only expects the Parthians or Indians to furnish a 'iustus triumphus'. He insists on dragging in a novel name, the Seres,

> sive subiectos Orientis orae
> Seras et Indos.[2]

One extremity of the world calls up the other. Hence conquest is announced there too,

> praesens divus habebitur
> Augustus adiectis Britannis
> imperio gravibusque Persis.[3]

Questions arise. Exotic names attract poets; and poets also like to appear alert to novelty and fashion. The government, at the lowest count, did not deprecate or discourage optimistic speculations. How far they reflect the policy of Caesar Augustus is another matter. Finally, attention should go to the tone and attitude of each writer. The cloud of make-believe varies in colour and density; and firm or prosaic statements may occur. Further, one poet will be eager to extol military glory, another less so.

The matter of Britain is easily disposed of, by paradox the more so in that the notion of an invasion has percolated into the pages of a sober historian. Cassius Dio reports it in three places. Already in the spring of 34 Caesar's heir, emulating his parent, set out with Britain as his destination, and he had got as far as Gaul when he turned back, prevented by rebellion among some Dalmatian tribes.[4] The alleged project, be it noted, falls in the middle of the two years of operations in Illyricum—which are a military plan, modest in design but achieving its purposes. One of them was to secure the Adriatic and the north-eastern frontier of Italy for the event of war with Marcus Antonius.

Next, in the summer of 27 Caesar Augustus departed for a British

---

[1] For Parthia and India in Propertius, below, p. 186.

[2] *Odes* I. 12. 55 f. On the Seres, Nisbet and Hubbard state that 'their conquest and that of India did not seem a wild dream to people of Horace's age'. Not quite justified by contemporary ignorance about the extent of territory eastwards from the Black Sea.

[3] *Odes* III. 5. 2 ff.   [4] Dio XLIX. 38. 2.

expedition.[1] But he spent some time in Gaul—and he reached Tarraco before the end of the year. According to Dio, he was baffled of Britain by the outbreak of rebellion in two regions. He therefore sent Terentius Varro against the Salassi, and himself dealt with the Cantabrians and the Asturians.[2]

Horace comes in providentially (so some may opine), implying a firm project in his prayer to Fortune, the goddess of Antium,

> serves iturum Caesarem in ultimos
> orbis Britannos.[3]

Which serves to date that ode: hardly later than 26 or 25.

So far rumour, predictions—and an invasion that was never intended.[4] Caesar Augustus, it is clear, left Rome in 27 with a firm design: to complete the conquest of Spain by subjugating a vast region between northern Portugal and the western Pyrenees. The two campaigns (26 and 25 B.C.) are the central episode in a ten years' war that lasted from 29 to 19 B.C.[5] After this time, Britain tends to fade from the pages of poets.[6] Britain may have recaptured some slight interest during the ruler's second sojourn in the provinces of the West (16–13 B.C.). If so, to no purpose. Legions set free from Spain now went to reinforce Illyricum and the Rhine.

Concerning Parthia, the aims and the methods of Caesar Augustus are also clear. Not war in the East but only attitudes of ostensible menace, and the perpetual advertisement of successes won through the arts of diplomacy. Britain and Parthia, the clamorous panegyrists were disappointed. But not the 'prudentes' at Rome; and the Princeps, renouncing those distant exploits, remained no less a 'praesens divus'.

However, the Augustan poets have recently come into serious and sharp debate. One thesis argues that their evidence lends support to the view that the foreign and imperial policy of Augustus was in the

[1] Dio LIII. 22. 5.   [2] Dio LIII. 25. 2.

[3] *Odes* I. 35. 29 f. Nisbet and Hubbard, however, wish to date this ode *c*. 35 B.C. (o.c. xxviii; 387).

[4] On I. 35. 30 Nisbet and Hubbard state 'the poets cannot have misinterpreted the intentions of the régime'.

[5] For this conception, scouting Britain, see *AJP* LV (1934), 293 ff.; *Legio VII Gemina* (León, 1970), 83 ff. = *RP* (1978), 825 ff.

[6] For catalogue and analysis of the passages about Britain see A. Momigliano, *JRS* XL (1950), 39 f. (discussing the *Panegyricus Messallae*).

main defensive.[1] The other sees Augustus as a world conqueror, without thought of any territorial limits to his ambitions.[2]

Both are extreme, it appears. The truth may lie, not half-way, but in a different conception or formulation.

Neither thesis seems to attach proper weight to Illyricum and the Danubian basin. Various reasons have contributed to oversight or dispraisal. In the first place, the ancient sources. In the northern campaigns of 12–9 B.C., the greater glory goes to Drusus—and much more space than for Tiberius in the narration of Cassius Dio. Not new conquests in Illyricum, but the suppression of revolts, that is the activity of Tiberius according to Dio.[3] And, in the sequel, the loss of Germany overshadows everything. Yet, it should seem, the great rebellion of A.D. 6–9 did more harm than the disaster incurred by Quinctilius Varus.

The invasions of Germany had been of subsidiary value in the Augustan plan of conquest in central Europe, at least until the design came to embrace Bohemia, culminating in the abortive campaign against Maroboduus in A.D. 6.[4] By contrast, it was necessary for Rome to win the land route from Italy to the Balkan regions and give the empire (dangerously elongated west and east) a broad territorial basis in its central zone.[5] To annexation a limit could be found, with suzerainty claimed beyond it, even if not capable of being enforced everywhere or in permanence. For example, Augustus proclaimed that he had compelled the Dacians 'to submit to the commands of the Roman people'.[6]

·　　　·　　　·

[1] H. D. Meyer, *Die Aussenpolitik des Augustus und die augusteische Dichtung* (*Kölner hist. Abh.* 5, 1961). See the review by W. Schmitthenner, *Gnomon* XXXVII (1965), 152 ff.

[2] P. A. Brunt, *JRS* LIII (1963), 170 ff. (discussing H. D. Meyer). Followed with enthusiasm by C. M. Wells, *The German Policy of Augustus* (1972), 3 ff. For criticism of the views of Wells, see H. v. Petrikovits, *Gött. gel. Anz.*, 1976, 163 ff.

[3] Dio LIV. 31. 2; 34. 3; 36. 2; LV. 2. 4. Nor does Dio name any native tribe conquered by Tiberius. The Pannonian Breuci were very important, cf. Suetonius, *Tib.* 9. 2.

[4] Policy towards Germany was 'kein festes klares und gleichbleibendes politisches Thema der augusteischen Zeit', according to D. Timpe, *Chiron* I (1971), 283.

[5] As maintained in *CAH* X (1934), 351 ff. and elsewhere (e.g. *Danubian Papers* (1971), 13 ff.). P. A. Brunt (o.c. 172) interprets 'the line Hamburg–Leipzig–Prague–Vienna' as a limit. But the passage puts the emphasis not on frontiers but on communications, o.c. 353, cf. 352; also 380: 'control of the route from the Elbe to the Danube'.

[6] *RG* 30, cf. Strabo VII, p. 305.

II. In putting emphasis on the lack of congruence between poetry and the facts, cursory attention has been given to the high and ample themes of imperial policy. Ovid may seem an anti-climax. Yet Ovid, so it happens, can supply military information about the last years of the reign.

When the Pannonians and Dalmatians rose in A.D. 6, Dacians and Sarmatians took the opportunity to cross the Danube and attack Moesia; and Caecina Severus, to repel them, had to turn back from Sirmium (which he had been able to protect from the rebels).[1] Further measures may have been taken in 9 or 10.[2] In 12, however, two towns far down the river and close to the delta succumbed to a sudden incursion but were recaptured by Roman troops. Ovid furnishes names and details.[3] That benefit accrued from his residence at Tomis. But one of the *Epistulae ex Ponto* may also have something of value to tell about the Rhine.

In a set piece written in 13 Ovid acclaimed and described the Pannonian triumph which Tiberius Caesar held on October 23 of the previous year.[4] Another poem in Book II (the second of two addressed to Cotta Maximus) expresses the hope that captive Germany may soon be led in triumph,

> sic fera quam primum pavido Germania vultu
> ante triumphantis serva feratur equos. (8. 39 f.)

Ovid invokes Livia, refers to the loss of Drusus, and utters the prayer that his brother may exhibit vengeance,

> sic tibi mature fraterni funeris ultor
> purpureus niveis filius instet equis. (8. 49 f.)

So far hopes and prayers. A poem in the next book, however, goes on to firm and fervid prediction (III. 4). It is addressed to a certain Rufinus, whose identity ought to excite curiosity.[5]

The change of tone is clear. In the interval something has happened. This poem acquires sudden importance in the light of military operations in 13 which it appears to disclose, or at least imply: not to be found in any other literary source.

---

[1] Dio LV. 29. 3.
[3] Below, pp. 81 ff. (discussing the friends of Ovid).
[4] *Ex P*. II. 1. For the date, above, p. 42.

[2] Below, p. 68.
[5] Below, p. 83.

After allusions to his own effort, namely the *Triumphus* in verse
(4. 3; 53 f.), the alert and pertinacious Ovid, undeterred by the
failure of two recent predictions (in 10 and in 11),[1] goes on to foretell
a second pageant, this time for victory in Germany,

> altera enim de te, Rhene, triumphus adest,
> inrita votorum non sunt praesagia vatum.   (4. 88 f.)

Ovid to be sure asserts that his prophecy proceeds from divine
inspiration,

> haec duce praedico vaticinorque deo.   (4. 94)

None the less, he is emboldened to invoke Livia by name and predict
a triumph with confidence. It is coming soon,

> quid cessas currum pompamque parare triumphis
>   Livia? dant nullas iam tibi bella moras.
> perfida damnatas Germania proicit hastas:
>   iam pondus dices omen habere meum.
> crede, brevique fides aderit: geminabit honorem
>   filius, et iunctis, ut prius, ibit equis.   (4. 95 ff.)

Optimism again, one may opine, and leave it at that. Or is there a
retarded reference to the campaign of 11 (the imperatorial salutation
of which had not so far been crowned by a German triumph)?[2] Yet
the language implies news of a recent victory and a war now ostensibly
terminated. The poem was written in the year 13, it is clear:
after the Pannonian triumph of the previous October (perhaps after
many months), and after Ovid's own *Triumphus*, which has now
reached the metropolitan reader (4. 53 f.). The natural inference
from the letter to Rufinus is a fresh German campaign in 13, although
none such is on attestation.

.   .   .

III. Where is evidence to be sought? A digression cannot be
avoided, which may lead into devious paths. According to Tacitus,
the German war had gone on, although not from desire of conquest
or to any great advantage.[3] That statement is no bar, and in any case,

---

[1] *Tristia* III. 12. 47 f.; IV. 2. 1 f.

[2] Velleius affirms that Tiberius ought to have celebrated a triumph (II. 122. 2).

[3] *Ann.* I. 3. 6: 'bellum ea tempestate nullum nisi adversus Germanos supererat, abolendae
magis infamiae ob amissum cum Quinctilio Varo exercitum quam cupidine proferendi
imperii aut dignum ob praemium.'

eager to make a start with the demise of Augustus, this historian, as is elsewhere all too clear, had not given enough study to the concluding epoch of the reign.[1]

Velleius was also hastening towards that climax. He has little to relate subsequent to the Pannonian triumph, apart from a brief reference to Germanicus, whom Augustus had sent to Germany, 'reliqua belli patraturum'.[2] That was in 13, the prince having spent the whole of the previous year at Rome as consul. Suetonius, pressing forward likewise, furnishes some facts: not many, however.[3]

Nor is there any warfare on record in Cassius Dio under that year. His narration needs to be carefully scrutinized. From the disaster of Quinctilius Varus to the death of Augustus it is meagre and compressed, even when two gaps in the manuscript are allowed for.

The first interruption occurs before the year 9 has terminated. It has engulfed the consuls of 10, with only one transaction preserved, as the last item in the year before the consuls of 11 are registered: namely the shrine of Concordia dedicated by Tiberius Caesar (LVI. 25. 1). The ceremony in fact took place at the beginning of the year (on January 16).[4]

The next two years are entire, but disclose only one campaign anywhere. In 11 Tiberius Caesar, accompanied by Germanicus, crossed the Rhine, but did not advance far into Germany. They fought no battle, they subjugated no tribe; and, after there celebrating the birthday of Augustus (September 23), they returned (25. 2 f.).

The space allocated to this year is narrow indeed (25. 1–8). The record of the next is also curt, and very peculiar. The consul Germanicus Caesar captures attention, naturally enough, not that his actions had any value or significance, so the author avows (26. 1).

However, Dio can even report minor particulars, such as the *Ludi Martiales*, held this time in the Forum of Augustus; and he notes a portico dedicated to the memory of the princes Gaius and Lucius (27. 5).

No word or hint however of the Pannonian triumph of Tiberius Caesar, held in October of this year, with emphatic pageantry. Which should stand, by the way, as a warning about the perils of

[1] Below, p. 197. [2] Velleius II. 123. 1. [3] Suetonius, *Tib.* 21. 1.
[4] Above, p. 29.

arguments from silence—or from the testimony of a historian writing two centuries later.

The second gap in Dio is crucial, and exacerbating. The narration breaks off in the summer of 13 (28. 6): an epitomator has an anecdote about the ruler's birthday in September.[1] The text does not resume until the chronicle of omens foretelling the death of Augustus (29. 4).

The gap extends from the summer of 13 to the summer of 14. Which transactions have been lost? Other sources help.

At the beginning of the year 13 Dio reported actions of state. The powers of Caesar Augustus were renewed for a further decennium, and Tiberius Caesar was given *tribunicia potestas* (28. 1). That being so, the historian, whose interest in constitutional matters is patent, and sometimes excessive, ought not to have missed the grant of an *imperium* over provinces and armies equal and equipollent to that of Caesar Augustus. Velleius and Suetonius attest.[2]

Further, the joint census they held, 'consulari cum imperio', as registered in the *Res Gestae*.[3] The *lustrum* was terminated about May 11, A.D. 14, so it appears.[4] In the course of the late summer Tiberius set out for Illyricum. That was noted, for a later passage in Dio speaks of his still being in Dalmatia (31. 1, not in fact accurate).[5]

Finally, and beyond any doubt, the despatch of Germanicus Caesar to the Rhine in 13, which is presupposed later on in the narrative. Military operations may also have fallen out, modest to be sure, but magnified. Nothing in the extant sources precludes.

·   ·   ·

IV. On the standard view, Germanicus went out without having been invested with *imperium proconsulare*. There stood the explicit and prepotent testimony of Cornelius Tacitus. Tiberius Caesar in the Senate made request for that grant: for Germanicus, but not for Drusus, who was present and consul designate for the next year.[6] That item of senatorial business occurred at the session of September

---

[1] Dio LVI. 29. 1 (from Xiphilinus).
[2] Velleius II. 121. 1; Suetonius, *Tib.* 21. 1.   [3] *RG* 8.
[4] For the date, Mommsen, *Res Gestae Divi Augusti*[2] (1883), 1 f.
[5] As shown by Tacitus, 'vixdum Illyricum ingressus' (*Ann.* I. 5. 3); and by Suetonius, 'statim ex itinere revocatus' (*Tib.* 21. 1).
[6] *Ann.* I. 14. 3.

17, A.D. 14, after the position of the new ruler had been recognized or confirmed. And it seemed appropriate and logical.[1]

On the showing of Tacitus, therefore, the first grant of that *imperium*, not a renewal.[2] Reflection should have insinuated some dubitations. A relevant factor of status and authority was neglected. Having to supervise two consular legates, each in charge of an army of four legions, Germanicus Caesar required a superior title and authority. That was visibly embodied in the twelve *fasces* against five for the *legatus Augusti pro praetore* (be he praetorian or consular);[3] and that *imperium* permitted an acclamation by the troops, conveying the claim to a triumph—which in the sequel might be delayed or even denied.

When C. Caesar went to the eastern lands in 1 B.C. he held the *imperium* of a proconsul.[4] Likewise Germanicus Caesar on a later occasion.[5] The provision was designed to preclude a clash of authority with Caesar's legate in command of the army in Syria, or to decide it. The princes ran into trouble, and so in turn did M. Lollius and Cn. Piso, with unhappy consequences for the government.[6]

So far the general argument in support of proconsular *imperium* for Germanicus Caesar, in and from the year 13.[7] A notorious enigma can now be approached, no longer in entire diffidence. It is the twenty-first and last acclamation of Caesar Augustus; and, parallel, the seventh of Tiberius Caesar. The twentieth had been earned by the campaign of 11.[8]

---

[1] Hence valid for an argument, as e.g. in *Tacitus* (1958), 411. That is, to show that discussion about the position of Ti. Caesar had terminated, the 'relatio consulum' being allowed to pass.

[2] If Germanicus had already held his *imperium*, he did not stand in need of a renewal—as Tiberius himself did not. No new powers were conferred on Tiberius.

[3] Therefore it would not have been necessary to specify his *imperium* as 'maius'. His competence, be it noted, covered Tres Galliae, cf. *Ann.* I. 31. 2.

[4] Dio LV. 10. 17 (from *Exc. Val.*).

[5] *Ann.* II. 43. 1, where the *imperium* is specified as superior to that of both imperial legates and proconsuls. Germanicus himself bore the title of proconsul, at least in two edicts (Hunt and Edgar, *Select Papyri* II (1934), no. 211).

[6] M. Lollius (it can be argued) while acting as 'comes et rector' of C. Caesar, was in fact governor of Syria, cf. above, p. 12.

[7] But not already in 11, as erroneously stated by Dio (LVI. 25. 2).

[8] For a table of the salutations of Augustus from 25 B.C., see T. D. Barnes, *JRS* LXIV (1974), 26. He rightly assigns XVIII to 8, XIX to 9 (ibid. 24): that is the Bellum Pannonicum (terminated by the Battle of the Bathinus) and the Bellum Delmaticum. It cannot be doubted that XX belongs to 11, although it appears conjoined with the *trib. pot.* date 9/10 on the

An occasion was not easy to discover in the years 12–14. Yet the Rhine was the only theatre of warfare. Some therefore opted for an exploit of Germanicus.[1] That touched the question of his salutations, two of which were registered before his decease.[2] Further, certain perplexities in the Tacitean account of his campaigns. A number of scholars were tempted to avoid entanglement and leave the decision in abeyance.

Accident now intervenes beneficially with the inscription of Fabricius Tuscus, an equestrian officer from Alexandria in the Troad, a Roman colony.[3] In the course of his activities (a long career), he carried out a recruitment of troops at the capital: 'trib. dilectus ingenuorum quem Romae habuit Augustus et Ti. Caesar'. That was in 6, that critical year, so it appears. Subsequently, when *praefectus equitum*, Tuscus was awarded military decorations 'a Germanico Caesare imp. bello Germanico'.

Germanicus, it follows, was exercising the prerogatives of a proconsul and had earned the title of 'imperator' before the decease of Augustus. Hence the plausible theory that the prince won a victory in 13, with a salutation for himself as well as for Augustus and Tiberius.[4]

The case seemed adequate, but a subsidiary item has been brought in. An epigram of Crinagoras acclaims a great victory of Germanicus, with masses of slain enemies.[5] The grandiloquent language embraces the Pyrenees, and the Alps that contemplate the sources of the river Rhine. Since Gaul in its wide expanse is mentioned by the poet (and nothing east of the Rhine), the recent editors suggest a Gallic insurrection quelled by the prince.[6]

---

splendid inscription from Cabo Torres in Asturias (*CIL* II. 2703). On which, cf. *Epigraphische Studien* VIII (1969), 125 ff. = *RP* (1978), 732 ff.

[1] Thus Mommsen (o.c. 17 f.), though his exposition lacks his normal clarity, and he twice refers to a salutation of Germanicus in 14. Gelzer was positive that the first acclamation of Germanicus must belong to 13 or early 14 (*RE* X, 439).

[2] *ILS* 176 ff.

[3] First published by G. E. Bean in J. M. Cook, *The Troad* (1973), 412, whence *AE* 1973, 501. See the full and excellent commentary by P. A. Brunt, *ZPE* XIII (1974), 161 ff.

[4] P. A. Brunt, o.c. 176 ff., with a table of salutations (177), and the conclusion, regarded as 'probable' (180); T. D. Barnes, o.c. 25 f.

[5] *Anth. Pal.* IX. 283.

[6] Gow and Page, *The Garland of Philip* II (1968), 234 ff. The poem is quoted, and their comments are not rejected, by T. D. Barnes, o.c. 25.

Trouble in Gaul about this time happens to be on record. But, be it noted, in the old *provincia*, Narbonensis, as well as in Gaul properly so called (that is, Tres Galliae, a sharp and patent distinction).[1] According to Velleius, there was a disturbance among the people of Vienna. It was composed by Tiberius, gently.[2] The incident, recorded by Velleius after the campaign of 11, belongs to the end of that year or early in 12.

Little support therefore from Velleius. For the rest, action against Gallic malcontents seems hardly an adequate pretext for the first salutation of Germanicus Caesar at a time when the Germans were in arms. Moreover, Κελτοί in a Greek writer can denote Germans no less than Gauls. The poem of Crinagoras (it is a better notion) celebrates victories of Germanicus in 14–16.[3]

This item was not needed. It might have been more useful to adduce the condition of Dio's text in 13/14: not as proof, but to assuage doubts.

.   .   .

V. Germanicus as 'imp. I' in 13, that helps to elucidate his campaigns as related by Tacitus—and clear up apparent obscurities about the second and last salutation. The matter throws light on an important topic: dissonance between Tiberius and Germanicus, its origin and its nature.

After dealing with the mutinies in the autumn of 14 Germanicus conducted the legions across the Rhine, on a foray against the unsuspecting Marsi. Massacre and booty, but even so no imperial salutation is registered (I. 50 f.). The news provoked various reactions in the mind of Tiberius Caesar, according to Tacitus: relief at the suppression of the mutiny, but disquiet engendered by the 'bellica gloria' of the prince. However, the Princeps reported the actions of Germanicus to the Senate, with generous praise of his 'virtus': more, in fact, than he could be held genuinely to credit (I. 52. 1).[4]

Next, the first item of the year 15 after the names of the consuls:

---

[1] For the distinction, *Tacitus* (1958), 456.

[2] Velleius II. 121. 1: 'cum res Galliarum maximae molis accensasque plebis Viennensium dissensiones coercitione magis quam poena mollisset'.

[3] Thus the judicious Cichorius, *Römische Studien* (1922), 307 f.

[4] Presumably based on the *Acta Senatus* (apart from the historian's comments).

a triumph is awarded by the Senate, 'decernitur Germanico trium-phus manente bello' (I. 55. 1). Coming where it does, the notice has caused perplexity. Though Cornelius Tacitus is duly conceded accuracy, he might have been inadvertent. That is, anticipating the result of operations conducted by Germanicus later in 15, when in fact he took an imperatorial salutation (58. 5).[1]

Recourse to a supposition of that kind now turns out to be an aberration. No triumph, it is clear, can be awarded without a saluta-tion, no salutation accepted without possession of the *imperium* of a proconsul. That axiom holds for Germanicus Caesar, as previously for the two Claudii, Tiberius and Drusus, in 12–9 B.C.[2]

Now Germanicus had previously acquired a claim, in 13, it can be affirmed.[3] But it had not then been followed by any decree awarding a triumph. That ensued at the beginning of 15 (by decision of Tiberius Caesar).

The consequence is important. It discloses the intent of Tiberius. The grant of a triumph was designed as admonition as well as honour: to elude the ambitions of the prince and deprecate the prosecution of warfare in Germany.

Germanicus was not deterred. The report of dissension among the Cherusci early in 15 gave a welcome opportunity, which could be held not to exceed his mandate. The first action was an expedition, culminating in the rescue of the chieftain Segestes, the father-in-law of Arminius (along with his daughter) from the rival faction (I. 55–8). As a result of this success, Germanicus was allowed to take an impera-torial salutation: 'nomenque imperatoris auctore Tiberio accepit' (58. 5). A second honorific admonition, it will be inferred. None the less, elaborate operations ensued in the course of the year, ending

[1] The solution of D. Timpe, *Der Triumph des Germanicus* (1968), 46, accepted by reviewers in *JRS* LIX (1969), 278; *CR* XX (1970), 348. Not an inadvertence of the historian, so he argued, but a deliberate displacement (o.c. 57).

[2] The position of Tiberius and Drusus in the years 12–9 has not always been properly estimated by scholars. See, for example, the annotation on *Ann.* I. 3. 1 ('imperatoriis nomini-bus auxit') furnished by the recent commentators, E. Koestermann (1965) and F. R. D. Goodyear (1973). The stepsons of the Princeps first received proconsular *imperium* after the campaigns of 11, to be valid for Drusus from January of the next year (Dio LIV. 33. 5; 34. 3). The general statement of Timpe was unfortunate: 'das imperium proconsulare ist für die Zählung der Akklamationen keine zwingende Voraussetzung' (o.c. 37).

[3] In 13, on the present argument. The campaign of 11 was proposed by D. Timpe, *Der Triumph des Germanicus* (1968), 37, cf. 45. That cannot be correct.

hazardously (59–71). Three consular legates were given the *orna-menta triumphalia* (72. 2), but nothing is said about the holder of the supreme command over the Rhine armies.[1]

The historian (it will be recalled) is supposed erroneous: the notice that Germanicus was voted a triumph in 15 should belong, not at the beginning of the year, but at the end, along with the decorations for the three consular legates.[2]

The notion was plausible, but not necessary, since Germanicus had already earned a salutation in 13. As for the second (and superfluous) salutation permitted by the Princeps in the course of 15, it was granted for achievements far from spectacular. None the less, the statement of Tacitus cannot be confuted. Therefore this was the second and last salutation of the prince.

Which might seem peculiar, in view of the campaign of 16, ending in a great battle at Idistaviso. As Tacitus reports, 'miles in loco proelii Tiberium imperatorem salutavit' (II. 18. 2).[3] No fresh acclamation for Germanicus, however. Tiberius now became 'imp. VIII'.[4]

The comportment of Tiberius is noteworthy. In 15 he allowed Germanicus to become 'imp. II', but he did not choose to add that salutation to his own total. After that, it may be conjectured, Germanicus received a quiet but firm intimation that he was to have no more salutations, even for a victory in the field—and in fact his triumph had already been earned in 13 and voted at the beginning of 15 (I. 55. 1).

.   .   .

VI. At the end of the year 16 Tacitus registers the dedication of a triumphal arch at Rome 'ob recepta signa cum Varo amissa ductu Germanici, auspiciis Tiberii' (II. 41. 1). The phrase is significant and valuable. It furnishes the reason or pretext for the attitude of Tiberius Caesar.

[1] Viz. Caecina Severus and P. Silius, commanders of the two armies; and L. Apronius (*suff.* 8), a legate on the staff of Germanicus.

[2] Thus D. Timpe, o.c. 46: 'probably justified' in the opinion of P. A. Brunt, o.c. 179; and accepted by R. Seager, *Tiberius* (1972), 81.

[3] Observe also that the victory dedication specified 'exercitum Tiberii Caesaris' (II. 22. 1).

[4] The historian, it follows, is correct in what he records about salutations and triumphs. For 'imp. VIII' cf. H. Gesche, *Chiron* II (1972), 339 ff.: arguing against the views of Timpe (o.c. 51).

To put the matter briefly. It depends on the relation of the *imperium* of Caesar Augustus to that held by proconsuls (and, in the sequel, to the *imperium proconsulare* of members of the dynastic group). Under the rule of the Triumvirs and in the first years of the new dispensation proconsuls had duly celebrated triumphs. None, however, after Cornelius Balbus in 19 B.C., although the proconsul may still take a salutation and add 'imp.' to his name: as did L. Passienus Rufus in Africa *c.* A.D. 2.[1]

The ruler, it is clear, had developed a doctrine: only he possessed the 'auspicia'. The formula emerges clearly for the first time in A.D. 6. A temple of Mars at Lepcis commemorated the victory won by a proconsul 'auspiciis imp. Caesaris Aug. . . . . ductu Cossi Lentuli'.[2]

The same principle, it can be argued, applied when princes had been invested with *imperium proconsulare*—but official doctrine is flexible. By a beneficent and fraudulent exception they were permitted to hold triumphs.

Therefore the war in Germany was fought 'auspiciis Tiberii Caesaris'. Further, Tiberius (it may be assumed), had already acquired the 'auspicia' along with authority over provinces and armies equal to that of Augustus, as conferred in 13. That was done (it is not rash to conclude) before the despatch of Germanicus to the Rhine.

.   .   .

VII. This excursus, evoked by a poem of Ovid (*Ex P.* III. 4), serves to illustrate the singular defects of the literary sources for the five years intervening between the disaster of Varus and the death of Caesar Augustus. And, by the same token, the hazards of argumentation. Various reasons have to be adduced to account for strange silences or omissions in Velleius and in Dio.

For dramatic effect, Velleius spread himself on Tiberius' coming to the Rhine in 10, and he thus exhausted the German matter. If Tiberius went there again in 13, that might disturb the sequence of his thought, the proportions of his emphasis. More so, the intrusion of a victory of Germanicus Caesar in that year. However it be, Velleius can omit

---

[1] *ILS* 120. The last was Junius Blaesus, the uncle of Seianus (III. 74. 4).
[2] *IRT* 301, cf. Velleius II. 116. 2; Dio LV. 28. 3 f.

things by inadvertence or displace the order of events without his normal and conscious designs of deceit. For example, he puts the enhanced *imperium* of Tiberius before the Pannonian triumph. Having already a seat in the Senate, and present at the triumph, he ought to have known.

Cassius Dio followed a source favourable to Germanicus, depreciatory of Tiberius. His silence about an action in 13 would be enigmatic—were it not for a textual hiatus in 13/14.

.   .   .

VIII. To resume. As has been shown, Germanicus' position on the Rhine in 13 required and entailed the grant of *imperium proconsulare*; and the last salutation of the ruler has to be accounted for. The venerable Princeps, whose long life never disdained publicity, would welcome laurels claimed by the grandson of his blood, however superficial the victory. Hence Germanicus 'imp. I', himself 'imp. XXI'. Tiberius, it may be conjectured, neither needed nor wanted his 'imp. VII.'

The poem dedicated to Rufinus now lends support. It hails victory and the near prospect of a triumph from Germany, Tiberius Caesar being assigned the credit.[1] Why not, even if the alleged victory in the field was won by Germanicus?

Ovid could be tactful on occasion—and he might also learn by experience. His panegyric on the Pannonian triumph was over-generous to Germanicus, and it predicted future military fame, at some length.[2] The last book of the *Epistulae ex Ponto* contains several poems written in 15 and 16. References to Germanicus' campaigns in those years are confined to a single poem, addressed to Suillius Rufus. They are slight and general.[3] There is no hint here or elsewhere of the triumph voted in 15.

Germanicus the poet has the large part.[4] Similarly in the new proem to the *Fasti* composed in 17. Nothing about warfare and glory. The appeal goes to the poet and orator.

As for Tiberius Caesar, nothing attests an absence from Rome and Italy in the course of the year 13—and nothing forbids. Only the

[1] *Ex P.* III. 4. 95 ff. (quoted above, p. 54).   [2] *Ex P.* II. 1 (cf. above, p. 41).
[3] *Ex P.* IV. 8. 73; 87 f.   [4] *Ex P.* IV. 8. 69–78.

ingenuous will discover arduous tasks in the supervision of a census. As has been shown, the written record of that year is meagre and miserable.

The dearth of precise information about his movements in 12 and 13 is indeed remarkable. At the end of the campaign of 11, after celebrating the birthday of Augustus in enemy territory, Tiberius and Germanicus returned, so Dio states, and moves on to another topic.[1] They returned to Rome, that is one interpretation.[2] Rather to their point of departure on the Roman bank of the Rhine.[3]

In that case, whereas the young prince went to Rome to assume the *fasces*, Tiberius stayed on for some months, on the Rhine and in Gaul. But not far into the year 12. According to Suetonius, he was soon back in Rome—'post biennium regressus'.[4] There are no grounds for giving Tiberius a third campaigning season in Germany in that year.[5]

Next, his occupations in 13, after the recent triumph. One hypothesis, fragile enough, takes Tiberius to Dalmatia, where a programme of road-building was in progress.[6] Better, Gaul and the Rhineland. The veteran might give suitable guidance to the young prince before leaving him in sole charge. Germanicus was now twenty-seven. Tiberius at that same age conducted an Alpine campaign, it is true. Not comparable to the responsibility residing in the command over eight legions. Tiberius might concede a token victory over non-aggressive natives, but he was anxious to prevent any resumption of the wars of conquest.

·   ·   ·

IX. At this point it will be expedient to recapitulate, even at the cost of repetition. Two heterogeneous pieces of evidence called for explanation. First, the enigmatic imperatorial salutation registered before the decease of Caesar Augustus, which cannot be assigned to any region other than Germany. Second, here adduced for the first

---

[1] Dio LVI. 25. 3: ἐπανῆλθον.

[2] Thus recently G. V. Sumner, *Harvard Studies* LXXIV (1970), 274. But he reckons A.D. 12 among the nine missions of Tiberius to Germany (*Ann.* II. 26. 3; on which cf. below, p. 65).

[3] Thus Gelzer in *RE* X, 494.

[4] Suetonius, *Tib.* 20. 1.

[5] Gelzer, however, assumed a third campaign, in 12 (*RE* X, 494). Likewise D. Timpe, o.c. 30.

[6] C. M. Wells, o.c. 240.

time, Ovid's poem of the year 13 addressed to Rufinus, and expecting in firm confidence a German triumph for Tiberius Caesar: the date is given, since the poem alludes to Ovid's *Triumphus*, written to honour the Pannonian triumph of the previous October and presumed now to be known to the reading public at Rome.[1] The poem to Rufinus may have been evoked by the news that Tiberius was on his way back to Rome.

If the two pieces of evidence are combined, alternative hypotheses offer. First, joint operations of Tiberius and Germanicus (not, to be sure, of any magnitude, and easily escaping historical record).[2] Second, an action of the ambitious young prince, carried out on his own initiative after Tiberius had departed. The latter hypothesis would comport consequences of some interest.

In the event, the campaigns on which Germanicus soon insisted, becoming elaborate, costly and hazardous, provoked in Tiberius annoyance and alarm. Tacitus furnishes the gist of several despatches he sent at the end of 16. The arguments of the Princeps were potent, and he took care to remind the prince of what experience could teach: 'se novies a divo Augusto in Germaniam missum plura consilio quam vi perfecisse. sic Sugambros in deditionem acceptos, sic Suebos regemque Maroboduum pace obstrictum'.[3]

The computation of those nine missions has not failed to engage the resources of scholarship. Five are clear (viz. 8 and 7 B.C.; A.D. 4–6). Next, though not a campaign in Germany, the rapid march of Tiberius to reach his brother before he succumbed (9 B.C.). There remained the years 10–12. Suetonius reckons his stay on the Rhine as two years: 'a Germania in urbem post biennium regressus triumphum, quem distulerat, egit.'[4] Should two campaigning years be there understood instead of three, a final and separate mission in 13 comes in very handy.

.   .   .

X. The foregoing remarks call up a campaign that had been forgotten. A useful reminder. The record of the many wars over the

---

[1] *Ex P.* III. 4. 53 f.
[2] That the poem to Rufinus has no mention of Germanicus admits of an explanation.
[3] *Ann.* II. 26. 3.
[4] Suetonius, *Tib.* 20. 1.

wide world is fragmentary. Operations not conducted (or supervised) by the ruler and his associates tend to suffer eclipse. The conquest of north-western Spain is the prime example and clear case. Caesar Augustus conducted in person the operations against the Cantabri in 26 B.C. This is the only campaign of which a record in detail survives, going back ultimately to the autobiography of the ruler.[1] The name of the Cantabri duly annexed the war (to the obscuration of the Astures); and the war was regarded as terminated at the end of the next year.[2] In fact, Janus was closed.

The subjugation of the North-West was nothing less than a ten years' war. Cassius Dio furnishes valuable testimony. He is the sole source for campaigns, with the names of generals, in 24 and 22 B.C.[3] Likewise for the operations of P. Silius Nerva (cos. 20 B.C.), which preceded and prepared the much advertised exploits of Tiberius and Drusus in the Alpine regions.[4]

Dio's summary of minor wars, recorded under 16 B.C., is very valuable. There might have been a corresponding section later on, somewhere in the decade 6 B.C.–A.D. 4 (there are three gaps in the manuscript, each of two *folia*). Reaching A.D. 6, he notes disturbances raging throughout the imperial dominions; and he proposes to confine himself to the most important actions.[5]

In Africa Cossus Cornelius Lentulus (cos. 1 B.C.) suppressed the rebellion of a large nomadic people and earned the *ornamenta triumphalia*. The Bellum Gaetulicum of this proconsul is elsewhere on attestation.[6] But no other writer reports the rising of the intractable Isaurians, in the zone of the Taurus from Cilicia north-west towards Pisidia. Of scant importance, no doubt—and long neglected by scholarly investigators in the recent time. For extraneous reasons their eager attention fastened on another operation in the same region, viz. the subjugation of the Homonadenses carried out by P. Sulpicius

---

[1] For the accounts of Florus and Orosius see *AJP* LV (1934), 302 ff.; *Legio VII Gemina* (León, 1970), 90 ff. = *RP* (1978), 833 ff.

[2] The official view is echoed by Livy XXVIII. 12. 12: 'ductu auspicioque Augusti Caesaris perdomita'.

[3] Dio LIII. 29. 1; LIV. 5. 1.

[4] Dio LIV. 20. 1, cf. D. van Berchem, *Mus. Helv.* XXV (1968), 1 ff.; F. Fischer, *Germania* LIV (1976), 147 ff.

[5] Dio LV 28. 2 ff.

[6] *IRT* 301 (Lepcis), quoted above, p. 62.

Quirinius (*cos.* 12 B.C.).[1] For the Isaurian War, a dedication at Attaleia comes into service. It reveals M. Plautius Silvanus (*cos.* 2 B.C.) as imperial legate. That is, governor, like Quirinius, of the province Galatia–Pamphylia.[2]

It is welcome and appropriate to allude in passing to the merits of Cassius Dio. Praise must be intermittent. On the notice of Isauri and Gaetuli follows a reference to campaigns conducted by Tiberius against the Germans in 5 and 6. It is curt and misleading. Not a word about the Marcomanni and their king Maroboduus, against whom was directed the elaborate operation of the second year, to crown the design of conquest in Central Europe. The invasion of Bohemia was rudely interrupted by the insurrection in Illyricum. The Greek historian was misled by his source, itself abridged. That is, the history of Aufidius Bassus, who apart from that work of history had composed a monograph. His *Bellum Germanicum* covered the campaigns from 4 to 16, so it may be argued.[3]

Preoccupation with Germany in ancient and in modern writers has detrimental consequences. It obscures the history of a vast area, the Danubian and Balkan lands. The dearth of evidence is especially deplorable for the aftermath of the conquest of Illyricum (Tiberius' campaigns in 12–9 B.C.) and the pacification of Thrace by L. Piso the Pontifex (12–10 B.C.). On those considerable actions a lull ensued. Veterans were dismissed from the legions, and Janus was closed (presumably in 8 or 7). However, operations resumed. The great march of Domitius Ahenobarbus (*cos.* 16 B.C.) is on record, from the Danube to the Elbe, shortly before A.D. 1.[4] And Cn. Cornelius Lentulus (*cos.* 14 B.C.) has to be fitted in somewhere, also M. Vinicius (*suff.* 19 B.C.).[5] The evidence is seen to be partial, in both senses of the

[1] Strabo XII, p. 569; Tacitus, *Ann.* III. 48. 1 (the obituary notice). The war probably belongs *c.* 4 B.C., cf. now B. Levick, *Roman Colonies in Southern Asia Minor* (1967), 203 ff.

On the supposition that Quirinius waged the war as governor of Syria, some scholars fancied that they had found a date for the Nativity. That is a governorship (and, to be sure, a census) earlier than, and distinct from, the position and actions of Quirinus in A.D. 6, when Judaea was annexed (Josephus, *AJ* XVIII. 1).

[2] *SEG* VI. 646. For the Isaurian War, *JRS* XXIII (1933), 27; *Klio* XXVII (1934), 139 ff.

[3] Cf. *Tacitus* (1958), 274 f.; 697. Dio (it appears) was going to furnish a brief summary of Germanicus' campaigns when he registered his triumph in 17. The text breaks off before that point.   [4] *Ann.* IV. 44. 2; Dio LV. 10a. 2.

[5] *Ann.* IV. 44. 2; Florus II. 28 f. (Lentulus); *ILS* 8965 (Vinicius). See now *Danubian Papers* (1971), 69 ff.; 36 ff.

term, when the Roman panegyrist is assessed as well as the Greek historian. Velleius omitted victories won by the rivals of Claudius Nero during the decade of his eclipse.[1]

Not long after Piso's war in Thrace, and probably in direct sequence, the legions of Macedonia were taken from the proconsul and put in charge of an imperial legate. The first legate of Moesia (as it was subsequently called) is therefore Cn. Lentulus: on record for operations against Getae and Sarmatians. Hence not a legate in Illyricum, though he has sometimes been supposed such.[2] According to Tacitus he earned 'triumphalia de Getis'.[3]

Next on record 'in Thracia Macedoniaque' are P. Vinicius (cos. 2) and P. Silius Nerva (suff. 3) from about 4 B.C. to A.D. 1.[4] They are praetorian in rank, no doubt because a legion had been removed to supplement the armies in the East. However, the legion came back. In 6 and 7 the consular Caecina Severus is attested as legate of Moesia (suff. 1 B.C.); and in 11 or 12 Poppaeus Sabinus (cos. 9) took up the command.[5] Another consular legate might fall in between, for a brief command, if the experienced Caecina Severus was called away at once by the emergency on the Rhine (where he is first discovered in 14). After the rebellion in Illyricum was quelled it would be expedient to punish invaders from across the Danube and adopt measures for further security—which, however, could not be effective far down the river.[6] The Romans had been very lucky. The army of Moesia could be used against the Pannonians. A serious rebellion in Thrace did not supervene until twenty years had elapsed.

[1] The only campaign he notices is that of M. Vinicius in Germany (A.D. 2–4), the grandfather of his patron (II. 104. 2).

[2] As in CAH X (1934), 367. The reconstruction there adopted should now be questioned or rejected, cf. Rom. Rev. (1939), 401; Danubian Papers (1971), 69 ff.

[3] Ann. IV. 44. 1. Therefore Moesia, in succession to L. Piso. It is a strange fact that his operations are not recorded by Dio.

[4] Velleius II. 101. 3. For Vinicius, cf. IGR I. 654 (Callatis), as corrected in AE 1960, 378. The passage in Velleius was unfortunately missed by A. Stein, Die Legaten von Moesien (1940), 13. For their position, not proconsuls of Macedonia but imperial legates, see JRS XXXV (1945), 109 f.; Danubian Papers (1971), 68 f.

[5] For Caecina, above, p. 53. Further, he and Plautius Silvanus fought a battle near Sirmium in 7 (Velleius II. 112. 4 ff.; Dio LV. 32. 3). They had five legions: that is, three belonging to the Balkan command, two brought by Silvanus from Galatia–Pamphylia. For Poppaeus Sabinus, Ann. VI. 39. 3.

[6] Compare the action of Lentulus (Florus II. 28): to be placed in the sequel to Piso's war in Thrace.

Sex. Aelius Catus (*cos.* 4) comes into the account, whom no writer registers in any capacity, apart from Strabo: Catus had recently taken fifty thousand Getae across the Danube and settled them in Moesia.[1] Strabo offers precious items of instruction for the history of the times, notably concerning kingdoms and provinces in the eastern lands. The only Roman general operating on Rhine or Danube noted by the geographer happens to be Aelius Catus. A fact which might inspire speculation.[2]

Once again, the fragmentary nature of the evidence must be brought out in sharp relief. Prose narratives being absent or defective, recourse is had to the poets, and the same passages from Horace tend to be cited or quoted, the obvious and familiar not always (it appears) engendering tedium. Horace reflects a number of the campaigns. It cannot be said that he furnishes information not elsewhere available, or serves to modify any dates. Nor does he choose to celebrate any victory won by a general of Augustus.[3] His ode to the address of Marcus Lollius discloses a man of noble character, despising money: to be remembered not as consul of a year but as long as justice and integrity endure.[4]

By surprise, the elegiac poet (normally averse from public transactions) happens at the end to have something to tell about warfare on the lower reaches of the Danube. Three of the poems deal with it.[5] Poppaeus Sabinus, however, receives no missive, or any mention. Pomponius Flaccus was in charge, a praetorian legate under Poppaeus. The poet's vivid account of these events is instructive, for a variety of reasons.

.   .   .

[1] Strabo VII, p. 303. The date is a problem: no indication in *PIR*[2], A 157. He was either praetorian legate shortly before A.D. 4 (cf. *Rom. Rev.* (1939), 401), or consular, that is 9 to 11 or 12. See *Danubian Papers* (1971), 69. No trace of Catus happens to be on clear record subsequent to his consulship.

[2] He was one of the Aelii Tuberones, of old plebeian nobility. For their link with Aelius Seianus see G. V. Sumner, *Phoenix* XIX (1965), 134 ff. Also below, p. 102.

[3] To be sure, Horace has 'Cantaber Agrippae, Claudi virtute Neronis/Armenius cecidit' (*Epp.* I. 12. 36 f.). There was no warfare in Armenia, but the other item may be useful. Agrippa's operations in Spain, terminating the conquest, are narrated by Dio under 19 B.C.: the book of Horace was published the year before, cf. 20. 27 f.

[4] Horace, *Odes* IV. 9.

[5] *Ex P.* I. 8; IV. 7 and 9. Below, p. 81.

The names of generals have a value far transcending mere operations in the field (sometimes trivial, or the routine duties of a governor in a turbulent territory). They can be put to good employ, they form a bridge, leading towards political and social history. Of the benefits of this approach, a number of studies in the recent age can stand as testimony. They throw light on the needs and vicissitudes of government at different times in the long reign of Caesar Augustus.

First, the men whom Caesar can use and trust. In the present pages, Lollius and Quirinius exemplify, men of no family, but earning promotion, or enforcing it. Experience counted, but bare competence might suffice, as witness Poppaeus Sabinus, appointed to Moesia soon after his consulship and kept there until the end of his days twenty-four years later. In the verdict of the percipient historian, 'par negotiis neque supra'.[1]

Before all, loyal devotion: 'pietas' towards Princeps and dynasty. Exhibitions of that virtue were not disdained by the highest in the land.

Second, rank and family. The *nobilitas* being now renascent in the renovated Republic of Caesar Augustus, it was a season when high aristocrats can still acquire the command of armies: a Piso, a Lentulus, a son of Messalla Corvinus, quite apart from others who were linked in some way to the dynasty, such as Domitius Ahenobarbus and Fabius Maximus. In the course of time, the prestige of birth yields to safe and steady merit. And Tiberius Caesar, a proud and arrogant aristocrat, but hostile to many of his own order (especially the smooth and subservient), lends encouragement to *novi homines*.

.   .   .

The letters from Pontus display a wide parade of persons, ranging from aristocrats of eminence (few of them, and select) to some minor senators, then poets, professors, and librarians: the latter on the margin of society, but not so regarded by Ovidius Naso. A friend of long date, Pomponius Graecinus (the brother of Flaccus), illustrates a rising family from municipal Italy. Along with predictable nonentities among the correspondents occur persons of eager talent and

[1] *Ann.* VI. 39. 3.

subsequent notoriety, such as Suillius Rufus, a power for evil under the successors of Tiberius, and the eloquent Junius Gallio, who took in adoption a son of Annaeus Seneca, the *rhetor* from Corduba. Furthermore, a new character: substance and shape may accrue to a certain Rufinus, who so far has eluded the ambit of erudite enquiry.

V

THE FRIENDS OF OVID

I. THREE poems in *Amores* carry the names of friends.[1] First, a certain Atticus. He receives 'Militat omnis amans' (1. 9), and later two pieces from Tomis (*Ex P.* II. 4; 7). Something emerges from the first. Atticus was a 'vetus sodalis' (4. 33), his critical judgement was brought to bear on Ovid's writing (13 f.), and they had travelled together (20).

It is sometimes assumed without question that Ovid's friend can be identified: he is the Curtius Atticus twice mentioned by Tacitus. A Roman knight of high station ('ex inlustribus'), he went with Tiberius Caesar to Capri—and was subsequently brought to ruin through machinations of Seianus.[2] Identity is far from certain. Brief attention should go to a Narbonensian family of early distinction, the Julii Attici. They produced a procurator and an author who wrote on viticulture, not without literary pretensions.[3]

Or again, an Antonius Atticus among the Augustan *rhetores*.[4] An origin from Narbonensis is not implausible. That province shows a fairly large number of Antonii (although, for source of the name, no Antonius holder of *imperium* can be certified under the Republic).[5]

---

[1] For Ovid's friends, notably those in the poems from exile, see G. Graeber, *Quaestiones Ovidianae* I (Elberfeld, 1881); S. G. Owen in his edition of *Tristia* I (1889, edn. 3, 1902), xxvii ff. There were also dissertations published in 1881 and 1883. Since that active decade the topic has lacked adequate treatment.

[2] *Ann.* IV. 58. 1; VI. 10. 2. Identity is assumed by E. Koestermann in his commentary (1963); R. Seager, *Tiberius* (1972), 203. No such suggestion, however, in *PIR*[2], A 1333; C 1609.

[3] *PIR*[2], J 186; 183. The former, M. Iulius C. f. Atticus, was 'proc. provinc. duarum' (*CIL* XII. 1854: Vienna), that is of Lugdunensis and Aquitania. The two volumes of the latter were 'composita facetius eruditiusque' (Columella I. 1. 4). His more famous disciple, L. Julius Graecinus of Forum Julii, was the son and son-in-law of imperial procurators (Tacitus, *Agr.* 4. 1).

[4] Seneca, *Suas.* II. 16 (not of any repute).

[5] For statistics, *Tacitus* (1958), 783. Like 'Atticus', the *nomen* 'Attius' is frequent in Narbonensis.

Next, Macer, recipient of the important letter which registers several of Ovid's writings (II. 18), to be assigned on the better showing to the second edition.[1] Macer recurs in Book II of *Ex Ponto*. Theirs was a close connection. Macer had been an intimate friend in the old days, and he was related to Ovid's wife (10. 10). In Macer's company and guidance they had once made a tour together, visiting both Asia and Sicily (10. 21 ff.). Finally, Macer wrote epic poetry, continuing the tale of Troy (10. 13 f., cf. IV. 16. 6).

Identity is clear. He is none other than Pompeius Macer, the son of Theophanes of Mytilene, who was the famous friend, agent, and historian of Pompeius Magnus. According to Strabo, Augustus made him procurator of Asia, 'and he now holds rank among the foremost friends of Tiberius.'[2] Further, Suetonius states that Augustus put him in charge of the libraries at Rome.[3] Finally, two poems in the *Greek Anthology* belong to Pompeius Macer.[4]

Most scholars believe that the procurator of Asia was a fairly close coeval of Ovid and of Tiberius Caesar.[5] Nor was there any difficulty in recognizing as his son Q. Pompeius Macer, praetor in A.D. 15.[6] Another piece of evidence about the family produces a dilemma. Narrating under the year 33 the catastrophe that overtook the descendants of Theophanes, Tacitus registers an 'inlustris eques Romanus', his daughter, and his son, a senator of praetorian rank.[7] So far so good. But Tacitus also states that Theophanes was the great-grandfather of the 'praetorius' and his sister.

The standard view accepts Tacitus.[8] That entails interpolating one more generation and a second Roman knight of consequence between Theophanes and the praetor of 15. Not all that easy. Indeed not possible, if one holds Pompeius Macer born about 43 B.C.: his son, the praetor of A.D. 15, cannot have been born later than 16 B.C. Not everybody is ready to acquiesce in the simple solution that the historian, for all his attention to ancestors, made a mistake concerning

[1] Above, p. 7.
[2] Strabo XIII, p. 618, where some have altered υἱόν to υἱωνόν. Not a good idea.
[3] Suetonius, *Divus Iulius* 56. 7.
[4] *Anth. Pal.* VII. 219; IX. 28. The subjects are the courtesan Lais and the fate of Mycenae.
[5] R. Laqueur, *RE* VA, 2099; R. Hanslik, XXI. 2276.
[6] *Ann.* I. 72. 3, cf. *ILS* 9349 (Q. Pompeius Macer).   [7] *Ann.* VI. 18. 2.
[8] *PIR*[1], P 472 f., and most scholars in the sequel. For example, Gow and Page, *The Garland of Philip* II (1968), 468 (on the Greek poems).

a period that had become remote.[1] It is no bar that his own time witnessed a consul from that family now resurgent, M. Pompeius Macrinus Theophanes (*suff.* 115).[2]

Third, Graecinus, who denied that a man could be in love with two women at the same time (*Am.* II. 10. 1). This is C. Pomponius Graecinus (*suff.* 16), brother of L. Pomponius Flaccus (*cos.* 17).[3] Graecinus now receives three pieces (*Ex P.* I. 6; II. 6; IV. 9). In the second he is described as a 'sodalis' (6. 5), and he has brothers (6. 16). The third is long (134 lines), and variously instructive, anticipating both Graecinus' consulship (IV. 9. 5) and that of his brother (9. 59 ff.). It also carries details about a military exploit of Flaccus on the Danube (9. 75 ff.), and his official position (9. 119).[4]

Pomponius Flaccus, the first *novus homo* to be *ordinarius* since Poppaeus Sabinus, came to the consulate through 'militaris industria'. He possessed other qualities. Velleius singles out his modesty and his 'simplex virtus'. Flaccus ended as governor of Syria, having enjoyed the friendship as well as the confidence of Tiberius Caesar. Along with L. Piso (*cos.* 15 B.C.) he drank a whole night through, and Tiberius cherished them both as 'iucundissimos et omnium horarum amicos'.[5]

As for Pomponius Graecinus, the exordium of the first poem carries open indications that have been ignored by students of history and literature. Graecinus is devoted to liberal studies, 'artes ingenuae', but there is something else,

> nec quisquam meliore fide complectitur illas,
> qua sinit officium militiaeque labor. (I. 6. 9 f.)

---

[1] For this solution, *Tacitus* (1958), 748 f. Accepted by G. W. Bowersock, *JRS* LI (1961), 116 f.; *Augustus and the Greek World* (1965), 41.

[2] For his consulate, previously assumed *c.* 101, see G. Barbieri, *Riv. stor. it.* LXVI (1954), 419; *MEFR* LXXII (1970), 263 ff.; R. Syme, *Historia* XIV (1965), 348 f. = *Danubian Papers* (1971), 231 f.

[3] W. Eck, *RE* Supp. XIV (1974), 439 f. (Flaccus); 440 f. (Graecinus): both omitted previously. The youth of senatorial family C. Pomponius Graecinus (*CIL* XI. 5809: Iguvium) may be a son of the *suffectus* of 16: the formulation of the inscription makes it unlikely that he lived to enter the Senate. There was a third brother (*Ex P.* II. 6. 16): perhaps Pomponius Labeo, praetorian legate in Moesia under Poppaeus Sabinus (*Ann.* IV. 47. 1; VI. 29. 1). No link is known, or has been surmised, with the next consular Pomponii, viz. Q. Pomponius Secundus (*suff.* 41) and his brother Publius (*suff.* 44), the famous dramatist.

[4] Below, p. 83 (praetorian legate in Moesia).

[5] Velleius II. 129. 1: 'nati ad omnia quae recte facienda sunt simplicique virtute merentis semper, numquam captantis gloriam'; Suetonius, *Tib.* 42. 1 (the drinking bout). Appointed governor of Syria in 32, Flaccus died soon after (*Ann.* VI. 27. 2 f.).

That is to say, warfare. Furthermore, at the time of Ovid's disaster he was absent from Rome, 'nam te diversa tenebat/terra' (6. 1 f.).[1] Graecinus was therefore in one of the military zones. Perhaps in Illyricum, serving as a *legatus* under Tiberius (though Ovid nowhere brings him into relation with the Pannonian triumph).

A *novus homo*, Graecinus is not likely to accede to the *fasces* before the age of forty-two—and he may have been half a dozen years older.[2] Precision is not to be had. Still, it may be worth pointing out that if Graecinus became consul at forty-two, his year of birth would be 28 B.C. Hence *Am.* II. 10 could not belong to the first edition. Neither does II. 18 (to Macer), as is argued on other grounds. There remains I. 9 (to Atticus). There is a chance that no poem in this first edition was equipped with a name. That is to say, the only contemporary person in it was 'Corinna', if she be a person.

Only one other friend gets an entry in the *Amores*. It is Sabinus (in the poem to Macer), returned from distant lands and bringing with him a harvest of poetry, namely responses to the *Heroides* (II. 18. 27 ff.). As emerges later, he did not live long (*Ex P.* IV. 16. 16). The *cognomen* 'Sabinus' is too common to lead anywhere.[3]

. . .

These friends are 'sodales', congenial spirits brought together by a community of tastes and temperament, to form a kind of confraternity. Thus Ovid in the autobiographical piece that rounds off Book IV of his *Tristia* speaks of Propertius,

iure sodalicio quo mihi iunctus erat.   (10. 46)

There follow the names of the poets Ponticus and Bassus, who

dulcia convictus membra fuere mei.   (10. 48)[4]

These two, it will be added, occur in the first book of Propertius.[5]

---

[1] These inferences from Ovid are not drawn by W. Eck, *RE* Supp. XIV, 440 f.

[2] Presumably the elder of the two, without such high favour and merits as Flaccus. However, Graecinus became a *frater arvalis* in 21 (*CIL* VI. 2023).

[3] Three Augustan *rhetores* have that cognomen: Asilius, or rather Asellius (*PIR*[2], A 1213); Clodius (C 1184); Gavius (G 109).

[4] For 'convictus', *Tr.* I. 8. 29; *Ex P.* IV. 3. 15; for 'convictor', *Ex P.* IV. 3. 15 (first in Cicero, once (*Ad fam.* XVI. 21. 5), then in Horace, *Sat.* I. 4. 96; 6. 47).

[5] Below, p. 98.

On the whole 'sodales' belong to the same generation and social milieu. But not always. Ovid was able to claim young Cotta Maximus as a 'sodalis' (*Tr.* IV. 5. 1).

The *Amores* enlist no persons of high rank as patrons or protectors. If Pomponius Graecinus was already a senator when addressed in *Am.* II. 10, nobody would have seen him as a potential consul.

It is therefore something of a surprise when the 'magna nomina' emerge in Ovid's poems many years later. Messalla Corvinus, it is asserted with palpable truth, had encouraged the youthful Ovid; and he had entrance into the great mansion well before the birth of the younger son (about 14 B.C.). Further, Ovid composed a wedding song for Paullus Fabius Maximus (*Ex P.* I. 2. 131 f.).

. . .

II. The letters in the *Tristia* eschew names, ostensibly to avoid embarrassment. The writer operated 'positis pro nomine signis', as he declares at the outset (I. 5. 7), and he kept up the convention or pretext until the end of the series. Despite the absence of the names, there is no concealment in the epistles to the sons of Corvinus: to Messallinus (IV. 4), and to Cotta Maximus (IV. 5; V. 9).

Otherwise the 'signa' are not clear for posterity. One individual can perhaps be discerned in three poems. He is one of Ovid's 'sodales', he wears a ring on his finger with the image of the poet (I. 7. 6 ff.). Further, he receives a manuscript of the *Metamorphoses* (7. 11 ff.): he is instructed to prefix the edition, if he so wishes, with six verses (7. 35 ff.). That is to say, not only a friend but an editor and publisher. The edition emerges again (III. 14. 15 ff.); and this poem opened with

> cultor et antistes doctorum sancte virorum,
> quid facis ingenio semper amice meo?

Finally, this man receives the last book of the *Tristia*, to be added to the four preceding,

> hunc quoque de Getico, nostri studiose, libellum.   (V. 1. 1)

Perhaps Ovid's friend Brutus, who was charged with *Ex Ponto* I–III.[1] Perhaps somebody else.

---

[1] Below, p. 80.

For the rest, erudite ingenuity or fancy has free scope.[1] Five items may engage a mild interest on sundry counts.

I. 5: a dear friend who stands in the front rank of Ovid's 'sodales', who was the first to console and fortify the poet when the blow fell.

II. 9: a younger man, of promise as an orator (9. 48; 57).

III. 5: not a close friend, but he came to Ovid after the calamity (5. 5 ff.) and defended his cause later on (5. 17 f.).

III. 6: a 'sodalis' of long date, 'nobis usu iunctissime longo' (6. 19). His loyalty and candour are known to Augustus, 'cognita sunt ipsi, quem colis, ista viro' (6. 8). Therefore a person of high station.

V. 2: this friend is incited to make a bold approach to Caesar, 'quid dubitas et tuta times? accede rogaque' (2. 37). The poem has a second part (2. 45–78), introduced by a direct appeal to the ruler: 'alloquor en absens absentia numina supplex' (2. 45). Therefore likewise a man of rank.

.   .   .

III. With the year 12, Ovid becomes more alert and confident. Books I–III of *Ex Ponto* were written, so it appears, before the autumn of 13, and then published as a unit. The correspondents now have names, eight of them in Book I. Five fresh names emerge in Book II, none in Book III. Book IV, however, with poems extending from summer 13 to summer 16, offers eight new characters.

In all, twenty-one persons, along with three left to be divined:

III. 6: addressed as a 'sodalis', and 'longo mihi proximus usu' (6. 53). The poem refers to the 'Ara Iustitiae Augusti' (25 f.)[2]

III. 7: indistinctive, and perhaps held over from *Tristia*.

IV. 3: reproaches to an old friend, 'vetusta / paene puer puero iunctus amicitia' (3. 11 f.). They had once been very close, 'ille ego convictor densoque domesticus usu' (3. 15). He is denounced as 'perfide' (3. 17).

The names and persons afford various instruction. It may be helpful to classify them. First of all, by order of their emergence.

---

[1] For conjectures, mainly deriving from predecessors, see A. L. Wheeler (Loeb, 1924), xiv f.; J. André (Budé, 1968), xxxii. The latter scholar assigns *Tr.* III. 6 (and perhaps V. 4) to Atticus; I. 5 and V. 9 to Celsus (here held identical with A. Cornelius Celsus); III. 14 (and perhaps I. 7) to Julius Hyginus (who gets no letter in *Ex Ponto*).

[2] Above, p. 41.

A. Brutus I. 1; III. 9; IV. 6.
   Fabius Maximus I. 2; III. 3.
   Rufinus I. 3; III. 4.
   Cotta Maximus I. 5, 9; II. 3, 8; III. 2, 5, 8.
   Graecinus I. 6; II. 6; IV. 9.
   Messallinus I. 7; II. 2.
   Severus I. 8.
   Flaccus I. 10.

B. Atticus II. 4, 7.
   Salanus II. 5.
   Cotys II. 9.
   Macer II. 10.
   Rufus II. 11.

C. Sex. Pompeius IV. 1, 4, 5, 15.
   Severus IV. 2.
   Vestalis IV. 7.
   Suillius IV. 8.
   Albinovanus Pedo IV. 10.
   Gallio IV. 11.
   Tuticanus IV. 12, 14.
   Carus IV. 13.

At the outset, two phenomena excite attention. First, the eight names selected for Book I, two of them at first sight enigmatic, viz. Rufinus and Severus. Second, the eight that come in with Book IV, reflecting a change of approach on the part of the poet.

Next, it will be convenient to segregate three high aristocrats, Paullus Fabius Maximus and the sons of Messalla Corvinus.[1] And Sex. Pompeius deserves for various reasons a separate rubric.[2] That leaves seventeen names. They may be classified under four heads, viz. relatives; friends from the old days; miscellaneous; friends of Germanicus Caesar.

. . .

IV. Relatives. The uncle of Ovid's wife gets an epistle, concluding the second book. He is named and acclaimed in the last line as

maxima Fundani gloria, Rufe, soli. (II. 11. 28)

[1] Ch. VII and Ch. VIII.   [2] Ch. IX.

This Rufus, by the way, is the only correspondent to be assigned an 'origo'. Now a man called L. Tampius Rufus occurs in the inscription of L. Tampius Flavianus (consul suffect for the second time in 76) discovered at Fundi.[1] Attention was duly drawn to that fact long ago.[2] It does not lead anywhere. 'Rufus' is among the six most common *cognomina*. It is no surprise to find a Rufus along with Proculus, Sabinus, and Severus in Ovid's list of poets (IV. 16). Nor is it clear that Fundi can stand as the *patria* of the senatorial Tampii.[3]

A municipal worthy can rise to a peak of renown in his own city either as a 'senator populi Romani' or as a man of letters.[4] A Rufus occurring in Ovid's catalogue was a poet in the Pindaric manner (IV. 16. 28). So was a certain Titius, on the staff of Tiberius in 20 B.C.[5] Some equate them.[6] Who can tell? It might be more attractive to raise the 'maxima gloria' of Fundi a little higher and confer it upon a senator and consul. There is that remarkable *novus homo* L. Passienus Rufus (*cos.* 4 B.C.) whose father was reckoned among the foremost speakers of the early Augustan epoch, in the vicinity of Messalla and Pollio.[7] For his *patria*, however, various reasons rule out Fundi, including the shape of his name.[8] But there is nothing against the orator C. Vibius Rufus (*suff.* 16), even though the common *cognomen* discourages.[9] And Vibii can occur anywhere.

Next, 'studiis exculte Suilli' (IV. 8. 1). This is P. Suillius Rufus (*suff. c.* 43), already (in 15 or 16) showing promise as an orator. It emerges that he has married the daughter of Ovid's wife (8. 11 f.; 90). But that is not the main reason for the letter. Suillius was a devoted adherent of Germanicus Caesar (8. 22 f.), and he belongs to that rubric.

· · ·

[1] *ILS* 985. For the second consulship see now *AE* 1968, 7.

[2] *PIR*[1], T 6.

[3] Flavianus might have had a villa there: he was one of the 'divites senes' (Tacitus, *Hist.* II. 86. 3). For numerous Tampii of early date at Praeneste, F. Münzer, *RE* IVA, 2149. But observe also *ILS* 2992 = *ILLRP* 195 (Aquileia).

[4] Cf. below, p. 96.

[5] Horace, *Epp.* I. 3. 9 f. Note also Titius, a friend of Tibullus (I. 4. 73).

[6] Schanz–Hosius, *Gesch. der r. Lit.* II[4] (1935), 153. But not in *PIR*[1], T 195.

[7] For the orator, W. Kroll, *RE* XVIII, 2096.

[8] For the *nomen*, W. Schulze, *LE* 105; 213. Etruria looks plausible. There is a specimen at Clusium (*CIL* XI. 2376 = *CIE* 868).

[9] Below, p. 84.

V. Friends from the old days, notably practitioners in the schools of rhetoric, and some poets. Of them, Atticus, Graecinus, and Macer occurred already in the *Amores*.

The front and head of this category is Brutus, perhaps the recipient of three poems in *Tristia*.[1] In the collection *Ex Ponto* I–III he has the first poem and the last; and he may have been charged with the publication of those books (cf. III. 9. 51 ff.). The last poem to his address, written after the decease of Augustus, discloses rhetorical power in the courts of law,

> ut qui, quid valeas ignoret Marte forensi,
>   posse tuo peragi vix putet ore reos.   (IV. 6. 29 f.)

Brutus, it has been supposed, may be identical with the *rhetor* Bruttedius Brutus, named by the elder Seneca.[2] The *nomen* is rare, he may be a near relative of the prosecutor Bruttedius Niger, the notice of whom in Tacitus advertises brilliant talent, ruthless ambition—and a bad end in store for an adherent of Aelius Seianus.[3]

Next Gallio (IV. 11), whom Ovid consoles for the loss of his wife. That is, Junius Gallio: a powerful speaker named frequently by Seneca, who includes him in his set of four champions.[4] The others are Porcius Latro, Albucius Silo, Arellius Fuscus. In the year 32 Gallio fell foul of Tiberius Caesar through an imprudent proposal. Tacitus has a full and vivid account of the incident: an angry denunciation from Caesar, with Gallio expelled from the Senate and relegated.[5] Gallio, it will be recalled, took in adoption Novatus, the eldest of Seneca's three sons, who became proconsul of Achaea and consul (*suff.* 55).[6]

Then come several poets.[7] First, Severus, introduced as 'vates magnorum maxime regum' (IV. 2. 1), compare 'carmen regale' (16. 9). Patently the epic poet Cornelius Severus, on adequate record else-

---

[1] Above, p. 76.   [2] *PIR²*, B 156, cf. 171.

[3] *Ann.* III. 66. 4, cf. *Tacitus* (1958), 326 f.; 368. Mentioned four times in Seneca—and he is the Bruttidius of Juvenal X. 83.

[4] *PIR²*, J 756. For the 'tetradium' of rhetors, *Controv.* X, praef. 12 f. For Gallio as a friend of Ovid, and also (it appears) of Tiberius, see *Suas.* III. 7.

[5] *Ann.* VI. 3. 1 ff. Gallio chose the pleasant retreat of Lesbos, but was brought back and put under official custody.

[6] L. Junius Annaeus Gallio (*PIR²*, J 757).

[7] Ovid's long catalogue (IV. 16) is discussed and annotated in Schanz–Hosius, o.c. 269 ff.

where.[1] Seneca transmits his lines on the death of Cicero.[2] Although 'versificator quam poeta melior', he was awarded high rank by Quintilian, with special praise for Book I of his *Bellum Siculum*.[3]

Next, Albinovanus Pedo (IV. 10), addressed by *nomen* (10. 4) and by *cognomen* (10. 63). He had written about Theseus (10. 65), cf. 'sidereusque Pedo' (16. 6). Something more can be said about him, in relation to Germanicus Caesar.

Another old friend is Tuticanus (IV. 12), addressed as

> paene mihi puero cognite paene puer. (12. 20)

A poet himself (12. 27 f., cf. 16. 27), he had corrected Ovid's manuscripts (12. 25). By patronage of Augustus, Tuticanus had risen to senatorial rank (12. 39 f.). The *nomen* is rare; and, as Ovid explains, not easily brought into verse (12. 5 ff.).[4] The second poem to Tuticanus (14) is not revealing.

Carus is also a 'sodalis' (IV. 13. 1), and he had written about Hercules (13. 11 f., cf. 16. 7).[5]

Finally, another Severus, who has early entrance (I. 8).[6] Addressed as 'iucunde sodalis' (8. 25), but the letter betrays no interest in oratory or poetry. Severus had a villa in the Alban Hills, and may come from Umbria (8. 67). This *cognomen* offers no guidance.

· · ·

VI. Miscellaneous friends. After a time Ovid sends a poem to Cotys, the Thracian king (II. 9).[7] They are neighbours now; and the young monarch, formed by 'ingenuae artes' (9. 47), himself composes verses (9. 51 ff.). Although he is 'Marte ferox' (9. 45, cf. 55 f.), Ovid calls up no military exploit. Such there had been recently, as disclosed by Ovid's poem to Severus (I. 8), written before the winter of 12/13 (cf. 8. 27 f.). The Getae in a sudden raid had captured

---

[1] *PIR*[2], C 1452. See now H. Dahlmann, 'Cornelius Severus', *Mainzer Abh.* 1975, no. 6.

[2] *Suas.* VI. 26.

[3] Quintilian X. 1. 89.

[4] For Tuticanus, C. Cichorius, *Römische Studien* (1922), 324, with his emendation to produce the name on the title of *Anth. Pal.* V. 48; for the distribution of the *nomen*, T. P. Wiseman, *New Men in the Roman Senate 139 B.C.–A.D. 14* (1971), 268.

[5] It is stated (wrongly) in *PIR*[2], C 455 that Carus is named in *Tr.* III. 5. 17 f.

[6] Amalgamated with Cornelius Severus in the Oxford text (1925).

[7] *PIR*[2], C 1554, the son of Rhoemetalces (*PIR*[1], R 50). The 'ingenium' of Cotys was 'mite et amoenum' (*Ann.* II. 64. 2).

Aegissus, a town not far from the delta of the Danube. The king, 'memor magni generis', intervened promptly and inflicted a defeat (8. 11 ff.).

Two other poems describe operations in this region (IV. 7 and 9), which he described, perhaps with exaggeration, as

> haec est Ausonio sub iure novissima, vixque
> haeret in imperii margine terra tui.   (*Tr.* II. 199 f.)

Ovid now acquires unexpected value. The events are nowhere else on even the faintest record.[1]

Some scholars, it is true, adduce Orosius who refers to a 'Dacorum commotio' as occurring 'sub extrema Augusti senectute', the Gates of War being opened in consequence. Not valid. Orosius, part ignorance, part deceit, put the advent of universal peace in 2 B.C., with Janus closed thereafter for a dozen years. Which may go where it belongs.[2]

Two notable poems. First, with Vestalis (IV. 7), a novel and extraneous character crops up, who, like Cotys, would have been beyond Ovid's ambient but for his exile on the shore of Pontus. Vestalis is addressed as 'Alpinis iuvenis regibus orte' (7. 6), as 'progenies alti fortissima Donni' (7. 29). The labels do not deceive. This man is the son of the native prince M. Julius Cottius, whose name stands on the arch at Segusio and is perpetuated in the designation of a small province, the Alpes Cottiae.[3]

A military exploit of Vestalis is acclaimed: his share in the recapture of Aegissus from the invaders (7. 21). Perhaps the victory of Cotys was imperfect.[4] However, the poem goes on to describe how a Roman officer, Vitellius, brought troops down the Danube (7. 27 f.). Vestalis, it is stated, was a *primus pilus* in a Roman legion (7. 49). That is, a man of equestrian status, as is not anomalous in this age. In the sequel he ascends to an administrative post. Ovid describes it,

> ut positis reddas iura sub axe locis.   (7. 2)

The inference is easy. Julius Vestalis might have been a *praefectus*

---

[1] For these transactions see especially A. Stein, *Die Legaten von Moesien* (1940), 15 ff.

[2] Orosius VI. 22. 1, see further above, p. 26.

[3] *ILS* 94 (Segusio): for Cottius, *PIR*², J 274; Vestalis, J 621. For the family see now the exhaustive study of C. Latta, *Athenaeum* LIV (1976), 37 ff.

[4] There is a gap in the text after I. 8. 19.

ripae Danuvii.[1] Better, he was in charge of the coast of Pontus as *praefectus orae maritimae*.[2]

Second (L. Pomponius) Flaccus (*cos.* 17). The evidence comes from the long poem addressed to his brother Graecinus in the course of the year 16, the latest poem in Book IV to convey a date (IV. 9). Flaccus had recently held authority over the region (9. 75, cf. 119). He was active in the campaign of the year 12,

> hic raptam Troesmen celeri virtute recepit
> infecitque fero sanguine Danuvium.   (9. 79 f.)

That is to say, the Getae had captured not only Aegissus but Troesmis, of later fame as the camp of the legion V Macedonica.[3] The legate of Moesia in charge of the Balkan army was C. Poppaeus Sabinus (*cos.* 9), from 11 or 12 onwards.[4] Flaccus was a legate of Sabinus; and he later reverted to that post in the year 19, although now of consular rank.[5]

Flaccus himself after an early entrance (I. 10) received no direct appeal. That poem conveyed no personal detail, no sign of ancient friendship or community in polite studies. But Flaccus was the brother of Graecinus, there lies the explanation.

Finally, to round off the rubric, Rufinus (I. 3; III. 4). Like Flaccus, he is early on show, and like Flaccus, without appeal to common interests, or to a long allegiance. He should have excited curiosity.

.   .   .

VII. Rufinus was endowed with the gift of eloquence (I. 3. 11); he had written to Ovid and imparted 'praecepta' like a medical man

---

[1] For an early example, *AE* 1926, 80 (Pisidian Antioch). The man had previously been tribune in IV Scythica (one of the two legions of Moesia) and *praefectus equitum*.

[2] *CAH* X (1934), 805, cf. *PIR*², J 621 ('probabiliter'). For a long doxology of opinions, W. Reidinger, *RE* VIIIA, 1778.

[3] The recapture of Troesmis is generally put in 15. Thus *PIR*¹, P 538; A. Stein, o.c. 19; A. Betz, *RE* VIIA, 592; D. M. Pippidi and D. Berciu, *Din Istoria Dobrogei* I (1965), 298. For the year 12, R. Syme, *JRS* LVI (1966), 63; *Danubian Papers* (1971), 47 f. There is no sign that Pomponius Flaccus was still in Moesia in 15; and (P.) Vitellius was with Germanicus in that year (*Ann.* I. 70. 1).

[4] *Ann.* VI. 39. 3 (the obituary, under the year 35). This command (that is, the removal of the legions from the proconsul of Macedonia) had been set up at a much earlier date. Probably after the Thracian War of L. Piso (in 12–10 B.C.), cf. *Rom. Rev.* (1939), 400, n. 6; *Danubian Papers* (1971), 69 f.; *Akten des VI. Int. Kongr. für. gr. u. lat. Epigraphik* (Munich, 1973), 596 f. Also above, p. 68.

[5] *Ann.* II. 66 f.

(3. 5 ff.; 27). The therapeutic note is emphasized (3. 92), and it recurs in the second poem (III. 4. 7 f.).

There is something else. Ovid had written his *Triumphus* to commemorate the ceremony of October 23, A.D. 12. He describes his poem as

> est opus exiguum vestrisque paratibus impar.   (III. 4. 5)[1]

And lower down he says in depreciation

> si duce non facta est digna corona tuo.   (4. 64)

From this language the deduction is not flimsy that Rufinus had occupied a due place in the triumph of Tiberius Caesar ('dux tuus'). That is, Rufinus had seen service during the war in Illyricum from 6 to 9. If he survived, prospects opened for a good career.

To expedite the argument (and anticipate its conclusion), something must first be said about C. Vibius Rufus. For the years 15 and 16 the historian Dio furnishes an account that permits comparison with Tacitus, results being worse than predictable. Dio offers a lot of trivial and anecdotal material. The most entertaining item happens to be useful. A consul, Vibius Rufus, had acquired the curule chair of Caesar the Dictator. Also the widow of Cicero, as though desirous of oratory for an inheritance.[2]

The lady is clearly that young Publilia, an opulent heiress whom Cicero, her guardian, married towards the end of 46 B.C., after he had discarded Terentia.[3] Moreover, an inscription found near Tusculum, but strangely neglected, discloses a freedman of the married couple: 'M. Publilius Publiliae et C. Vibi Rufi l. Strato'.[4]

Vibius Rufus, consul suffect in 16, went on to be president of a newly instituted board, namely the Curators of the Tiber, a few years later.[5] After which he fades out.

---

[1] On 'paratibus' observe that the word comes to extend from the mustering of troops (Sallust, *Hist.* I. 88) to military or regal pageantry.

[2] Dio LVII. 15. 6.

[3] Cf. Drumann–Groebe, *Gesch. Roms* VI (1929), 612 ff. Denied by W. Hoffman, *RE* XXIII, 1918.

[4] *CIL* XIV. 2556. Dessau was below his usual self when he stated in *PIR*[1], V 396: 'vix huc pertinent Vibii Rufi Tusculani XIV, 2590 cf. 2556 seq.' Further, M. Publilius Strato recurs on an inscription with the date of 33 (*Eph. Ep.* IX, p. 407, no. 679 = *AE* 1907, 78).

[5] *ILS* 5925. By error adduced as the first college in *Rom. Rev.* (1939), 403. It had for president L. Caninius Gallus (*suff.* 2 B.C.), cf. *ILS* 5893.

About his *cognomen* there is a double discrepancy on the consular records.[1] First, on the *Fasti Antiates Minores* he stands as 'C. Vibius Libo'. An error of the engraver, who has repeated 'Libo', the *cognomen* of the *ordinarius* on the preceding line, viz. L. Scribonius Libo. Second, the *Ostienses*, a better product. Rufus here appears as '[C. Vibius] Rufinus'. In this instance the lapicide had already in his mind the termination of the *cognomen* he was going to inscribe on the next line, that of C. Pomponius Graecinus.

The coincidence in error is peculiar, but such things happen. It is unfortunate that standard works register the consul as 'C. Vibius Rufus Rufinus'.[2] Not plausible.

Now a senator called C. Vibius Rufinus stands on clear and triple attestation. But each item has produced a problem, and they all interlock.

First, the colleague of M. Cocceius Nerva in August of an uncertain year.[3] The jurist Nerva, the grandfather of the Emperor, was certainly consul before 24, when he became *curator aquarum*.[4] At first sight, the pair goes conveniently into 21 or 22, where there is room for them.[5] Some scholars, however, opt for the vicinity of 40.[6] In that case Nerva is the Emperor's father, not known to have been consul—and the jurist must in any event have a place in the early Tiberian years.

Second, C. Vibius Rufinus, proconsul of Asia.[7] For Asia and Africa Tiberius tried for a time to keep to an interval of ten years from a man's consulship.[8] But some perturbations arose—and then the Princeps left the proconsuls in office for a sexennium.[9] After the tenure of P. Petronius (*suff.* 19), from 29 to 35, there are problems concerning the next few years. Cotta Messallinus (*cos.* 20) should belong in 35/6, so it appears.[10] If Rufinus was consul suffect in 21 or 22,

[1] A. Degrassi, *Inscr. It.* XIII. 1, p. 303 (the *Fasti Antiates Minores*); p. 185 (*Fasti Ostienses*).
[2] Thus R. Hanslik, *RE* VIIIA, 1979: the article is variously defective. Also, however, in Degrassi, o.c., p. 215 (but in the indexes he is '[C. Vibius] Rufinus'); and likewise in Degrassi, *I Fasti consolari* (1951), 8.
[3] *CIL* VI. 1539; 9005 = *ILS* 1795.   [4] Frontinus, *De aq.* 102.
[5] Thus Groag, quite firmly, in *PIR²*, C 1225.
[6] A. Degrassi, *Epigraphica* VIII (1946), 37; *I Fasti consolari* (1952), 11; R. Hanslik, *RE* VIIIA, 1981.
[7] *Forsch. in Ephesos* III. 113, no. 23.   [8] Below, p. 160.
[9] Dio LVIII. 23. 5.   [10] Below, p. 131.

he might go in 36/7; and C. Sulpicius Galba (*cos.* 22) was in fact debarred from the sortition in 36.[1] It has been maintained that no space is available for a proconsulate of Rufinus in this period.[2] However, the difficulties raised might not be insuperable.

Third, C. Vibius C. f. Rufinus, legate of Germania Superior: attested in 43 and in 45.[3] Objections have been raised on grounds of age. Not valid. It is enough to adduce C. Vibius Marsus (*suff.* 17) succeeding P. Petronius (*suff.* 19) in Syria, in or about the year 42.[4]

Recognized as Vibius Rufinus, Ovid's young friend Rufinus thus acquires an identity and a career.[5] Further, nothing forbids identification with the Vibius Rufinus who wrote about trees and herbs and flowers.[6] That avocation is by no means incompatible with the governorship of provinces.

It remains to provide Rufinus with a parent. Who but C. Vibius Rufus, consul suffect in 16?

The short interval between their consulships is no bar. Observe, for example. C. Cestius Gallus (*cos.* 35) and his homonymous son (*suff.* 42), or P. Suillius Rufus (*suff. c.* 43) and M. Suillius Nerullinus (*cos.* 50). The phenomenon is patent: an elderly or retarded father, a son benefiting by several years in access to the *fasces* through the new rank of the family.[7]

Rufinus, as Ovid's poem shows, had been active in Illyricum: presumably as quaestor or legate of quaestorian rank. Therefore Rufinus may well have had occupation in other military regions before his consulship.[8] Nor is attachment to Germanicus Caesar precluded. It might help to explain why he emerges, like Vibius Marsus, as an army commander under Claudius.

The father finds abundant mention for his performance in the schools of rhetoric: he followed the 'antiquum genus', his manner

---

[1] Tacitus, *Ann.* VI. 40. 2.

[2] Chr. Meier in the Anhang to W. Kunkel, *Herkunft u. soziale Stellung der r. Juristen* (1952), 378 ff. Note also Groag on Caligulan consuls in *PIR²*, A 1242 (C. Asinius Pollio, *cos.* 23).

[3] *ILS* 7076; 2283.   [4] Josephus, *AJ* XIX. 316.

[5] Ovid's Rufinus is identified with Vibius Rufus (*suff.* 16) by R. Hanslik, o.c. 1981.

[6] A source of Pliny in six books, and registered as *PIR¹*, V 394. Ovid's friend gets no separate entry: he is there noted, with 'plane incertum num huc pertineat'.

[7] Cf. C. Caelius Rufus, praetor in 13, consul in 17 (*PIR²*, C 141).

[8] Military experience is inferred for Pomponius Graecinus, from Ovid's language (above, p. 75).

tended to the crude and popular.[1] A Vibius Gallus is also there on show, a wild man who ended by going off his head.[2] Vibii are so frequent, so widely distributed throughout Italy that, in default of a clear clue, no path leads to their local origin. These years are also inhabited by Vibius Marsus (*suff.* 17) and the two brothers from Larinum, Postumus and Habitus (*suffecti* in 5 and 8).[3]

So far old Vibius Rufus, once the husband of Publilia M. f., and his son Vibius Rufinus.[4] Cornelius Tacitus, distrustful of the historians, had recourse to the *Acta Senatus*, with manifest advantage. A glance at the *Fasti* of the early Tiberian years would have done no harm.

.   .   .

VIII. Friends of Germanicus. The young prince was on the Rhine with Tiberius in 11, and he is accorded discreet mention in the splendid piece acclaiming the modest operations of that year (*Tr.* IV. 2). First, subsumed with Drusus the son of Tiberius,

> et qui Caesareo iuvenes sub nomine crescunt.   (2. 9)

Second, introduced by his father's name and reference to the *cognomen*,

> Drusus in his meruit quondam cognomina terris
> quae bona progenies digna parente tulit.   (2. 39 f.)[5]

After that, he is absent until *Ex Ponto* II. 1 (of early 13).

Consul in 12 at the age of twenty-five, Germanicus went to the Rhine the next year. Not alone, but in the company and under the supervision of Tiberius Caesar, so it may be conjectured. Further, that year witnessed a campaign against the Germans.[6] The prince was left in the command, prosecuting military enterprises in the autumn of 14 and in the course of the next two years.

---

[1] Seneca, *Controv.* I. 2. 23; IX. 2. 25.

[2] Ibid. II. 1. 25: 'quod toties simulabat ad verum redegit.'

[3] Marsus is attested as 'inlustris studiis', but only by one writer (*Ann.* VI. 47. 2). Neither Marsus nor Rufus is admitted to the list of T. P. Wiseman, *New Men in the Roman Senate* (1971).

[4] Of Rufus R. Hanslik opines that he survived 'bis gegen das Ende der Regierung des Tiberius' (o.c. 1981).

[5] As the last word of the couplet 'fuit' appears in standard modern texts: Teubner, 1911; OCT, 1914; Loeb, 1924; Budé, 1968. G. Luck, however, in his edition (Heidelberg, 1967) prints 'tulit', the conjecture made by two scholars in the seventeenth century: as I was not aware when submitting 'tulit' to three excellent Latinists at Harvard on January 5, 1976.

[6] Ch. IV.

The emphatic piece celebrating the Pannonian triumph (*Ex P.* II. 1) invokes 'Fama' for the report of precise details (1. 19 ff.), acclaims Tiberius Caesar (29 ff.), and passes to exploits of Germanicus, who is hailed by name (49). There follows, at some length (55–68), the hope and prediction of a triumph for Germanicus.[1]

The poem was written early in 13, perhaps when Germanicus had already set out for the Rhine. It is the nearest Ovid comes, in the letters *Ex Ponto*, to a personal dedication to the prince. He was over-eager, so it appears. In the sequel, he adopts a more discreet approach —through friends of Germanicus Caesar.

Before long Ovid is found writing to a certain Salanus (II. 5). Not, so he has to confess, one of his own intimates of long date, 'quamvis modico tibi iunctus ab usu' (5. 7). But Salanus likes Ovid's poetry, and he will receive a copy of his *Triumphus* (5. 33). The point and purpose of the solicitation is disclosed. Salanus these many years has been the teacher of the prince,

> tu comes antiquus, tu primis iunctus ab annis.   (5. 43)

The person is on record as Cassius Salanus.[2]

Ovid before the year 13 ended was coming to distrust the 'magna nomina'. Book III shows the last poem to Cotta Maximus (III. 8), the last to Paullus Fabius Maximus (III. 3). In Book IV only two of the previous friends recur, viz. Brutus (IV. 6) and Graecinus (IV. 9). Instead, eight new characters. Four of them are poets: (Cornelius) Severus, Albinovanus Pedo, Tuticanus, Carus. They illustrate Ovid's changed approach to persons of influence.

Carus stood in his own right as a poet. But Ovid's poem, written in the winter of 14/15 (IV. 13. 40), goes on to reveal the fact that Carus was tutor to the sons of Germanicus (13. 47 f.).

Then there is the epistle dedicated to Albinovanus Pedo in the summer of 14 (IV. 10. 1). It contains a long catalogue of the rivers that flow in the Pontus (10. 45 ff.), but no mention of Germanicus Caesar. Had Pedo then been on the Rhine, an allusion would be easy and attractive. Pedo happens to be on attestation in the next year, commanding cavalry in the land of the Frisians.[3] Furthermore, Pedo wrote a poem, of which an extract survives, describing the

---

[1] Above, p. 41.   [2] Pliny, *NH* XXXIV. 47.   [3] *Ann.* I. 60. 2.

terrors of navigation in the northern Ocean.[1] The occasion was the disastrous end of the campaign of 16.[2]

Finally, and of prime value, Suillius (IV. 8). The pretext for his induction is the fact that he had married the daughter of Ovid's wife. But Ovid quickly brings in his devotion to the prince,

> di tibi sunt Caesar iuvenis. tua numina placa.
> hac certe nulla est notior ara tibi.   (8. 23 f.)

From which he goes on to address Germanicus (8. 31 ff.). He appeals as one poet to another, and proclaims that any further efforts of his talent will be consecrated to the prince,

> siquid adhuc igitur vivi, Germanice, nostro
> restat in ingenio, serviet omne tibi.   (8. 65 f.)

Germanicus is both a general and a poet,

> nam modo bella geris, numeris modo verba coerces.   (8. 73)

Finally, it may be vouchsafed to Ovid to acclaim his exploits,

> unde tuas possim laudes celebrare recentes.   (8. 87)

The poem belongs to 15 or 16. Ovid, though so often exuberant in prophecy, refrains from expatiating on the military glory of Germanicus and the sure prospect of a triumph. He has learned discretion.

The age of P. Suillius Rufus and his career now come into the reckoning. Suillius, so Tacitus is careful to record, had been quaestor to Germanicus.[3] For that post a wide range offers at first sight, from 12 to 19. An acephalous inscription found at Antioch honours a man who had been 'q. Germanici Caesaris'.[4] It is generally assigned to Suillius. His next post was 'leg. Ti. Caesaris Aug.'. That is, legate of a legion, presumably in Syria. Moreover, since Suillius was condemned for taking bribes in 24 and sent into exile, conjecture may put his praetorship in the previous year.[5] And further, his quaestorship in 15. Suillius happens not to be named anywhere among the friends or officers of Germanicus either on the Rhine or in Syria. Several returning from Syria, notably P. Vitellius and Q. Veranius, were active at the indictment of Cn. Piso in 20.[6] But not Suillius,

---

[1] Quoted by Seneca, *Suas.* I. 15. Pedo is attested as a friend of Ovid in *Controv.* II. 2. 12.
[2] *Ann.* II. 23 f.   [3] *Ann.* IV. 31. 3; XIII. 42. 3.   [4] *ILS* 8967.
[5] *JRS* LX (1970), 28 = *RP* (1978), 806.   [6] *Ann.* II. 74. 2; III. 10. 1; 13. 2; 17. 2.

despite his 'pietas' and his opportunism. Perhaps he was still absent in Syria.

Suillius came back from exile after the death of Tiberius, and became consul (*c.* 43).[1] He earned evil repute as a prosecutor, the associate of L. Vitellius and the loyal friend of Claudius Caesar—and in his turn he was brought to ruin in 58.[2]

Suillius engages interest on various counts. Let it be added that he was one of the children of Vistilia, the lady of the six husbands.[3] Some have argued, but wrongly, that he is one of the six.[4] Further, M. Suillius Nerullinus (*cos.* 50) is a son born to him by Ovid's step-daughter. Some opine that the *cognomen* was selected to advertise loyal devotion to the Claudii.[5]

．　　．　　．

IX. Twenty-one correspondents have thus been apportioned. It will be suitable to register two other names from *Ex Ponto*, viz. Celsus and Vitellius.

Ovid condoles with Cotta Maximus for the loss of a true friend called Celsus (I. 9). Celsus had been faithful to Ovid at the time of the catastrophe, encouraging him to expect help from Cotta and from Messallinus (9. 25 ff.). As for identity, he may well be the Albino-vanus Celsus who was 'comes' and 'scriba' of Tiberius in 20 B.C. Horace sent him a letter and in another place administered a gentle warning about proclivities to plagiarism.[6] Presumably close kin to Albinovanus Pedo.[7]

A certain Vitellius brought a detachment of Roman troops down the Danube in the year 12 (IV. 7. 27). On the general and reasonable assumption this is P. Vitellius.[8] He is next heard of on the Rhine, in

---

[1] The year 41 is now accorded preference by W. Eck, *Historia* XXIV (1975), 342.

[2] *Ann.* IV. 31. 3: 'quem vidit sequens aetas praepotentem, venalem et Claudii principis amicitia diu prospere, numquam bene usum'. For his prosecution and banishment, *Ann.* XIII. 42 f.

[3] Pliny, *NH* VII. 39. Thus *PIR*[1], S 700, followed in *JRS* LX (1970), 31 f. = *RP* (1978), 811 f.

[4] C. Cichorius, *Römische Studien* (1922), 432; M. Fluss, *RE* VA, 722; R. Hanslik, *RE* XXI, 2356 (discussing P. Pomponius Secundus, one of Vistilia's sons).

[5] It might be maternal. For 'Neronius' and 'Nerullius', cf. W. Schulze, *LE* 67 f.; 442.

[6] Horace, *Epp.* I. 3. 15 ff.; 8. 2.   [7] Thus *PIR*[2], A 478 f.

[8] As in *PIR*[1], V 502, where, however, his action is put in A.D. 6–8: followed in the verbose article *RE* IXA, 385 ff.

charge of two legions at the end of the campaign of 15. P. Vitellius was an orator of some note—at least his speech at the prosecution of Cn. Piso was known to posterity.[1]

. . .

X. Sorted out by categories, the correspondents yield manifold instruction for social history. As concerns rank, after the four *nobiles* come four senators who were to reach the *fasces* (the two Pomponii, (Vibius) Rufinus, Suillius) and two other senators (Gallio and Tuticanus). For the rest, a variegated company. The *Epistulae* of Horace are a close parallel; and, infinitely richer, Pliny's collection. Not all of the literary 'circles' on show through the ages, from Scipio to Symmachus, can stand up to scrutiny. That of Pliny, however, is both variegated and authentic.[2]

The danger is to take such a group for typical or fully representative. Other circles existed, and many of them overlapped. Benefit can accrue from bringing to light people or coteries absent from the list of Pliny's friends.[3]

Similarly for Ovid. In early fame as a poet and assiduous in the schools of rhetoric, he would enlist a wide ambit of friends and fanciers, even had he lacked grace and amenity. Again, talent and wit opened the salons of high society to a man of good family in his own town, one of the 'domi nobiles'.

Forfeiting use and value in the period of the wars, eloquence took refuge in the schools and prospered in a fatal fashion. Liberated from the writing of his history, Asinius Pollio paraded as a declaimer no less than as an orator; and so did Messalla Corvinus, his junior by a decade (no public employment after 26 B.C.). Young Ovid was no doubt attentive to their performances. He also heard among the early Augustan exponents Rubellius Blandus, on record as the first Roman knight to give instruction in rhetoric, and the famous 'Passienus pater', the father of the consul.[4]

Aristocrats as well as orators may lurk among friends not labelled

---

[1] Pliny, *NH* XI. 187.

[2] A. N. Sherwin-White in his commentary (1966), 11 ff.; 65 ff. When discussing the epistolary genre (ibid. 1 ff.), he omits mention of Ovid. For the friends of Martial and Statius, P. White, *Harvard Studies* LXXIX (1975), 265 ff.   [3] *Tacitus* (1958), 87 f.

[4] For Rubellius Blandus, see Seneca, *Controv.* II, praef. 5; Tacitus, *Ann.* VI. 27. 1.

by name in the *Tristia*. One might wonder, for example, about P. Vinicius (*cos.* A.D. 2), a speaker of distinction and a man of precise taste. He declaimed frequently, he came out with a firm pronouncement: every orator, he declared, should have Ovid by heart.[1] Or another Vinicius, his father's cousin L. Vinicius (*suff.* 5 B.C.), a ready speaker and a young man of fashion: Caesar Augustus raised objection to his frequentation of Julia at the pleasure resort of Baiae.[2]

Ovid is named a dozen times in the repertory of the elder Seneca, with amicable appreciation. But also a number of sharp or revealing verdicts on his manner: he was too clever, he was prone to labouring a point.[3] Seneca also furnishes a sample of his performance.[4]

The declaimers were legion, a demoniac legion.[5] One of the most fervent fanatics was Porcius Latro, a close friend and fellow citizen of Seneca.[6] Ovid admired him, though their styles were diverse; and Ovid also got teaching from Arellius Fuscus.[7] Junius Gallio, another member of the famous 'tetradium', receives at last an epistle from Pontus (IV. 11). Others in the host of rhetoricians may have been represented anonymous in the *Tristia*, or even a grammarian, such as the learned Julius Hyginus, whom some called 'Polyhistor': he became head of the Palatine Library.[8] Likewise some from the company of poets mustered at the end (IV. 16).

[1] Seneca, *Controv.* X. 4. 25. P. Vinicius was proconsul of Asia *c.* 7, and still alive in 20 (*Ann.* III. 11. 2).

[2] Suetonius, *Divus Aug.* 64. 2. Augustus' elegant compliment on his oratory is quoted: 'L. Vinicius ingenium in numerato habet' (*Controv.* II. 5. 20). Not heard of after his consulship.

[3] *Controv.* II. 2. 8 f.; 12. See especially S. F. Bonner, *Roman Declamation* (1949), 143 ff.

[4] *Controv.* II. 2. 9 ff.

[5] For the catalogue, H. Bornecque, *Les Déclamations et les déclamateurs d'après Sénèque le père* (1902), 143 ff.

[6] *PIR*[1], P 638. For the Spanish declaimers, H. de la Ville de Mirmont, *Bull. Hisp.* XII (1910), 1 ff.; M. T. Griffin, *JRS* LXII (1972), 5 f.; 12. Porcius Latro and Statorius Victor are from Corduba (perhaps also Marullus), Gavius Silo from Tarraco. The towns of Junius Gallio and Clodius Turrinus are not certified.

Papirius Fabianus, the rhetor turned philosopher, looks Spanish, cf. M. Griffin, o.c. 16. One may add Cornelius Hispanus, on frequent mention, and (Fabius) Quintilianus (cf. *PIR*[2], F 57). And there might be grounds for suspecting Licinius Nepos as well as Fulvius Sparsus. Again, one or other in the obscure trio Paternus, Moderatus, Fabius in *Controv.* X, praef. 13: Fabius cannot be (as commonly assumed) the famous consular, cf. below, p. 143. Finally, Pacatus looks provincial.

[7] *Controv.* II. 2. 8.

[8] Suetonius, *De gramm.* 20: 'familiarissimus Ovidio poetae et Clodio Licino, consulari historico'. Nor should one omit C. Maecenas Melissus (*PIR*[1], M 31), put in charge of the library in the Porticus Octaviae.

Of members of Ovid's family (apart from his wife), her uncle, Rufus of Fundi, has an epistle (IV. 11), that character who may well excite speculation.[1] And Suillius Rufus (q. c. 15) earns a place, not for his marriage (contracted c. 12), but for his devotion to Germanicus Caesar (IV. 8).

Ovid's own daughter gets left out. She was twice married, with children from each husband (*Tr.* IV. 10. 75 f.). In the year 8 she was abroad, in Africa.[2] A son-in-law of Ovid is on later record, a certain Cornelius Fidus: Domitius Corbulo called him 'a plucked ostrich'.[3]

The *Epistulae Ex Ponto* convey information so varied and abundant that one may regret that there is not more of it. At the same time, a warning against arguments from silence. Authors omit facts which a later inquirer expects to find on register and exploit for erudite investigations: they omit the known or what is irrelevant to present purposes. For example, no hint in four poems of Ovid that Sex. Pompeius was related to the dynasty; and from the letter to Gallio one would not gather that he was one of the princes of rhetoric.

Nor is the place specified where a man happens to be at the time.[4] Thus the epistle to Pomponius Flaccus in 12 (I. 10). He was not so far away from Ovid, being legate in Moesia under the consular Poppaeus Sabinus. However, the reader might know or assume that Suillius Rufus (IV. 8) was on the Rhine with Germanicus in 15 or 16.

To pursue this line would be obtuse and pedantic. Ovid, despite his predicament, and his propensity to take an argument too far, became aware that he could engender tedium and annoy his correspondents (III. 7. 1 ff.).

---

[1] Identical, it is conjectured, with the elderly orator C. Vibius Rufus (*suff.* 16), cf. above, p. 79.

[2] *Tr.* I. 3. 19. She finds a mention in the *Fasti*. Seeking a propitious day for the nuptial ceremony the parent consulted the wife of the Flamen Dialis and learned that the first half of June was no good (VI. 219 ff.).

[3] Seneca, *De const.* 17. 1: 'in senatu flentem vidimus Fidum Cornelium Nasonis Ovidii generum cum illum Corbulo struthocamelum depilatum dixisset.' Presumably the general (*suff.* ?39), not his father, as assumed in *PIR*², C 1360.

[4] For parallel, observe that although Pliny writes to a number of army commanders he never specifies the province. Cf. *Latomus* XXIII (1964), 755 ff. = *Danubian Papers* (1971), 249 ff.

VI

PATRONAGE AND LETTERS

I. To investigate the provenance of authors is an alluring pastime in any age. For Rome the appeal is enhanced, since Rome from the outset lived by imported talent. In the operation it is expedient to know what one can expect to find and how to use the results.[1]

Many local origins are not verifiable, or, registered by some casual notice, they furnish a fact that could never have been divined from the writing itself. The *patria* of Lucretius evades all search. No impediment to the understanding of the poem. Elsewhere fallacy or fantasy may obtrude. Verona's poet and the man from Mantua have evoked opinions about race and geography in Transpadane Italy; and some speak of Celts.[2]

Ovid helps to dispel these notions. Ovid came from a martial people that stood in the forefront for freedom when confederate Italy seceded in 91 B.C. As he declares,

> Paelignae dicar gloria gentis ego.
> quam sua libertas ad honesta coegerat arma,
> cum timuit socias anxia Roma manus.   (*Am.* III. 15. 8 ff.)

Who would have guessed that origin for the urban and metropolitan poet, if he had not himself been so generous of information? Of external testimony there is only Martial's distich and the *Chronicle* of Jerome.[3] Each mentions only the Paeligni, whereas their territory had three urban centres: Corfinium, Sulmo, Superaequum. Again, it will suitably be recalled that only Jerome discloses the town and country of Sallust.[4]

The *patria* and the place of a man's birth do not always coincide—least of all with the higher in social rank. That is evident for Claudius

---

[1] For judicious remarks, see now M. Bonjour, *Terre natale* (1975), 88 f.; also, for anthology of opinions about Ovid in relation to his *patria*, ibid. 210 ff.

[2] Thus H. W. Garrod, *The Oxford Book of Latin Verse* (1912), xix ff.

[3] Martial II. 41. 1 f.; Jerome, *Chron.* p. 158 H.

[4] Jerome, *Chron.* p. 151 H.

Caesar, but not always recognized when Hadrian or Constantine is under review.

'Sulmo mihi patria est', to be sure—and Ovid in fact saw the light of day at Sulmo.[1] The municipal Roman possessed two *patriae*. For Ovid Rome as *patria* is not just a government or a state or a symbol of power. It can be the city itself, since in a dream

> aspicio patriae tecta relicta meae. (*Ex P.* I. 2. 48)

One might ask (or rather not ask) what is Paelignian in Ovid. For poets, origin and status is not the first thing. Their true pedigree is their predecessors in the art and manner, and their writing is their best biography.

It is another matter with historians. Antecedents and condition can hardly fail to have some influence on their social and political opinions. Likewise experience of affairs, since at Rome the historian tends to belong to the governing class, and is normally a newcomer. The town and region affect his ambitions, and may even determine his success. Groups and factions, allegiance and 'clientela' are pervasive.

The central theme in the history of Rome is the enlargement through the ages of the senatorial order. It was expounded by Cornelius Tacitus in his version of the oration delivered by Claudius Caesar, culminating in emphatic climax with the Cornelii Balbi from Spain, and with Narbonensis: 'nec minus insignis viros e Gallia Narbonensi transivisse'.[2]

Even when the precise ascertainment of a *patria* is ruled out, the position is not desperate. Discarding the notion that Tacitus must derive from an ancient house of the patriciate, recent enquiries turn to the new and dynamic territories of the Roman West. Transpadane Italy duly finds its advocates.[3] Better, Narbonensis. Various criteria can be adduced, and even the negative. The historian's friend, an enthusiast for regional pride, fails to bring Tacitus into relation anywhere with 'illa nostra Italia'.[4]

---

[1] *Tr.* IV. 10. 3, cf. 5.

[2] *Ann.* XI. 24. 3. The author's unobtrusive testimony to himself, it may be presumed: cf. also III. 55. 5; IV. 60.

[3] Regarded as possible by G. E. F. Chilver, *Cisalpine Gaul* (1970), 104 f.; and argued with conviction by E. Koestermann, *Athenaeum* XLIII (1965), 163 ff. This view earns commendation from S. Borzsák, *RE* Supp. XI, 379 ff.

[4] Pliny, *Epp.* I. 14. 4.

The agents and clients of the aristocratic Caesars end by extruding them; and the process goes on with municipal Italy giving way before Spain and Narbonensis. Exuberant divagations may evoke influences from race, region, and even climate.[1] To no purpose. Whatever be the *patria* or the province, it is social status and education that matter—and the talent of the individual.

Some relevance can be claimed to Ovid, and to the friends of Ovid. As it happens, Ovid shows no eagerness to bring in, by statement or allusion, the local origin of his correspondents.

There is one exception, and it is emphatic,

> maxima Fundani gloria, Rufe, soli.   (*Ex P.* II. 11. 28)

A question was worth the asking, how a municipal worthy can merit a label of that pretension. Two answers avail. Either excellence in polite studies or entrance to the governing class.[2]

.   .   .

II. The poet who when young had visited the great cities of Asia, with Pompeius Macer for guide and companion, might have mentioned the island of Lesbos—and Mytilene, a name that had already secured entry into Roman poetry. Though Ovid had a vivid and pictorial imagination, the journey leaves few traces discernible in his poetry.[3]

By chance an anonymous friend of long date turns up in his *Fasti*, when

> hospitis antiqui solitas intravimus aedes.   (IV. 687)

He was domiciled at Carseoli, on the Via Claudia Valeria, and he retailed ritual and folklore concerning foxes. Ovid was on the way back to his 'natalia rura'.

Of the Paeligni and Sulmo, of meadows, orchards, and streams, Ovid has frequent and affectionate mention, to find parallel in Latin poetry only with the man from Bilbilis in distant Tarraconensis. In the cults and antiquities of his own people (by origin in fact Illyrian),

---

[1] As W. Weber, *CAH* XI (1936), 325.
[2] Above, p. 79.
[3] For the *Metamorphoses*, cf. H. de la Ville de Mirmont, *La Jeunesse d'Ovide* (1905), 160 ff.

Ovid betrays no interest.[1] Martial furnishes in abundance the names of rivers and of mountains in his country. There are none in Ovid. Not even the river Aternus or the great mountain mass to the east above the plain of Sulmo and Corfinium.[2]

Men from families of substance and repute in the *municipia* went away to the metropolis, lured by ambition or profit, or by a free and elegant way of living. They did not forget their home. To the potency of local attachments, Cicero bears eloquent but candid testimony: not only the *patria*, but the whole Volscian territory.[3] On the other hand, Sallust (so far as extant) does not disclose Amiternum and the Sabine country. Relevance and reticence accord well with the writing of history.

At Rome new alliances formed between families from the same town or region, or old affinities were reinforced, despite the attractions of high birth in a bride. The expense deterred, and the perils. Again, the immigrants might select for their villas the same suburban vicinity. The best evidence for such habits emerges at a later date, with the provincial aristocrats who come in from the western lands.[4]

Along with clubs and salons, the schools of rhetoric exhibit a predictable function. Ovid was eminently sociable, and loyal to friends. It comes as a disappointment that no man from Sulmo can be certified among the company honoured with missives from the Pontic shore. There was a certain Q. Varius Geminus who passed into record as an orator of marked attainments. His verdict on P. Vinicius was remembered; and the great Cassius Severus admired his manner.[5] The inscription set up in honour of Geminus declares him the first of the Paeligni to acquire the rank of senator at Rome.[6]

.   .   .

[1] For their provenance, Festus, p. 248 L: 'Paeligni ex Illyrico orti. inde enim profecti ductu Volsimi regis' etc. Nomenclature confirms. Ovid, however, states that their 'proavi' are Sabine (*Fasti* III. 95). Their triple division may excite interest, 'pars me Sulmo tenet Paeligni tertia ruris' (*Am.* II. 16. 1), cf. E. Norden, *Altgermanien* (1934), 184. But one might have been spared the fable of Solymus, the eponymous founder of Sulmo (*Fasti* IV. 79).

[2] The ancient name of the Maiella, about 2,800 m. above sea level, has not been preserved.

[3] Cicero, *De legibus* I. 3 (Arpinum): *Pro Plancio* 22 (the Volscian country).

[4] Cf. *Tacitus* (1958), 602 f. (Spaniards at Tibur).

[5] *PIR*[1], V 187.

[6] *ILS* 932 (Superaequum). Note also the young man about to enter the Senate after equestrian service (*ILS* 2682: near Corfinium). The Mussidii, perhaps from Sulmo (*PIR*[1], M 550 ff.), present problems, cf. T. P. Wiseman, *New Men in the Roman Senate* (1971), 273.

III. Reference has already been made to 'sodalitates'. Some perhaps sharply delimited against other groups, others intersecting, as is clear in a later age when scrutiny is brought to bear upon the friends of Cornelius Tacitus and Plinius Secundus. And there would be rivalry and rifts in any concourse of literary gentlemen.

Ovid shared a 'sodalitas' with Propertius. Which permits and encourages a rapid comparison. Book I of Propertius is dedicated to Tullus, a close coeval, so it may be presumed. There are two other 'sodales' in that book. Ponticus, who composed an epic on the tale of Thebes, receives two poems, Bassus one.[1] Neither is alluded to in the sequel, but both are registered after Propertius in Ovid's autobiographical piece concluding *Tristia*, Book IV,

> Ponticus heroo, Bassus quoque clarus iambis
>   dulcia convictus membra fuere mei.   (10. 47 f.)

For all that, neither happens to earn a mention in the plethoric catalogue at the end. Identification is baffled. Nothing can be done with the *cognomen* 'Bassus'. But 'Ponticus' is rare, it invites inspection—but cannot repay it, at least for students of Propertius.[2] There are also two pseudonyms.[3]

By contrast, Tullus is a recognizable character, and notable for more reasons than one. Tullus went to Asia in 30 or 29, on the staff of his uncle (I. 6. 19 f.). This proconsul is with confidence identified as L. Volcacius Tullus (*cos.* 33 B.C.).[4] The Volcacii, it can be argued, came from Etruscan Perusia, neighbour city to Asisium—from the walls of which the siege operations could be discerned, and the fatal conflagration in February of 40 B.C.

---

[1] Propertius I. 7 and 9 (Ponticus); 4 (Bassus).

[2] It is absent from the repertorium of I. Kajanto, *The Latin Cognomina* (1965). The notion that the Ponticus to whom Juvenal VIII is addressed reflects a triumphal ancestor is endorsed by G. Highet, *Juvenal the Satirist* (1954), 113, cf. 272. Lesser persons annex *cognomina* of this type, for example the obscure Cestius Macedonicus of Perusia (Appian, *BC* V. 49. 204). On the other hand, Cn. Domitius Ponticus, legate to the proconsul of Africa in 77/8 (*IRT* 342) may be a new senator from the province Bithynia–Pontus.

[3] Demophoon (II. 22) and Lynceus (II. 34). The latter is treated in a hostile fashion. The former is generally held identical with Tuscus, the lover of Phyllis (*Ex P.* IV. 16. 20), as was Demophoon, the son of Theseus. For Lynceus as the poet Varius Rufus, J. P. Sullivan, *Propertius* (1976), 79. For pseudonyms in Augustan poetry, J.-P. Boucher, *Latomus* XXXV (1976), 504 ff.

[4] Now attested as proconsul on the revised text of the calendar decree of 10/9 B.C., Ehrenberg–Jones, *Documents*[2] (1955), 98, l. 42.

That hypothesis depends on the interpretation to be put upon the words in which Propertius addressed Tullus when proclaiming his own Umbrian origin,

> si Perusina tibi patriae sint nota sepulcra,
> Italiae duris funera temporibus.   (I. 22. 3 f.)

Not all accept it.[1] These Volcacii might be domiciled at Tusculum.[2]

.   .   .

IV. Book I also carries four pieces to the address of a friend named 'Gallus'.[3] This man calls for inspection, which must be preceded by segregation. First, Gallus a relative or neighbour of Propertius, who escaped from Perusia but fell victim to an assassin, lying unburied somewhere in the mountains of Etruria.[4] Second, Gallus, a centurion who fell in battle protecting his eagle: his brother Lupercus, an equestrian officer, also succumbed on that occasion.[5] Their mother, Arria, is mentioned there. Speculation has not neglected the mishap on the Rhine incurred by Marcus Lollius in 17 B.C.[6]

As in other contexts, the common and indistinctive *cognomen* begets despair, the implausible, or worse. In fact, a notion recently published makes play with none other than Cornelius Gallus: poet, general in the wars, and first viceroy of Egypt, who ended his life by suicide in 27 B.C.[7]

Not but that a clue offers. Gallus can get no help from birth and rank in the pursuit of love,

> nec tibi nobilitas poterit succurrere amanti:
> nescit Amor priscis cedere imaginibus.   (I. 5. 23 f.)

If the language be accorded its proper meaning, the friend of Propertius, even if not of the ancient *nobilitas*, is at least the son of a consul.

---

[1] Thus T. P. Wiseman, *New Men in the Roman Senate* (1971), 276 f.

[2] Cf. *JRS* LIII (1963), 60 = *RP* (1978), 565.

[3] Propertius I. 5; 10; 13; 20.

[4] I. 21. 7, cf. 22. 7.

[5] IV. 1. 93 ff.   [6] Above, p. 4.

[7] D. O. Ross, *Backgrounds to Augustan Poetry: Gallus, Elegy and Rome* (1975), 82 ff., cf. 102. This fancy was eloquently promulgated by F. Skutsch, *Gallus und Vergil* (1905), 145; it was regarded with favour by H. J. Rose, *A Handbook of Latin Literature* (1936), 289 ; and J. P. Sullivan sees 'nothing impossible' (o.c. 33). Similarly K. Quinn concurs in his long review of the book of D. O. Ross (*Phoenix* XXX (1976), 295).

These scholars perhaps neglect Propertius' claim to have witnessed an encounter between Gallus and the mistress of Gallus (I. 10. 1). When and where did that happen?

To assert descent from kings and gods was common form among the better sort in the cities; and poetic licence escapes into sheer fantasy when a patron is praised or the ruler equated with divinity and hailed as a conqueror to the world's end. Moreover, genuine frauds in genealogy existed, some known and condoned, others shown up by malice or exact scholarship. For a poet to attribute falsely a noble extraction to his friend, whether equestrian (as was Cornelius Gallus) or a minor senator, would expose them both to ridicule or contempt.

Discarding idle fancies, rational conjecture may impart instruction, though not proof. Two options may be presented. If either fails acceptance, or both, some benefit may still accrue to the study of Roman society.[1]

First, why not a Caninius? This family is on attestation in the senatorial order a century and a half earlier. Recently there was L. Caninius Gallus, holding the *fasces* in 37 B.C. No action of his finds record before or after that year. Curiosity cannot be suppressed. He may well be the Caninius Gallus revealed by an entertaining notice: he prosecuted the consular C. Antonius (in 59 B.C.), and then married his daughter. If so, a youthful prosecutor—and husband of the Triumvir's cousin.[2]

The consuls imposed by the Triumvirs exhibit sharp contrasts: either action and ambition rewarded by swift promotion, or elderly relics. The bar of age falls by ten years, as witness M. Valerius Messalla Corvinus, born in 64, consul in 31. The innovation persists under the Republic of Caesar Augustus, restricted (as was deemed proper) to *nobiles*. No writer attests it. Facts bring proof, notably L. Piso (*cos.* 15 B.C.), dying in 32 at the age of eighty.[3]

At the other extreme, men well on in years such as the obscure Sex. Pompeius (*cos.* 35 B.C.).[4] And under the new dispensation the *novus homo* cannot often expect to be consul short of forty-two.

Therefore a Caninius Gallus can easily be evoked and postulated,

---

[1] The more so since this Gallus finds no lodgement in *PIR²*. Another item is 'Licinia P. f. Galli', buried in the sepulchre of the Crassi (*CIL* VI. 21308): noted in *Rom. Rev.* (1939), 310. The entry of her husband Gallus (*PIR²*, G 54) unfortunately omits her patronymic. It is important. There were not many Licinii Crassi with that *praenomen*.

[2] Valerius Maximus IV. 2. 6. His father was held to be the prosecutor, the tribune of 56 B.C., cf. *Rom. Rev.* (1939), 200. But the age of the son (*cos.* 37) precludes.

[3] *Ann.* VI. 10. 3.   [4] Below, p. 158.

between the consul of 37 B.C. and his homonym, *suffectus* in 2 B.C.[1]
There is no deception. Other examples attest a missing generation in
families of the *nobilitas*, both now and later. The young friend of
Propertius either died before consular years, or renounced well in
advance, like Volcacius Tullus. Which will not occasion surprise
or discomfort.

The Caninii may be an old family of Tusculum, the home of so
many senators and consuls. C. Caninius Rebilus (*suff.* A.D. 37) paid
honour to that community by holding the office of aedile; and the
name of Taurus Caninius is also to be discovered at Tusculum.[2] By
the emphatic *praenomen* the nomenclature suggests a *nobilis*—and a
link with the family of the Augustan marshal T. Statilius Taurus
(*cos.* II 26 B.C.).

Second, an Aelius Gallus. The notorious man of this name is the
Prefect of Egypt next in succession to Cornelius Gallus.[3] He took in
adoption a son of Seius Strabo, an equestrian notable from Etruscan
Volsinii. His own parentage has failed to excite curiosity. One is impelled towards C. Aelius Gallus, a writer on jurisprudence of the age
preceding.[4] Not a senator, so far as is known.[5] None the less, this
Aelius Gallus might belong to a noble family that had lapsed from
the career of honours. An illustrious parallel offers in that age. The
jurist Ser. Sulpicius Rufus (*cos.* 51 B.C.) belonged to the patriciate:
his grandfather a senator of no consequence, his father merely a
knight in status.[6]

The Aelii, an old plebeian *gens* of the nobility noted for proficiency in the law, had fallen on evil days long since. There were
two branches at least, the Paeti and Tuberones, the latter renowned
for frugality. After a long interval the Aelii recapture the consulship
with L. Aelius Tubero (*cos.* 11 B.C.) and his brother Sex. Aelius Catus

---

[1] The two consuls are assumed without question father and son in *PIR*², C 389 f. On the
hypothesis here presented, Propertius' friend would not be the father of the consul of 2 B.C.

[2] *CIL* XIV. 2622; 2620.

[3] *PIR*², A 179. There is uncertainty about his *praenomen*. Probably 'Lucius' rather than
'Marcus'.

[4] On whom, cf. *RE* I, 492 f. A scholar rather than a jurisprudent. None the less, he might
have found a mention somewhere in W. Kunkel, *Herkunft u. soziale Stellung der r. Juristen*
(1952): if only for the chance of a relationship with the decayed consular family.

[5] This man, or a son, might be the C. Aelius Gallus honoured at Athens by a statue made
by a certain Praxiteles (*IG* II². 4117): for problems of dating, see the annotation on 4181.

[6] Cicero, *Pro Murena* 16.

(*cos.* A.D. 4), the sons of Q. Tubero, the jurist and historian.[1] Catus by his *cognomen* recalls the primeval jurist Sex. Aelius Paetus Catus (*cos.* 198 B.C.).

Furthermore, the great Aelius Seianus, the son of Seius Strabo, has a link with the Tuberones. His father adopted one of them, viz. L. Seius Tubero (*suff.* 18).[2]

So far so good. Let the relevance to Sex. Propertius now emerge. A poem reveals Aelia Galla married to a Postumus. He left her to go away to the wars,

> Postume, plorantem potuisti linquere Gallam.   (III. 12. 1)

Postumus may (or may not) be identical with C. Propertius Q. f. Postumus, a senator known from an inscription.[3] Further, a small item. A Paetus happens to be registered in the poems, who perished on a journey to Egypt (III. 7). Possibly an Aelius Paetus: the *cognomen* is ancient in that family, and may have been revived recently. Sex. Aelius Catus (*cos.* 4) gave his daughter the name 'Aelia Paetina'.[4]

Finally, on the flank of the argument, yet perhaps not lacking pertinence, a link not hitherto detected. Of generals active along the zone of the northern frontiers, the geographer Strabo happens to mention only Aelius Catus, the legate of Moesia, as has already been put under emphasis in another place.[5] Now Strabo was a friend of Aelius Gallus, with whom he made a tour in Upper Egypt.[6]

Conjecture therefore becomes permissible. The Gallus who gets four poems from Propertius may be an Aelius Gallus. That is, brother, son, or nephew of the Prefect of Egypt; and Aelia Galla, wife of the senator Propertius Postumus, may be his sister.

---

[1] *PIR²*, A 274; 157. The parent, noted there, might have deserved a separate entry.

[2] On which link see G. V. Sumner, *Phoenix* XIX (1965), 134 ff. (with a stemma); G. W. Bowersock, *Augustus and the Greek World* (1965), 129 f.

It may be remarked in passing that not all of Sumner's conjectures about the family and relationships of Aelius Seianus are acceptable. For example he denies to Seius Strabo and gives to Caecina Tuscus the inscription *ILS* 8996 (Volsinii).

[3] *ILS* 914 (Rome), patently of early Augustan date. Neither this senator nor Aelia Galla is discussed by Bowersock (o.c. 129).

[4] *PIR²*, A 305 (the second wife of Claudius, subsequent to the decease of Plautia Urgulanilla).

[5] Strabo VII, p. 303; cf. above, p. 69.

[6] Strabo II, p. 118; XVII, p. 806; 816. Bowersock suggests that he took the name of his patron—and even that he may have been called 'Aelius Strabo' (o.c. 129).

And, at the end, one will not miss the last Aelius Gallus. He was in peril, and he perhaps perished, after the destruction of Aelius Seianus on October 18 of the year 31.[1] Enticing perspectives open. It is time to cut them short.

. . .

V. The few names on attestation of Propertius' friends show a municipal aristocrat in relations of amity with two members of consular houses, Tullus and Gallus. The contrary would surprise. At the other extreme, the world of letters exhibited variegation in width or depth, descending through mixed or overlapping strata. It resembles the late epoch of the Republic, or, better, continues it: decayed aristocrats, debauched grammarians, influential bankers and freedmen, ladies of easy virtue and elegant accomplishments.[2] The surviving specimen was P. Vedius Pollio, the opulent friend of Caesar Augustus, in whose honour he constructed a shrine at Beneventum.[3]

Ovid, like other poets, would not hold anxiously aloof. He was alert, humane, and humorous, a paragon of 'facilitas' and 'comitas' if ever there was one. Those qualities, it is true, might become detrimental. Ovid possessed 'comitas honesta', based on a character pliant but not feeble.[4]

Ovid came of a healthy stock (his old father died at the age of ninety), but he was not robust in body or immune from maladies.[5] Nor had he submitted to military service in youth when aspiring to embark on the career of a senator.[6] Ovid was not given over to drink or dissipation—or to a variety of other diversions that may sap the mind rather than the body. Ovid believed in energy and the virtue of hard work.[7]

Foreign religions exerted a strong seduction in the world of women. Ovid duly produces a poem for Corinna, interceding with Isis.[8] It need not be taken seriously. Nor does he betray signs of being

---

[1] *Ann.* V. 8. 1. Sumner states that 'Aelius Gallus must be Seianus' elder son' (o.c. 141). Not necessarily.

[2] See now J. Griffin, *JRS* LXVI (1976), 87 ff. This elegant paper demolishes conventional questions about the relationship between life and letters in Augustan Rome.

[3] *ILS* 109. For Vedius Pollio, *JRS* LI (1961), 21 ff. = *RP* (1978), 518 ff.

[4] The phrase is applied to Seneca by Tacitus (*Ann.* XIII. 2. 1).

[5] His father's age, *Tr.* IV. 10. 77 ff.; his own physique, ibid. 37, cf. V. 2. 2 f. etc.

[6] *Tr.* IV. 1. 71.   [7] Below, p. 227.   [8] *Am.* II. 13.

addicted to magic or astrology, although the science of the stars won favour and adepts among men of powerful and penetrating intelligence, such as the poet's close coeval, Claudius Nero.

A variety of doctrines that had come to adhere to the venerable name of Pythagoras carried a certain appeal to the curious or the mystically minded. In the last epoch of the Republic erudition or rank in society lent credit. The notable figure was Nigidius Figulus; and Terentius Varro cannot be denied a tendency, perhaps at a late stage in his long existence.[1] Furthermore, Numa Pompilius was believed a disciple, although chronology refuted the patent fabrication. Numa came from the Sabine country. Varro was a sceptic in religion, but local patriotism may have induced Varro and others to exploit an attractive link. At least Vatinius was assailed by Cicero with allegations of necromancy; and the oration of a pseudo-Cicero incriminated Sallust.[2]

The sage of Samos and Croton is on conspicuous show in the *Metamorphoses*, Book XV. That should not deceive. Pythagoras is a structural device for bringing Greek mythology into relation with the legendary history of Italy, because of good king Numa; and Pythagoras might lend ostensible support at the end to the long sequence of transmutations.

While some of the beliefs or practices covered by the label of Pythagorean were innocuous, such as the avoidance of beans in diet or the wearing of a black toga, others were arcane or dubious. They incurred suspicion or were denounced as pernicious.[3] Ovid, however, may have inclined to sympathy with the teachings of the Sextii, 'nova et Romani roboris secta'.[4] One of its exponents was the excellent Papirius Fabianus, who made a name for himself in declamation before being captivated by higher studies.[5] Sextius the founder, it may be noted, declined to embark on the senatorial career.[6]

---

[1] K. Latte, *Römische Religionsgeschichte* (1970), 289 ff. Suetonius labelled Nigidius 'Pythagoricus et magus' (Jerome, *Chron.* p. 156 H).

[2] Cicero, *In Vatinium* 14; 'Cicero', *In Sallustium* 15. For the notion that Sabines were prone to mysticism, *Sallust* (1964), 8.

[3] Not all were as harmless as the vegetarianism that disturbed young Seneca's parent (*Epp.* 108. 22). It was a season when foreign superstitions were under attack.

[4] Seneca, *NQ* VII. 32. 2; *Epp.* 59. 7: 'Graecis verbis, Romanis moribus philosophantem'. For the Sextii, M. T. Griffin, *Seneca* (1976), 37 ff.

[5] *PIR¹*, P 85. For his style, Seneca, *Epp.* 100. 5.   [6] Seneca, *Epp.* 98. 13.

In so far as revealed by the poems, Ovid's mind is lucid and rational. About the gods of the Roman State he shared the opinions of the educated class:

expedit esse deos, et, ut expedit, esse putemus.[1]

Ovid came too late to be enlisted in promoting the Augustan restoration of the ancient cults. In which he may be counted fortunate. It was long after the decisive and emotional years (Actium and its aftermath) that Ovid thought of composing his *Fasti*. Not a good idea. The *Metamorphoses* accorded with his talents.

. . .

VI. Well aware of envy and detraction ('livor'), Ovid is generous in tribute to other poets, notably Gallus, Tibullus, Propertius. Through Gallus the writers of elegiac verse lead back to Catullus. That derivation might have been manifest in other writers now lost. Ovid furnishes a long catalogue of poets. No fewer than thirty, four of them anonymous (*Ex P*. IV. 16).[2]

The list, it may be noted, carries only three tragic poets, one comic.[3] There appear to be about nine composers of mythological epics.[4] A dozen of these poets are elsewhere on mention, mostly of the briefest. For the rest, only names. But with six exceptions, only *cognomina*; a list of this length could not fail to carry five of the most common and indistinctive.[5] Identification is baffled, likewise the seductive search for origins and family.

Rising and prospering, the educated class in the western provinces had been making a splendid contribution to polite studies. Above all, the Transpadane zone, when Gallia Cisalpina was still governed by a proconsul. Spain should not be left out of the reckoning, with its rich harvest of rhetors, or Narbonensis, truthfully described by a man from Italia Transpadana as 'Italia verius quam provincia'.[6] Cornelius Gallus came from the 'vetus et inlustris Foroiuliensium colonia'.[7]

---

[1] *AA* I. 637, cf. Pliny, *NH* II. 26: 'deos . . . credi ex usu vitae est.'

[2] One of them (16. 27) is identifiable as Tuticanus, cf. 12. 27 f.

[3] *Ex P*. IV. 16. 29 ff. Namely Turranius, Varius (Rufus), (Sempronius) Gracchus. The comedian is (Maecenas) Melissus, a polygraph (*PIR*[1], M 31).

[4] Ibid. 16. 5 ff., beginning with (Domitius) Marsus, 'magnique Rabirius oris'.

[5] Viz. Priscus (twice), Proculus, Rufus, Sabinus, Severus.   [6] Pliny, *NH* III. 31.

[7] As argued in *CQ* XXXII (1938), 39 ff. = *RP* (1978), 38 ff. The town in Friuli has been

On Ovid's list only 'Montanus' looks provincial, viz. Julius Montanus, a poet remembered for a friendship with Tiberius Caesar that failed to prosper.[1] However, a word might go to Julius Florus, a member of the 'studiosa cohors' that accompanied Claudius Nero on his mission to the eastern lands in 20 B.C.[2] Perhaps from Tres Galliae rather than from Narbonensis. The 'principes' of that country were making rapid progress, in eloquence at least. Another Julius Florus not much later earns high praise from Quintilian.[3] However, it was too early, it appears, for many of them to figure in the repertory of the elder Seneca. Of persons there named, only two are Julii, viz. the poet Montanus and the declaimer Bassus, the latter on frequent mention and approved by Albucius Silo.[4]

Further, the notables of Tres Galliae not only command regiments of native cavalry. They may be found in the regular 'militia equestris' or even in financial posts. The name of Iccius will be suitably recalled.[5] Birth, wealth, and liberal studies would before long lead the notables of Gaul to seek admittance to the Roman Senate.[6]

.   .   .

VII. A proper study of life and letters during the four decades of Augustus' reign will allocate generous space to Greek writers.[7] Once again, the note is continuity, impaired by the wars and by the danger that the imperial dominions might split into two halves (which geography as well as language indicated, Illyricum not yet conquered), but resuming after the victory of Caesar's heir. Though proclaimed a crusade in defence of Rome and Italy, the war of

advocated by some scholars—and even Forum Iulii Iriensium (Voghera) by J.-P. Boucher, *Caius Cornelius Gallus* (1966), 11.

[1] Seneca, *Epp.* 122. 11: 'tolerabilis poeta et amicitia Tiberii notus et frigore'. For the parent Seneca, 'egregius poeta' (*Controv.* VII. 1. 27).

[2] Horace, *Epp.* I. 3. He also received II. 2. Perhaps identical with the declaimer Florus, who had been an auditor of Porcius Latro (*Controv.* IX. 2. 23 f.).

[3] Quintilian X. 3. 13: 'in eloquentia Galliarum, quoniam ibi demum exercuit eam, princeps'.

[4] *PIR²*, J 204.

[5] Horace, *Odes*, I. 29; *Epp.* I. 12. To *PIR²*, J 15 might have been added a reference to Iccius, one of the first men among the Remi (Caesar, *BG* II. 3. 1).

[6] Tacitus' version of the Claudian oration suitably introduces 'iam moribus artibus adfinitatibus nostris mixti' (*Ann.* XI. 24. 6).

[7] G. W. Bowersock, *Augustus and the Greek World* (1965), 122 ff.

Actium brought no disadvantage to the vanquished or lasting animosity on either side. The chief adherents of Marcus Antonius passed without pain into the 'clientela' of Caesar Augustus: kings and tetrarchs and the aristocracy of the cities.[1] Princeps at Rome, 'imperator' to the armies, Augustus rules as a monarch in the eastern lands.

The return of peace launches an invasion: poets, thinkers and professors, eloquent ambassadors, medical men, and various charlatans. In the eager forefront stand Strabo of Amaseia and Dionysius of Halicarnassus. Strabo acquired the patronage of Aelius Gallus, a high equestrian dignitary; and Dionysius dedicated a treatise on Thucydides to a Roman historian, the parent of Q. Aelius Tubero (*cos.* 11 B.C.).[2] As for *rhetores*, the elder Seneca furnishes a mass of names; and some perhaps were expatriates returning.[3] The schools of declamation thus illustrate aspects of unity in the two cultures.

The conspicuous patron of Greek poets was Piso the Pontifex, inheriting the elegant proclivities of his father. Chief among them were Antipater and Crinagoras.[4] The latter produced a number of small pieces honouring members of the dynasty.[5] Another poet, Diodorus, did not omit the stepson of the Princeps.[6]

The Hellenic tastes of Claudius Nero are seldom accorded due weight and emphasis.[7] They are multifarious (works of art as well as letters) and they deserve a long disquisition. For present purposes, summary indication must suffice.

Suetonius has a precious chapter documenting his addiction to 'artes liberales'.[8] For his poems in Greek, Tiberius took as models Euphorion, Rhianus, and Parthenius. So fervent was his predilection that he put their portraits along with their writings in the public

---

[1] Cf. *Rom. Rev.* (1939), 300 f.; *Tacitus* (1958), 506 f.

[2] Not the consul, as in *PIR²*, A 102, cf. Bowersock, o.c. 130.

[3] Not L. Cestius Pius of Smyrna (*PIR²*, C 694). But perhaps Argentarius (A 1038): to be identified with the author of Greek epigrams, cf. Reitzenstein, *RE* II, 712.

[4] See especially the long chapter in C. Cichorius, *Römische Studien* (1922), 294 ff.

[5] Cichorius, o.c. 306 ff. Notably Germanicus. For *Anth. Pal.* IX. 283 see above, p. 58. For Crinagoras see now Gow and Page, *The Garland of Philip* II (1968), 210 ff.

[6] *Anth. Pal.* IX. 219. Note also Apollonides (IX. 287), who dedicated to Tiberius his commentary on the *Silloi* of Timon (Diogenes Laertius IX. 109).

[7] That is a defect in the otherwise useful book of R. Seager, *Tiberius* (1972), cf. remarks in *Historia* XXIII (1974), 490 f. For Tiberius' philhellenism, Bowersock, o.c. 77; 133 f.; B. Levick, *Tiberius the Politician* (1976), 17 f.; A. F. Stewart, *JRS* LXVII (1977), 76 ff.

[8] Suetonius, *Tib.* 70.

libraries beside the authors of classic rank. Hence a fashion in scholarly circles, with eager competition for patronage.

Seven years spent on Rhodes confirmed the philhellenic tastes of Claudius Nero. Then, finally, the retreat to another island. With him went one senator only, Cocceius Nerva, the consular jurist (perhaps a close coeval), and a knight of distinction, Curtius Atticus. For the rest, a troop of scholars, Greeks for the most part, 'quorum sermonibus levaretur'.[1] Sombre and frugal banquets on Capreae were enlivened by erudite or frivolous discourse on problems in mythology.

The character and the tastes of Claudius Nero were formed and reinforced by a spirit of opposition to his environment. None the less, he ought not to be held a total anomaly in Augustan Rome. Others may have refused to award favour and preference to the poets annexed by Maecenas and earning approbation from the Princeps. Velleius can be put to good employ as a guide to Tiberius Caesar. Among the literary glories of the age he reckons Ovid, but not Horace.[2]

. . .

VIII. Little survives of Latin prose from this epoch. The aftermath of the wars produced memoirs, perhaps a whole crop. Messalla Corvinus presented his record in warfare and politics, no doubt with noble and patriotic pleas to explain changes of allegiance. Another renegade who wrote was inferior in rank and repute, the agile Q. Dellius.[3] Corvinus coined for him a label of dispraisal;[4] and Horace came out with an elegant and superfluous piece of admonition—Dellius should practice equanimity in his season of retreat.[5]

To recount recent transactions was a perilous undertaking. The lava was still burning beneath the ashes, so Horace reminded Asinius Pollio.[6] Livy had gone to the most ancient history for comfort, to

---

[1] *Ann.* IV. 58. 1.

[2] Velleius II. 36. 3: 'princeps carminum Vergilius Rabiriusque et consecutus Sallustium Livius Tibullusque et Naso'. For Rabirius cf. Ovid's praise in *Ex P.* IV. 16. 5 (quoted above, p. 105 n. 4). For the significance of the omission of Horace, cf. now R. J. Goar, *Latomus* XXXV (1976), 43 ff.

[3] *PIR*[1], D 29 (omitted from the second edition).   [4] Seneca, *Suas.* I. 7.

[5] Horace, *Odes* II. 3: neatly placed, following Asinius Pollio and Sallustius Crispus, to evoke the age of tribulation, and changes of side.

[6] Horace, *Odes* II. 1.

take him away 'a conspectu malorum quae nostra tot per annos vidit aetas'.[1] But Livy's long task brought him to the twenty years of tribulation.

Livy came to history from eloquence, perhaps even from some study of philosophy. Such at least was the tone and trend of certain books he left behind him.[2] Livy is an isolated figure in the social life of the age. He spent most of his time, it would seem, at his native Patavium. He is absent from the rhetorical debates which the elder Seneca compiled. Nor does any anecdote disclose Livy in the company of other authors or patrons of literature. The two stories that survive show him on a footing of candid amity with members of the dynasty.

Caesar Augustus styled him a 'Pompeianus'.[3] No rebuke was intended. And Livy indeed performed a signal service. He rendered harmless the annals of the late Republic.

Further, Livy directed Claudius, the brother of Germanicus, towards a vocation suitable for a youth whom the family wished to seclude from public life.[4] Claudius proposed to begin with 44 B.C. But that choice, he saw, would entail writing 'neque libere neque vere'. And he was warned off by his mother and his grandmother. He therefore began when the wars ended, 'a pace civili'.

Claudius reached the age of twenty in A.D. 11. Three years previously he had suffered a disappointment. They took away his betrothed, Aemilia Lepida, because her parents had given grievous offence to Augustus.[5] The study of history, it appears, can be deemed to offer consolation even in early youth.

In this season the mentor himself was verging towards the term of a long life. By the year of his birth Livy is bracketed with Messalla Corvinus in the *Chronicle* of Jerome. But the consulate of Corvinus (31 B.C.), and other facts concerning Corvinus, disallow the year. Therefore, not 59 B.C., but 64, as was established close on a century

---

[1] Livy, Praef. 5.

[2] Seneca, *Epp.* 100. 9: 'scripsit enim et dialogos, quos non magis philosophiae adnumerare possis quam historiae, et ex professo philosophiam continentis libros.' It is not clear that these products belong to an early stage in the historian's life.

[3] *Ann.* IV. 34. 3.

[4] Suetonius, *Divus Claudius* 41. 1.

[5] Ibid. 26. 1. See further below, p. 208.

ago.[1] The corollary, however, namely Livy passing away in 12, not in 17, is far from having won general acceptance.[2]

The last instalment of Livy's work, the nine books devoted to the Republic of Caesar Augustus from 28 B.C. to 9 B.C., are an epilogue, so it may be conjectured.[3] Further, not begun before A.D. 4. For a good reason. And the choice of the terminal point was well advised. To end with Drusus dying on campaign beyond the Rhine enabled the historian to celebrate the glory of conquest and the fame of the Claudii.

Contemporary annals had their limitations and their hazards. Curiosity may well be aroused about the quality of those nine books. Another historian, Cremutius Cordus, who began with 44 B.C., narrated the reign of Caesar Augustus, and even held recitations in his presence, so it is recorded.[4] Both Cordus and Livy may be subsumed in the verdict of Cornelius Tacitus: 'temporibusque Augusti dicendis non defuere decora ingenia, donec gliscente adulatione deterrerentur.'[5] Though Tacitus when embarking on the *Annales* had not devoted adequate study to the previous reign, not even to its concluding decade, he would know about Cordus. The eloquent historian did not miss the great orator Cassius Severus.[6]

The distant past was safer. L. Arruntius (*cos.* 22 B.C.), who had been one of the admirals at Actium, wrote about the first war against the Carthaginians in a style that carried to excess the manner of Sallust.[7] That was also the theme of a certain Alfius, as the solitary notice in a grammarian attests.[8] Rather, perhaps, an epic poem. That permits assigning a name to one of the performers on Ovid's list.[9] Alfius Flavus won fame in the schools by precocious talent, which, so some opined, would vanish in due course: yet Flavus did not for-

---

[1] H. Schulz, *De Valerii Messallae aetate* (Prog. Stettin, 1886), 6.

[2] It was not drawn in *Tacitus* (1958), 337, where Livy dies in the same year as Ovid. See, however, the argument in *Harvard Studies* LXIV (1959), 40 ff. = *RP* (1978), 414 ff.; and also *Sallust* (1964), 13 f. The notion that Livy did not outlive Augustus is regarded with favour by R. M. Ogilvie, in his Commentary to I–V (1965), 6. The problem of Livy's age is ignored in *PIR*[2], L 292.

[3] Above, p. 2.

[4] Suetonius, *Tib.* 61. 3; Dio LVII. 24. 3.   [5] *Ann.* I. 1. 2.

[6] *Ann.* I. 72. 3 (his prosecution for *maiestas*).   [7] Seneca, *Epp.* 114. 17 ff.

[8] Festus, p. 150 L.

[9] *Ex P.* IV. 16. 23: 'quique acies Libycas Romanaque proelia dixit'. Cf. the full discussion of Cichorius, o.c. 58 ff.

feit all his vigour, though it was debilitated through sloth and the writing of poetry.[1]

Nor should C. Clodius Licinus be omitted.[2] He in fact put his inception at the end of the Second Punic War, the third book being cited for an incident in 194 B.C.[3] A general comment made by Tacitus about ancient history finds illustration: 'neque refert cuiusquam Punicas Romanasne acies laetius extuleris.'[4] The sentence leads up to the prosecution of Cremutius Cordus.

.   .   .

IX. Along with Licinus, another prose author invites mention, for a reason at first sight extraneous, namely their consulships. It is C. Valgius Rufus.[5] He makes an early entrance into literary and social life, in a group of poets and senators in 35 or 34 B.C.[6] Messalla Corvinus was of the company; and in the panegyric which celebrates the consulate of Messalla, one other name is exalted,

Valgius, aeterno propior non alter Homero.[7]

No epic poem of this person stands anywhere on record, but he wrote some elegies and epigrams. Also prose, on a variety of topics: on rhetoric, on grammar, and so on. His work on botany was dedicated to the Princeps. A devotional sentence from the preface has happily been preserved.[8]

The surprise is the honour to which he acceded, the only *novus homo* (apart from the *ordinarius* Sulpicius Quirinius and the last *suffectus* of this peculiar year, namely L. Volusius Saturninus) to hold the *fasces* in a period of nine years (15–7 B.C.).[9] On March 6 of 12, the day on which Augustus assumed the office of *pontifex maximus*, Valgius is discovered as consul, taking the place of the colleague of Quirinius. Barbatus Appianus had died, one of the Appii Claudii

---

[1] Seneca, *Controv*. I. 1. 22. Cestius Pius accused him of imitating Ovid, 'qui hoc saeculum amatoriis non artibus tantum sed sententiis implevit' (ibid. III. 7).

[2] *PIR*[2], C 1167; C. Cichorius, *RE* IV, 77 ff.

[3] Livy XXIX. 22. 10.

[4] *Ann*. IV. 33. 4.

[5] *PIR*[1], V 169; H. G. Gundel, *RE* VIIIA, 272 ff.

[6] Horace, *Sat*. I. 10. 81 ff.

[7] 'Tibullus' IV. 1. 180.

[8] Pliny, *NH* XXV. 4: 'incohata etiam praefatione religiosa ut omnibus malis humanis illius potissimum principis semper mederetur maiestas.'

[9] No surprise or curiosity is expressed in *RE* VIIIA, 272 ff.

adopted by a Valerius Messalla.[1] It was an unhealthy year. Marcus Agrippa died towards the end of March, and one of the *suffecti* later on, namely C. Caninius Rebilus.[2]

Even so, Valgius Rufus was very lucky. No credit earned by science of the law, public eloquence or warfare explains the exceptional promotion. The influence of Messalla Corvinus might be divined—and perhaps that of Ti. Claudius Nero, who was consul the year before.[3]

.   .   .

X. Clodius Licinus is the subject of an attractive notice transmitted by Suetonius: the 'consularis historicus' succoured the polymath Julius Hyginus, who passed his last years in dire impoverishment.[4] A melancholy fate for one of the higher librarians, and perhaps the sequel to some scandal or action of political imprudence.[5]

Hyginus is here described as a friend of Ovid. He is not elsewhere registered as such. Which is a warning about negative inferences about the range of his friendships. There are others. For example, Ovid did not think of writing to Sex. Pompeius until 13, the year preceding his consulship.

The history of Clodius Licinus is cited by Livy in Book XXIX, at an early stage in his own composition. The passage has been an occasion of perplexity.[6] It is patently a subsequent insertion. But subsequent by how much, that is the question. The incident (it concerns Q. Pleminius) is introduced well in advance—and it is retold in similar language under 194 B.C. where it belongs.[7] On that showing, the passage looks authentic.[8]

---

[1] Barbatus (*PIR*[1], V 89), married to a niece of Augustus, the younger Claudia Marcella (*PIR*[2], C 1103).

[2] *PIR*[2], C 391: otherwise unknown, but a *nobilis*.

[3] The last *suffectus* of 12 B.C. was L. Volusius Saturninus: related in some way to Claudius Nero, cf. *Rom. Rev.* (1939), 424.

[4] Suetonius, *De gramm.* 20.

[5] Compare Q. Caecilius Epirota, allegedly adulterous with Attica, the wife of Marcus Agrippa: he fled for protection to Cornelius Gallus, and that was among the 'gravissima crimina' brought up by Augustus against the Prefect of Egypt (Suetonius, *De gramm.* 16). About this time Agrippa acquired a new wife, the elder Marcella (*PIR*[2], C 1102).

[6] Livy XXIX. 22. 10.   [7] Livy XXXIV. 44. 6 ff.

[8] As urged on stylistic grounds by Conway and Johnson ad loc. (OCT, 1935). Some scholars have maintained an interpolation. Thus C. Cichorius, *RE* IV, 78. See, however, F. Münzer, *Hermes* XLVII (1912), 162 ff.; *RE* XXI, 222.

Therefore Licinus may have written a long time before his consulship, which fell in the second half of A.D. 4; and like Valgius he won
public recognition late in life.

The type and classic model of the senatorial annalist is a man of
mature years who takes to history after the active career has terminated, often for consolation or apologia, and not seldom bitter and
censorious. For the consulship of Licinus no support other than his
history can be adduced—unless perhaps Claudius Nero, who became
Ti. Caesar in June of the year.

Another *novus homo* became consul suffect three years later, viz.
Lucilius Longus: a person of no known distinction, but abnormally
honoured with a public funeral. This Lucilius was the sole senator to
accompany Claudius Nero when he went away to Rhodes.[1]

. . .

The prestige of polite letters was advertised and enhanced by the
public honour accruing at the end to Valgius Rufus and Clodius
Licinus. Valid for a Roman historian, the claims of 'bonae artes' seem
strained when extended to a poet and miscellaneous compiler.

Along with his elder brother, P. Ovidius Naso received the *latus
clavus*.[2] The brother died in the year 24/3, and Ovid renounced the
career after holding two minor magistracies.[3] He states his reasons,
which are clear and adequate. There is no call to adduce a transaction
that darkened the political horizon: the conspiracy of Varro Murena.

However, the fancy is not idle that if Ovid had found the life of
a senator not incompatible with the writing of verse (the duties were
not exacting, but time was wasted, and money), he might have ended
by holding the twelve *fasces* as consul suffect. Ovid reached fifty in
A.D. 8. Or at a later age still, as witness the paradoxical Vibius Rufus
(*suff.* 16), who was coeval with Ti. Caesar, if not somewhat older.
If the new Princeps was hesitant to concede full approbation, albeit
a friend to poetic studies, the influence of Messalla's sons cannot
tolerate underestimation.

---

[1] *Ann.* IV. 15. 1 f. Tiberius had a long memory for loyalty, cf. III. 48 (the obituary of
Sulpicius Quirinius).

[2] *Tr.* IV. 10. 27 ff., cf. below, p. 182.   [3] Ibid. 34, cf. *Fasti* IV. 384.

VII

THE SONS OF MESSALLA

I. MERE access to the Senate was not difficult in the last epoch of the Free State. The high assembly mustered a mass of nonentities, by origin municipal and well deserving the label 'homo novus parvusque senator'. In a period so rich in varied documentation, about one-third of the total escapes all record.

Senators and knights, they are two orders but one class: on brief definition the officer class, from which in the earlier time the Senate was an offshoot. The 'senator populi Romani' is marked off by the 'dignitas' of the governing order, but wealth and education procure social parity for knights—as do birth and family, since many men of adequate substance and repute lacked incentive to enter the Curia.

The dynasts annexed the eager talents of agents like Pompeius Theophanes and Cornelius Balbus (both foreign born), the wars of the Triumvirs enhanced their value, and the new order of Caesar Augustus conferred rewards and status through the creation of official posts. Prefects of Egypt and commanders of the Guard carry weight and authority far excelling the ordinary magistrate or proconsul. A straight line runs from Aelius Gallus and Seius Strabo to the predominance of Aelius Seianus.

At the same time, Caesar's friends continue to exercise 'potentia' in the counsels of the ruler. When C. Maecenas lapsed from favour after the crisis of 23 B.C., Sallustius Crispus slipped into the vacant place. Dying at an advanced age in A.D. 20, Crispus earned an obituary notice that consecrates the talents and potency of both ministers.[1]

As befits a master of statecraft, Crispus seems remote and inscrutable. Horace favoured him with an ode. It advertises the distaste Crispus felt for money, unless it be put to useful purposes—and it conveys a gentle admonition towards the virtues of temperance and

---

[1] Tacitus, *Ann*. III. 30. 2. Crispus was ignored by Suetonius and Dio.

benevolence.[1] There is also a Greek epigram in his honour: Crinagoras extols the three shrines of Fortuna that stood close to the
opulent gardens near the Porta Collina.[2] That is all. Though Crispus
was the grand-nephew and heir of the historian, no anecdote brings
him into relation with orators and men of letters. Perhaps Crispus
cared very little for poetry and its adepts.

. . .

II. Poets did not need much persuasion to celebrate in their different modes the victories of Caesar's heir, the blessings of peace and
stability, the revival of religion and the moral life. Augustus wanted
the best exponents, and he secured them.[3]

No other patron could hope to compete. Asinius Pollio had forfeited Virgil long since. Abandoning warfare and politics, Pollio
took to literature: first tragedy, then history. Finally, most of his
energies went to the practice of eloquence. The name of Pollio
occurs frequently in the pages of the elder Seneca, with appraisal of
his manner and report of his verdicts on sundry declaimers.

In the later season of a long life, Pollio seems to have lost interest
in the fostering of Latin poetry. Nor, though the arts of peace had
returned, and also the prestige of birth and station, can many notable
or active patrons be certified among the consulars.

The illustrious Fabius Maximus may be conceded, but Piso the
Pontifex appears confined to the Greeks. That is, unless he is the Piso
of the *Ars Poetica*,

pater et iuvenes patre digni. (24)

Argument tends to be circular, involving as it does the date of the
poem and the identity of the persons, neither by itself admitting
proof.[4] On the earlier dating (*c.* 18 B.C.), which some favour, old Cn.
Piso (*suff.* 23) would fit, with two sons, the consuls of 7 and 1 B.C.
But if the *Ars Poetica* be regarded as the latest work of Horace
(*c.* 10 B.C.), the Pontifex acquires marked priority. Search for the
sons is baffled, it is true. That is no bar. A son might perish short
of his consulship or pass by adoption into another family. The

---

[1] Horace, *Odes* II. 2, cf. W. M. Calder, *CP* LVI (1961), 175 ff.
[2] *Anth. Pal.* XVI. 40, cf. Vitruvius III. 2. 2.   [3] Suetonius, *Divus Aug.* 89. 3.
[4] Cf. below, p. 178.

disappearance of young *nobiles* whom birth designated for office can readily be documented.[1]

Neither Piso, be it noted, gets an ode from Horace. That category of person in the literary life of Augustan Rome may afford instruction and amusement.[2] Some coteries inclined to selection and exclusion; and, as in other ages, various groups should be allowed for that have not benefited from the hazards of record and survival.

A great name remains, that of Messalla Corvinus. He earned an ode from Horace, discreet and unobtrusive, with no mention of renown in warfare or excellence in oratory.[3] Instead, Corvinus is addicted to 'Socratici sermones'. No impediment, the poet avers, to enjoying vintage wine, as old Cato did.[4]

Corvinus shared primacy with Pollio among the orators of the time.[5] Some of the younger men took him for model, such as Claudius Nero.[6] But the enduring fame of Corvinus accrued through the poets to whom he extended favour and support. In the first place, Albius Tibullus. But Valgius Rufus will not be omitted;[7] and, to descend, the Corpus Tibullianum (which by good fortune does not have to be discussed in this place). The products of his own pen, verse as well as prose, were numerous and varied; and he had a poetess for niece, the daughter of the younger Ser. Sulpicius Rufus.[8]

. . .

Ovid in his autobiographical piece explains that Tibullus died too soon for friendship to develop,

> Vergilium vidi tantum: nec avara Tibullo
> tempus amicitiae fata dedere meae.   (*Tr.* IV. 10. 51 f.)

---

[1] Observe Paullus Aemilius Regillus, quaestor of Tiberius (*ILS* 949); M. Claudius Marcellus Aeserninus, praetor in 19 (*PIR*², C 928); Messalla Barbatus, the son of Barbatus Messalla Appianus (*PIR*¹, V 88).

[2] Those receiving odes or epistles from Horace 'include all the greatest names of the Augustan Age' according to L. P. Wilkinson, *Horace and his Lyric Poetry* (1945), 53.

[3] *Odes* III. 21. Previously in *Sat.* I. 10. 29 and 85; and he has a passing mention in *AP* 371.

[4] The ode is in fact dedicated to the wine jar. Old Messalla Rufus (*cos.* 53 B.C.) was a hard drinker, cf., discussing Varro's treatise *Messalla de valetudine*, C. Cichorius, *Römische Studien* (1922), 233 ff.

[5] Thus, already, Velleius II. 36. 2.   [6] Suetonius, *Tib.* 70. 1.

[7] Above, p. 111.

[8] He is named in the company of Corvinus in 35 or 34 (*Sat.* I. 10. 86), but is not heard of in the sequel.

Tibullus died in 19 B.C. Ovid's earliest associates, as disclosed in *Amores*, are 'sodales', young men of his own age and standing. In the sequel, no other poems carry an address or dedication to a friend or to a patron until the latest season of his writing. It comes as a surprise to learn that young Ovid was a welcome guest in mansions of the highest aristocracy, that Messalla Corvinus encouraged his earliest efforts. The revelation emerges, explicit and repeated, in letters Ovid sent to the sons of Messalla.[1]

.   .   .

III. The elder is M. Valerius Messalla Messallinus, consul in 3 B.C. The full style of the younger is revealed by a Greek inscription set up when he was proconsul of Asia: M. Aurelius Cotta Maximus Messallinus.[2] He was a Valerius Maximus adopted by an Aurelius Cotta; and he took over the *cognomen* 'Messallinus' on the decease of his brother.[3] For convenience he will hereinafter be styled 'Cotta Maximus' or 'Cotta'.

There has been some uncertainty about the precise identity of Cotta. As the consuls of the year 20 Tacitus registers 'M. Valerius et M. Aurelius' (*Ann.* III. 2. 3), and the latter recurs soon after as 'Aurelius Cotta consul' (17. 4). But a Cotta Messallinus was already on show in 16, named before six ex-consuls (II. 32. 1), and he appears in four places later on.

Borghesi held them identical, and so did Dessau.[4] But there was expert and weighty dissent, causing perplexity.[5] However, a piece of extraneous evidence now comes in. The name of Cotta can be detected in an inscription, showing him praetor in 17.[6] It was therefore as praetor-designate that he spoke his 'sententia' after the trial of the alleged conspirator Scribonius Libo.

Tacitus was inadvertent. Perhaps even worse, not aware that M. Aurelius Cotta and Cotta Messallinus were one and the same person. Though accurate in his work, and alert to the *Acta Senatus*,

---

[1] *Tr.* IV. 4. 27 ff.; *Ex P.* I. 7. 27 f.; II. 2. 97; 3. 70 ff.

[2] *Forsch. in Ephesos* III. 112, no. 22.   [3] Velleius II. 112. 2.

[4] Dessau said 'si vere est ut esse videtur' (*PIR*[1], V 90).

[5] Groag allotted separate entries, *PIR*[2], A 1487 f. But Degrassi held them identical, *Epigraphica* VIII (1946), 38.

[6] On the *Fasti Arvalium* (*Inscr. It.* XIII. 1, p. 297), cf. *JRS* XLVI (1956), 18 = *Ten Studies in Tacitus* (1970), 52.

Tacitus may not have looked at the consular list for the early Tiberian years.[1]

Next, their ages. Each may be presumed to accede 'suo anno' to the *fasces* (and Cotta was in fact praetor in 17, consul in 20). For the elder, no problem of competition to face. The decade 16–7 B.C. had witnessed a fine run of aristocrats. In 5 and 4 there were *suffecti*, the first since 12. Moreover, Messallinus was able to hold the *fasces* for the full twelve months. Likewise Cotta in A.D. 20, with for colleague his own nephew, M. Valerius Messalla: the sole and unique year without a *suffectus* during the whole reign of Tiberius Caesar. In each case, special favour has operated. The elder brother, it follows, was born in 36 B.C., the younger in 14.

A poem of Tibullus shows Messallinus inducted into the *quindecimviri sacris faciundis*.[2] Nothing forbids putting it in 21 or 20 B.C.— and everything commends. A *nobilis* can annex a priesthood in extreme youth, even when putting on the *toga virilis* about the age of fifteen. Observe, for example, the case of Paullus Fabius Persicus (*cos.* 34). He takes the place of his deceased parent in the confraternity of the Arvales in the summer of 15.[3] His birth can be assigned without discomfort to 2 or 1 B.C.

Not but that discrepant dates for the age of Messallinus have recently been conjured up. In a standard work of erudition it is asserted, not once but twice, that his birth must fall in 39 B.C.[4] This decree reposes on somebody's belief that the Tibullan poem can be proved written in 24 B.C., so it appears. Another scholar, arguing for 43 B.C., betrays himself. He fancied senatorial status to be requisite for a priesthood—and he wanted to prolong the life of Tibullus beyond 19 B.C.[5] These opinions, it is unfortunate, have not been accorded the treatment they deserve. Erudite fantasy leads to psittacism, to the end that a resplendent aristocrat is refused that consulship 'suo anno' to which he was destined from the day of his birth.

·　　　·　　　·

[1] Cf. above, p. 87.　　　　　　　　　　　　　　　　　　　　　[2] Tibullus II. 5.
[3] *AE* 1947, 52.
[4] R. Hanslik, *RE* VIIIA, 134; 139 ('muss'). This view is accepted by J. Scheid, *Les Frères arvales* (1975), 55, cf. 124 etc. Note also, arguing for 41 B.C., J. Morris, *Listy Filologické* LXXXVII (1964), 326.
[5] E. Bickel, *Rh. Mus.* CIII (1960), 97 ff. See also above, p. 3.

IV. Twenty-two years separate the consulates of the two brothers. Which raises a question, the marriages of Messalla Corvinus. One lady may at once be sent packing, namely the elderly 'Terentia M. Ciceronis'. According to Jerome, she was lodged in turn with Sallust, Cicero's enemy, and with Messalla Corvinus, and so 'quasi per quosdam gradus eloquentiae devoluta est.'[1] The fable has found fanciers.[2] There is an entertaining parallel, Vibius Rufus taking over Publilia.[3] Jerome's story may well excite curiosity. It was perhaps the product of manifold confusion—and it might have queer ramifications concerning either the historian or his grand-nephew. The two were liable to be amalgamated in the defective scholarship of late Antiquity.[4]

On the standard view Corvinus had for wife first a Calpurnia, then an Aurelia.[5] The evidence calls for close scrutiny. There are several uncertainties—and many Messallae.

First, a Calpurnia M. f. Messallae revealed by an inscription.[6] But one might expect 'Calpurnia Corvini'. That nomenclature happens to occur on a tile.[7] It might, however, belong to a wife of Messalla Corvinus (*cos.* 58), the great-grandson of the orator.[8]

The daughter of a Marcus Calpurnius carries some appeal. Calpurnii with that *praenomen* are not at all common. Alternatives offer. First, a putative daughter of M. Piso, the elder son of Cn. Piso (*cos.* 7 B.C.).[9] Next, in consideration of a wife for Messalla Corvinus, a daughter of either M. Piso, praetor in 44 B.C., or M. Calpurnius Bibulus (*cos.* 59).

A daughter of M. Piso is attractive, it cannot be denied.[10] More so, a daughter of Bibulus. She would be a granddaughter of Marcus

---

[1] Jerome, *Adv. Iov.* I. 48.

[2] E. Meyer, *Caesars Monarchie und das Principat des Pompejus*[3] (1922), 164; L. Pareti, *La congiura di Catilina* (1934), 204.

[3] Above, p. 84. [4] Thus Pseudo-Acro on *Odes* II. 2.

[5] R. Hanslik, *RE* VIIIA, 134. Dessau in *PIR*[1], V 90 appears to have assumed only one marriage.

[6] *ILS* 5989: the orator's wife according to Dessau in *PIR*[1], V 90.

[7] Published in *Bull. Comm.* 1889, 208 = Bloch no. 249. Not noted in *RE* VIIIA, 134.

[8] Cf. Groag in *PIR*[2], C 322, whose hesitations extend to the Calpurnia of *ILS* 5989.

[9] *PIR*[2], C 296.

[10] She would be a sister of M. Licinius Crassus Frugi (*cos.* 14 B.C.) who was a Calpurnius by birth, adopted by M. Licinius Crassus (*cos.* 30 B.C.). For the stemma, *JRS* L (1960), 17 = *RP* (1978), 503.

Cato, and sister to that Bibulus who was prominent with Corvinus, his coeval, in the cause of the Republic. After the defeat at Philippi they transferred their allegiance to Marcus Antonius, and they kept to it for some years.[1]

L. Calpurnius Bibulus died in 32 while governing Syria for Antonius.[2] Corvinus in the meantime had come to discern the appeal of the better cause, as he was later to designate it.[3] The date of his metamorphosis has been a subject of enquiry and debate. Much of it misguided, but of some benefit to historical investigations.[4] A *nobilis* enjoyed freedom of action or decision such as was denied to a *novus homo*. He could manœuvre for a long time between the rival dynasts.

Changes of side in a civil war often ruptured the matrimonial tie. If Corvinus' first wife was in fact a sister of Bibulus, there was room for him to acquire another attachment before espousing the lady who in 14 B.C. bore him his second (or second surviving) son.

Next, therefore, the mother of Cotta. She presents a problem of name and identity. It concerns a pair of Ovidian passages. In epilogue to his last poem, Ovid alludes to the extraction of Cotta Maximus,

> maternos Cottas cui Messallasque paternos,
> Maxime, nobilitas ingeminata dedit.   (*Ex P.* IV. 16. 43 f.)

Corvinus, it follows, had married an Aurelia. The last Aurelius Cotta on direct record (*pr.*?54) is heard of for the last time in 49.[5] On the standard view, Messalla's wife is a sister of this M. Cotta, who took in adoption Valerius Maximus, his sister's son.[6]

Since, however, that adoption occurred in 14 B.C. at the earliest, questions of age and of survival intervene to discountenance the opinion.[7] It is better to postulate an unattested son of M. Cotta (*pr.*?54). It is no anomaly that the last descendants of noble houses leave no trace.

---

[1] Appian, *BC* IV. 136, 575 f.   [2] Appian, *BC* IV. 38, 162.

[3] Plutarch, *Brutus* 53.

[4] A date as early as 40 B.C. was assumed by J. Hammer, *Prolegomena to an edition of the Panegyricus Messallae* (New York, 1925), 25. That cannot be. For several highly vulnerable opinions see J. Carcopino, *Rev. phil.* LXXII (1946), 96 ff.: accorded warm acclaim by P. Grimal, *Mélanges Carcopino* (1966), 433.

[5] Caesar, *BC* I. 30. 2.

[6] *RE* VIIIA, 134. Groag has 'fortasse avunculo suo' (*PIR*², A 1488).

[7] A difficulty not discerned by scholars in the recent age.

That is not all. An earlier poem produced the following statement of Cotta's ancestry,

> adde quod est animus semper tibi mitis, et altae
>   indicium mores nobilitatis habent,
> quos Volesus patrii cognoscat nominis auctor,
>   quos Numa materni non neget esse suos,
> adiectique probent genetiva ad nomina Cottae,
>   si tu non esses, interitura domus.   (*Ex P.* III. 2. 103 ff.)

The reference to adoption by a Cotta in order to perpetuate the name is welcome, albeit superfluous. On the other hand, Numa proclaims descent from the Calpurnii—and that on the maternal side, so it is stated. Hence a perplexity, if Cotta's mother was in fact an Aurelia.[1] Where lies the explanation of this double ancestry? The easiest way out is to suppose that Cotta's maternal grandfather had married a Calpurnia.

It may be added in passing that another explanation is not excluded. The second wife of Corvinus might have been a Calpurnia, daughter of a Calpurnius who married an Aurelia. On that hypothesis, the adopting parent would be an uncle (not a brother) of Cotta's mother. Stranger things can happen in matrimony among the *nobiles* than two wives bearing the same *gentilicium*. Perhaps even a single marriage for an aristocrat.[2]

.   .   .

V. So far so good (if that is the correct expression).[3] It is time to investigate the two brothers. After his consulship Messallinus first turns up as legate of Illyricum in A.D. 6. He lost a pitched battle to the insurgents, but was able subsequently to overcome them by an ambush. Such is the brief statement in Cassius Dio.[4] Velleius reports a victory won despite the heavy odds, more than twenty thousand

---

[1] It was no doubt for this reason that Dessau, discussing Calpurnia M. f. Messallae (*ILS* 5989), stated 'fortasse hac ex uxore genuit M. Aurelium Cottam Maximum, cuius matrem a Numa oriundam fuisse ait Ovidius' (*PIR*¹, V 90).

[2] And further, for long intervals between births, observe children of Vistilia, the lady of the six husbands (Pliny, *NH* VII. 39), cf. *JRS* LX (1970), 30 f. = *RP* (1978), 811 f.

[3] It is only a hypothesis, be it recalled, that Corvinus married a sister of his friend and ally L. Bibulus.

[4] Dio LV. 30. 2.

of the enemy being routed; and Messallinus was honoured with the
ornamenta triumphalia.[1]

Messallinus gets three epistles from Tomis. The earliest, in Book
IV of *Tristia*, eschews the name but at once discloses the person
'positis pro nomine signis'. It opens with a compliment to noble
birth and noble character, and to eloquence inherited from the
parent,

> cuius in ingenio est patriae facundia linguae,
> qua prior in Latio non fuit ulla foro.   (*Tr.* IV. 4. 5 f.)

Then, without much delay, comes the plea for intercession with
Caesar. Ovid reassures Messallinus. Friendship cannot be regarded as
detrimental, and it goes back a long way,

> quo vereare minus ne sim tibi crimen amicus,
>   invidiam, siqua est, auctor habere potest.
> nam tuus est primis cultus mihi semper ab annis
>   (hoc certe noli dissimulare) pater,
> ingeniumque meum (potes hoc meminisse) probabat
>   plus etiam quam me iudice dignus eram;
> deque meis illo referebat versibus ore,
>   in quo pars magnae nobilitatis erat.   (4. 25 ff.)

Ovid thus makes appeal to the past, to the memory of the parent
whose habit it was to encourage the young poet and even to recite
his verses. Corvinus, it should seem, is no longer among the living:
one observes the tone, and the tenses ('probabat', 'referebat', 'erat').
The poems in *Tristia IV* were written in the year 11; and the next
book registers the winter of 11/12.[2]

The second poem occurs early in *Ex Ponto* (I. 7), and can be dated
to the year 12. No poem in *Ex Ponto*, Book I, alludes to the
Pannonian triumph of October 23.

That event is first noted in the next book, with II. 1; and II. 2
(namely the third to the address of Messallinus), with generous
tribute to the dynasty, also contains an account of the triumph.
Messallinus has his place in the procession (2. 81), and there is a

---

[1] Velleius II. 112.   2. Messallinus is further attested in the *consilium* of Augustus in 13
(*P. Oxy.* 2435).
[2] Ch. III.

discreet allusion to the laurel of his triumphal honours (2. 89 f.).
Nor is the deceased parent omitted,

> hoc pater ille tuus, primo mihi cultus ab aevo,
> si quid habet sensus umbra diserta, petit.   (2. 97 f.)

Exact scrutiny must now be directed to the second poem (I. 7), of
the year 12. The illustrious parent is again evoked,

> nec tuus est genitor nos infitiatus amicos,
> hortator studii causaque faxque mei:
> cui nos et lacrimas, supremum in funere munus,
> et dedimus medio scripta canenda foro.   (I. 7. 27 ff.)

Ovid had not only been among the mourners at the funeral of
Messalla Corvinus. He composed a dirge. Therefore Corvinus passed
away before Ovid departed from Rome in the early winter of the
year 8. On the repeated testimony of the poet, Corvinus is a defunct
person in 11—and even more so (be it said) in 12, when his obsequies
are registered.

The testimony appears plain and decisive. Yet it has been contested
and passed over. Argument has been advanced with confidence that
Corvinus lived on for five more years after the catastrophe of Ovid,
that he did not succumb until 13.[1] The scholar whose authority
continues to be invoked based his thesis on an interpretation of the
second poem to the address of Messallinus (I. 7).[2] He ignored the
first letter (*Tr.* IV. 4).

The case for 13 was supported by two pieces of extraneous evidence.
First, the *Chronicle* of Jerome: Messalla Corvinus dies when aged
seventy-two (at least according to some of the manuscripts).[3] That
supports Jerome's date for his birth, namely 59 B.C. Hence A.D. 13
for his death.

But there is an impediment. Jerome's date for the birth of Corvinus
is patently too late. That was discerned long ago by Borghesi, who
assumed that it belonged *c.* 64. Indeed, precisely in 64, it can be

---

[1] F. Marx, *Wiener Studien* XIX (1897), 150 ff. Accepted by Dessau in *PIR*[1], V 90.

[2] The argument is based on 'nec tuus est genitor nos infitiatus amicos' (7. 27): the only
occasion when Corvinus might be thought to disown Ovid was in 8, after the catastrophe.
Yet the statement may not be specific but general, referring to Corvinus' attitude through
the long years of friendship: the next line acclaims him as the inspirer of Ovid's poetical
genius.

[3] Jerome, *Chron.* p. 170 H, cf. *PIR*[1], V 90.

argued.[1] Hence the corollary, which applies also to Livy, to throw back the date of his death by five years.

The dates in Jerome are often erroneous, it is true, the figures liable to corruption. Therefore, with arguments based on different manuscripts, a recent scholar advocates 64 B.C.–A.D. 13 for the span of the orator's life. He declares his result to be 'firm and clear'.[2]

Second, a document. Messalla Corvinus held the post of *curator aquarum*. Frontinus furnishes the list, equipped with consular dates, from the appointment of Corvinus (in 11 B.C.) down to his own.[3] On that list the successor to Corvinus in 13 stands as Ateius Capito (*suff.* 5), his tenure lasting until 23, when L. Tarius Rufus follows (*suff.* 16 B.C.).

A consular date, that is serious.[4] How and why should the testimony of a conscientious administrator be called into question? Alternative explanations avail. First, the aqueducts of Rome were left without a *curator* for five years. That was Borghesi's notion.[5] Objection might be raised. At first sight, the *cura aquarum* appears important. Yet perhaps not so, even though consular. At least Tacitus never names any of its holders; and almost all of those on the list in Frontinus are *novi homines*, some acceding to the charge not long after their consulships. Furthermore, doubts about the gravity of official occupations may be conceived in any age. The reign of Claudius witnessed a *curator* absent for several years, being legate of Moesia.[6]

Second, the text of Frontinus. If the eminent consular (or his clerk) was diligent and accurate in compilation, the manuscript may have suffered in the transmission. In fact, one of the consuls of 23 was left out. Graver disturbances may lurk unsuspected. Disquiet should have been excited by Tarius Rufus, appointed in 23.[7] One of the admirals at Actium and suffect consul in 16 B.C., Tarius would be

---

[1] Above, p. 109.   [2] R. Hanslik, *RE* VIIIA, 136.

[3] Frontinus, *De aquis* 102.

[4] Hence, following *PIR*[1], V 90, the year 13 was adopted in *Rom. Rev.* (1939), 512. See, however, *Harvard Studies* LXIV (1959), 41 = *RP* (1978), 415. The editor's Addendum there inclines to the theory of F. Marx.

[5] Followed by J. Hammer, o.c. 9.

[6] *PIR*[2], D 70 (A. Didius Gallus, *suff.* 39). For the date of his consulship see now *AE* 1973, 138.

[7] It was felt by Dessau: 'nisi hic est diversus . . . scilicet filius eius' (*PIR*[1], T 14). But not by others, apparently.

over eighty at the time. Perhaps the order is incorrect, or the name of a *curator* (from 8 to 13) may have fallen out.

To conclude, abridging an argument that might well take up more space.[1] Jerome can be dealt with, painlessly. But it is not easy to go against a document. Nevertheless, the worse posture is obduracy against the testimony of a precise and lucid writer. In any event, the date of 13, commended by faith and by calculations, must be discarded. Corvinus was only an 'umbra' on October 23 of the previous year (*Ex P.* II. 2. 98).

. . .

That being so, there is little advantage in mere subsidiary or negative considerations. Yet two questions could be put, of some pertinence. First, if the decease of Messalla Corvinus occurred after Ovid went away in relegation, how could a poem be despatched from Tomis in time to be recited at the obsequies? Second, if Corvinus died in 13, why does no poem of that year console the sons for a recent bereavement?

. . .

VI. Messallinus lapses with *Ex Ponto* II. 2 (probably written in the spring of 13). The three pieces to his address fail to disclose any close personal relationship, common acquaintances, or liking for poetry. The reference to his military achievement is slender indeed. Birth and eloquence are extolled, and the preponderant appeal goes to the memory of the parent.

Very different the younger brother. Ovid knew him from the cradle (*Ex P.* II. 3. 72), he mentions in 11 his wife and new-born son (*Tr.* IV. 5. 27 ff.). Cotta himself, born in 14 B.C., was probably quaestor in 12, having taken a wife when aged about twenty-two. That is the common pattern in the *nobilitas*.[2]

Ovid also admits an allusion to Cotta's mother (*Ex P.* II. 3. 98). His oratory wins praise several times, also his verses. Finally, Cotta is not only acclaimed as the foremost of Ovid's friends. He is even a 'sodalis' (*Tr.* IV. 5. 1).

[1] See further a chapter in *The Augustan Aristocracy* (forthcoming).
[2] Progressively younger, however, princes in the dynasty. Thus Germanicus at eighteen or nineteen, his eldest son Nero at fifteen.

Cotta Maximus receives no fewer than nine missives. Not, however, any of the longest. They go to Ovid's wife, to Fabius Maximus, to Pomponius Graecinus.[1]

The earliest bears no name, like that to Messallinus, which precedes it. The poem addresses Cotta as

> O mihi dilectos inter pars prima sodales,
> unica fortunis ara reperta meis!   (*Tr.* IV. 5. 1 f.)

The second is likewise anonymous. Ovid regrets that Cotta refuses to let his name stand in any poem (V. 9. 1 f.), and expresses gratitude to Cotta, next to the ruler, for life and salvation,

> Caesaris est primum munus, quod ducimus auras:
> gratia post magnos est tibi habenda deos.   (9. 11 f.)

For the rest, for the seven in the first three books *Ex Ponto*, brief comment in passing must suffice, although most of them are variously instructive. The first is I. 5 (late in 12 or early in 13). The next condoles with Cotta for the loss of Celsus, a client and a true friend (I. 9).[2] It enlarges upon loyalty (with a moral for Cotta easily to be drawn), and it does not omit devotion to a patron, and to the master of the world,

> nam tua non alio coluit penetralia ritu,
> terrarum dominos quam colis ipse deos.   (9. 35 f.)

The third (II. 3) contains an allusion to Ovid's catastrophe. The previous epistle, to Messallinus, counselled discretion, safety, and silence,

> vulneris id genus est quod, cum sanabile non sit,
> non contrectari tutius esse puto.
> lingua, sile. non est ultra narrabile quicquam.   (II. 2. 57 ff.)

Now, however, the poet comes closer to precision than is his wont. Cotta's earliest reaction to the news was righteous anger (II. 3. 61). Then, when apprised of the 'cladis origo', Ovid's mistakes made him groan aloud, so it was reported (3. 65 f.). Next, after digression on long allegiance to 'vestra domus', with due tribute to the parent

---

[1] *Ex P.* III. 1 (his wife), 166 lines; I. 2 (Fabius), 150; IV. 9 (Graecinus) 134.
[2] Above, p. 90.

(3. 69 ff.), Ovid recalls their last meeting. It was on the island of Elba. In answer to Cotta's enquiry about the transgression, Ovid in apprehension could only proffer a confused and ambiguous avowal,

> inter confessum dubie dubieque negantem
> haerebam, pavidas dante timore notas. (3. 87 f.)

In the fourth poem Ovid renders thanks for a precious accession to his domestic shrine: silver statuettes of the three heavenly beings ('caelites'): Augustus, Livia, Tiberius (8. 1 ff.). The poet is thereby in a posture to introduce a long entreaty, a panegyric on the ruler of the world and his family, beginning with

> parce, vir inmenso maior virtutibus orbe,
> iustaque vindictae supprime lora tuae. (8. 23 f.)

Finally, the three pieces in *Ex Ponto*, Book III (2, 5, 8). They have one thing in common: no direct request that Cotta undertake intercession with Caesar Augustus. The author now saw that he had overplayed his hand.

In the exordium of the first poem Ovid expresses concern about Cotta, whether his letter reached its destination, whether Cotta is safe and well,

> namque meis sospes multum cruciatibus aufers. (III. 2. 3)

The word 'sospes' is suitable if Cotta was in the field or on a journey.[1] As has been shown, Cotta was probably quaestor in 12: service abroad the next year is in no way excluded.

However that may be, this poem is designed to illustrate and commend the virtue of friendship. An elderly native retails at some length the legend of Orestes and Pylades. The audience approved,

> nomen amicitiae barbara corda movet. (2. 100)

The next poem (III. 5) expatiates upon the eloquence of Cotta (he had sent Ovid a speech) and upon his poetry. The third and last is very short (only twenty-four lines). Desirous of requiting Maximus with a gift, the poet passes in review all that the territory of Tomis

---

[1] The emphatic word occurs five times in *Tristia*: applied twice to Augustus, twice to Tiberius (then in the field).

can offer and decides on a quiver full of Scythian arrows (8. 19 f.).
What Maximus deserved had been declared at the outset,

> dignus es argento, fulvo quoque dignior auro,
>   sed te, cum donas, ista iuvare solent.   (8. 3 f.)

Maximus, it appears, is in the habit of being generous with the
precious metals. The poem can therefore be taken as a response to
the silver statuettes sent by Maximus (II. 8. 1 ff.).[1]

The gift of arrows does not normally advertise amity. The poem
is elegant and negative.

Book IV offers no poem to the address of Cotta. Ovid renounced.
He was now concentrating his efforts elsewhere: Germanicus, the
friends of Germanicus, Sextus Pompeius.

. . .

However, Ovid brings in the name of Cotta Maximus in splendid
evocation at the end, concluding his catalogue, with emphasis on the
'ingeminata nobilitas', and acclaiming the orator and poet,

> Pieridum lumen praesidiumque fori.   (IV. 16. 42)

The tardy tribute may perhaps be interpreted as a veiled reproach.
The poem goes on to terminate with a despairing apostrophe to
unrelenting 'Livor'.

. . .

VII. As is evident from sundry quotations in the preceding pages,
Ovid puts on exhibit choice specimens of devotional language and
attributes of divinity attached to the dynasty. Messallinus is signalized
by 'pietas in totum nomen Iuli' (Ex P. II. 2. 21). Indeed, he is inspired
by a passionate love,

> nunc tua pro lassis nitatur gratia rebus,
>   principis aeterni quam tibi praestat amor.   (2. 47 f.)

These fervent effusions may arouse distaste and suspicion in the
reader, in any age. It will be more instructive to prosecute the favour
and rewards that accrued to the two brothers, and the degradation.

---

[1] This poem is denied to Cotta in the Index of OCT (1915), but entered under Fabius
with 'ac fortasse'.

Their behaviour illustrates a theme of continuity between the two reigns, not in the better sense.

When the Senate convened at its first session after the demise of Caesar Augustus to discuss arrangements for the funeral, honours in great variety were proposed, a number of them extravagant or trivial.[1] The historian Tacitus was careful to single out only two of them as noteworthy, namely the 'sententiae' expressed by Asinius Gallus and L. Arruntius. But he did not miss an extraneous item obtruded by Valerius Messallinus. The oath of allegiance, he said, should be renewed each year in the name of the ruler. On question from Tiberius Caesar, Messallinus returned a noble answer: in what appertained to the 'res publica' he would take no advice from any but himself, even at risk of causing offence. As the historian observes, that was the one type of adulation that had not yet been tried.[2]

Silence then obtains about Messallinus for six years. After Cn. Piso had been prosecuted, he proposed that a golden statue be set up in the temple of Mars Ultor. Caesar objected. Messallinus then came out with something else, to celebrate the avenging of Germanicus: public thanksgiving to be rendered not only to the Princeps but to the women of the dynasty.[3]

The last appearance of Messallinus presents him in a more amicable fashion. In 21 he spoke against a motion to debar the wives of provincial governors from accompanying their husbands. With marked and proper allusion to the eloquence of his parent, the historian produces an oration in reported discourse. Messallinus expounded gracefully the argument for tolerance and humanity, and, as times and manners change, for an abatement of traditional severities.[4]

On that note Valerius Messallinus fades out. No obituary notice from Cornelius Tacitus, despite his interest in the descendants of Messalla Corvinus. That device, put to good employ by the historian for more reasons than one, had first occurred to him in the previous year of his narration. Tacitus then exploited the death of a consular, L. Volusius Saturninus (and the public funeral, although he does not say so explicitly) in order to commemorate Sallustius

---

[1] Suetonius, *Divus Aug.* 100. 2 f.

[2] *Ann.* I. 8. 4. Tacitus' names and facts may here derive from inspection of the *Acta Senatus*: not envisaged by recent commentators.

[3] *Ann.* III. 18. 2 f.   [4] *Ann.* III. 34.

Crispus, a man of lower station but superior potency and historic value.[1]

There was a sequence, it may be surmised, of unhealthy seasons.[2] Tacitus was impelled powerfully towards other necrologies: Sulpicius Quirinius, the great *novus homo*, and Ateius Capito, the master of sacred and profane law, who dishonoured his science through subservience to the government.[3]

.   .   .

VIII. Next, the younger brother. Cotta (here styled 'Cotta Messallinus') makes his entrance in 16, among the seven men of rank who came out with proposals for thanksgiving or vengeance after the prosecution of Scribonius Libo. Tacitus registered their 'sententiae' for express damnation, to demonstrate that the malady of adulation had an early origin.[4] His declaration has not always been accorded credit, or even recognition, among scholars in the recent age.[5]

Cotta is next heard of in 20 when consul, helpfully introducing measures to condemn the memory of Cn. Piso.[6] Then, in 24, Cotta proposed that husbands be rendered culpable for derelictions committed by wives in a province.[7] That was an epilogue to the prosecution of Sosia Galla, an intimate friend of Agrippina—and also to that of her husband C. Silius, who had been legate on the Rhine under Germanicus Caesar.[8] Cotta was pursuing a feud against the family of Germanicus, in the manifest design to engage the favour of Tiberius. In the poems of Ovid neither brother, it will be recalled, is brought into close association with Germanicus.

It is therefore appropriate that, when Agrippina and her eldest son

---

[1] *Ann.* III. 30. 2. Tacitus, it may be argued, took the public funerals from the *Acta Senatus*.

[2] Cf. above, p. 116 n. 1.

[3] *Ann.* III. 48; 75. These persons echoed back to the previous reign, in which his interest had recently been aroused (III. 24. 2). See further below, p. 197.

[4] *Ann.* II. 32. 2: 'quorum auctoritates adulationesque rettuli ut sciretur vetus id in re publica malum.' The ostensible originality of Messallinus (I. 8. 3) no doubt had Augustan precedents.

[5] Tacitus' portrayal has been disallowed on allegation of anachronism: 'to attribute a similar servility and lack of spirit to men who had grown up during the Augustan age is simply to imagine the unbelievable', according to M. L. W. Laistner, *The Greater Roman Historians* (1947), 135.

[6] *Ann.* III. 17. 4.   [7] *Ann.* IV. 20. 4.   [8] *Ann.* IV. 18 f.

were incriminated in 29, Cotta should be in the forefront of the
attack, 'cum atroci sententia'.[1]

There follows a gap in the *Annales*. His next entrance, and his last,
shows him in trouble, but confident (and not in vain) that he will be
rescued by his dear friend, 'Tiberiolus meus'.[2]

.   .   .

In the sequel Cotta, consul in 20, acceded to the proconsulate of
Asia: for the tenure 35/6, so it is generally held.[3] He may have
survived into the next reign. But there is a chance that he died before
Tiberius—or even during his governorship.[4]

The last obituary notice in Book VI of the *Annales* is that of
Poppaeus Sabinus, dying at the end of 35 and thus concluding his
twenty-four years in Moesia.[5] The historian was now immersed in
other preoccupations, leading on to the next reign. He omits
(or postpones) a character of some note, namely Cossus Cornelius
Lentulus (*cos.* I B.C.), who died in 36 while holding the office of
praefectus urbi.[6] If Cotta in fact predeceased Tiberius Caesar, enough
had been said to show him up for ever.

.   .   .

IX. Messalla Corvinus and his family engaged the attention of
Tacitus for a variety of reasons. His *Annales* happen to furnish a
history of Roman eloquence from the Augustan masters Pollio and
Messalla (as exhibited in the performance of their sons) down to the
orators he had heard when a young man.

Grace and eloquence marked the style of Corvinus. Quintilian
duly applies the epithet 'nitidus', twice.[7] And Ovid, in address to the
elder son, has 'nitor ille domesticus' (*Ex P.* II. 2. 49). Introducing the
oration of Messallinus, Tacitus suitably defines him: 'cui parens
Messalla, ineratque imago paternae facundiae.'[8] The language recalls
his induction in Ovid,

cuius inest animo patrii candoris imago

---

[1] *Ann.* V. 3. 2.   [2] *Ann.* VI. 5. 1.

[3] *IGR* IV. 1508; *Forsch. in Ephesos* III. 112, no. 22. Cf. above, p. 85.

[4] His decease in office would be convenient: there are difficulties about the lodgement of
C. Vibius Rufinus (*suff.* 21 or 22), cf. above, p. 86.

[5] *Ann.* VI. 39. 3.   [6] *PIR*² C 1380.   [7] Quintilian I. 7. 35; X. 1. 113.

[8] *Ann.* III. 34. 1.

followed by

patriae facundia linguae.   (*Tr.* IV. 4. 3 ff.)

That Tacitus at this stage in the composition of the *Annales* had been reading Ovid is by no means excluded.[1] But the thing may well be a commonplace.

There was another side to the oratorical precellence of Messalla Corvinus. Some found him prolix and lacking in bite.[2] Nor was the past career of the aristocratic opportunist exempt from questioning. An invented oration in Tacitus exhibits Messalla along with Pollio as a profiteer from the wars, owing enrichment both to Antonius and to Caesar's heir.[3] The great mansion on the Palatine had previously belonged to Antonius.[4]

However, what history transmits is more than favourable. Corvinus' own memoirs are one reason, at least for certain episodes. They come out clearly and fully in Plutarch's biography of Brutus, where the narration of Philippi carries his name in five chapters; and he is prominent in Appian's account of the Bellum Siculum.[5]

Self-praise or apologia was normal. But no writer of memoirs could touch Velleius Paterculus. After the battle the 'fulgentissimus iuvenis' preferred to be saved 'beneficio Caesaris'; and to Caesar no victory was happier than that act, which Corvinus duly requited, as an 'exemplum hominis grati ac pii'.[6] It was in fact to Antonius that Corvinus applied.

Traces can be discerned of an unfriendly tradition. Not so much malignity as silence about certain exploits. In the narration of Cassius Dio, Corvinus is absent from the field of Philippi, from the Bellum Siculum, from the victory at Actium; even the campaign in Aquitania, which earned a triumph, is omitted. It cannot therefore be assumed that Dio ought to have given a mention to his public funeral.[7]

Under the new dispensation, Corvinus paraded attitudes of independence. In 26 they persuaded him to take up the office of

---

[1] Cf. above, p. 47 (on III. 24. 4).   [2] Quintilian X. 1. 113, cf. IV. 1. 8.
[3] *Ann.* XI. 7. 2.   [4] Dio LIII. 27. 5 (he shared this palace with M. Agrippa).
[5] Plutarch, *Brutus* 40–2; 45; 53; Appian, *BC* V. 102. 425–113. 472.
[6] Velleius II. 71. 1.
[7] Therefore one cannot base an argument on the large gap in Dio's account of the year 8 (four folia missing).

praefectus urbi. After a few days Corvinus resigned, asserting that the office was anomalous, that he could not see what he was expected to do.[1] The excuse may be held valid. Corvinus, it is clear, was reluctant to be enticed into public and conspicuous involvement. His act of renunciation did him no harm.

Corvinus in due pride continued to affirm that Cassius had been his general.[2] That was no impediment, rather to be taken as a re-inforcement of concord and stability when forty years after the Battle of Philippi the Senate heard him propose in moving language that Caesar Augustus should assume the appellation of 'pater patriae'.[3]

What in Corvinus might be condoned or even praised, as due deference to the Princeps and a graceful recognition of changing times, comes out in the sons as abasement before power, an anxious and timorous comportment that was manifested already, and so painfully, in Ovid's poems from exile.

The theme of the *Annales* is decline and fall: liberty and the dynasty of the Caesars, and also the old aristocracy. Restored by Caesar's heir to wealth and prestige, the *nobiles* became clients of the Caesars: 'obsequium' passed into 'adulatio'.

The high aristocrat, it is true, can still aspire to the command of an army and gain the *ornamenta triumphalia* (the triumph being now denied). And civic virtue was not lacking, as witness consulars excellent in honour and judgement like Piso the Pontifex and Marcus Lepidus. There was another side to the *nobilitas*: arrogance and pretension, vice and sloth.

The Valerii seem to stand in the ascendant: three consulships in the vicinity of the War of Actium, and three more later, during the principate of Caesar Augustus. Their splendour was of no long duration. The last consul in the line of Messalla, in 58, took subsidy from Nero. Tacitus in extenuation speaks of 'paupertas innoxia'.[4]

---

[1] Tacitus, *Ann.* VI. 11. 3; Jerome, p. 164 H. This peculiar item is absent from the main historical tradition. Jerome got it from the *De viris illustribus* of Suetonius. Not inconceivable as the source of Tacitus.

[2] *Ann.* IV. 34. 4 (in the oration of Cremutius Cordus).

[3] Suetonius, *Divus Aug.* 58. 2 (quoting his words).

[4] *Ann.* XIII. 34. 1. That is, a son of M. Valerius Messalla, consul with his uncle Cotta in 20 —and not known apart from the fact of his consulship.

On this blameless character follow two other members of the decayed *nobilitas*, who had dissipated their patrimony in riotous living, namely Aurelius Cotta and Haterius Antoninus. The latter is a grandson of the fluent facile orator whom Tacitus dismissed in curt dispraisal.[1] The former when an infant was saluted by Ovid, with the hope and vow that he may reproduce the virtues of his father, the younger son of Corvinus,

> sic iuvenis similisque tibi sit natus, et illum
> moribus agnoscat quilibet esse tuum.   (*Tr.* IV. 5. 31 f.)

[1] *Ann.* IV. 60 (quoted below, p. 229).

VIII

PAULLUS FABIUS MAXIMUS

I. SULLA the Dictator was eager to bring back the primeval *nobilitas*, the substance and adornment of a renovated oligarchy. A patrician himself, Sulla discovered and promoted members of that order. Caesar and Caesar Augustus indulge the same predilection.

Long intervals interrupted a number of families. The Valerii Messallae had been absent from the *Fasti* for one hundred years when in 61 the father of Messalla Corvinus became consul. As for the Fabii, a void since Allobrogicus and Eburnus, consuls in 121 and 116. The latter left no descendants, and the son of Allobrogicus was a notorious wastrel.[1] The line of the great Cunctator was in danger of lapsing.

However, a grandson of Allobrogicus emerges as aedile in 57, namely Q. Fabius Maximus.[2] He would be eligible for the consulship of 51.[3] It fell in fact to another member of the submerged patriciate, the jurist Ser. Sulpicius Rufus.

Strong support from Caesar may be surmised for Sulpicius Rufus, and in due course Fabius came out as an adherent. He held a command in Spain, earning a triumph and a consulate in the autumn of 45. Fabius, however, died on the last day of the year, to be eclipsed by the notoriety of his brief substitute, Caninius Rebilus. Two sons inherited, Paullus and Africanus. Their consular dates (11 and 10) permit the assumption that the elder was born in 46, or perhaps in 45.[4]

The exorbitant *praenomina* advertise pride of ancestry and a new fashion in the *nobilitas*.[5] In the middle years of the previous century

---

[1] Cicero, *Tusc.* I. 81; Valerius Maximus III. 5. 2.

[2] *RE* VI, 1701 f. For the stemma of the Fabii, ibid. 1777 f.

[3] For his career, see G. V. Sumner, *Phoenix* XXV (1971), 251 f.

[4] For 46 B.C., *RE* VI, 1781.

[5] For a full treatment see *Historia* VII (1958), 172 ff. = *RP* (1978), 361 ff. The Fabii are lineal descendants of Aemilius Paullus—but not of the Scipiones.

the Fabii were saved from extinction by the device of adoption from families in alliance or at social parity. An Aemilius entered their house (*cos.* 145), and a Servilius (*cos.* 142). The Scipiones had also been in trouble. In each case sons of old Aemilius Paullus brought succour. Q. Fabius Aemilianus (*cos.* 145), the parent of Allobrogicus, is in fact the brother of Scipio Aemilianus.

.   .   .

II. Of Africanus Fabius Maximus, consul in 10 B.C. with Iullus Antonius for colleague, the record is sparse indeed. Consul, proconsul of Africa, and holder of a priesthood, those are the only labels of identity.[1] His name occurs in no literary source of his time, or of any time, unless it be alluded to in a passage of Seneca, where Caesar Augustus is evoked, administering a salutary rebuke to Cinna Magnus, an alleged conspirator. Even if Cinna succeeds, the Princeps points out, certain great noblemen will not put up with him. Since the episode is fictitious, nothing more need be said—not even to disparage the names conjured up by Seneca.[2]

The proconsulate of Africanus claims a certain interest. Coins of cities in Africa show his name and his portrait, with three types of legend. One of them, a coin of Hippo, on the obverse presents the head of Tiberius with 'Claudio Neroni Hippone libera'.[3] Which is peculiar and revealing. It has generally been taken to reflect the elevation of Claudius Nero through the acquisition of the *tribunicia potestas* on June 26 of 6 B.C. Hence 6/5 for the tenure of Africanus— and in any event a later date is patently ruled out. Perhaps, however, 7/6: the second consulship and the German triumph put the stepson of the Princeps in high prominence.

By contrast to Africanus, the conspicuous brother. Wealth and variety of information offers.[4] Paullus Fabius Maximus first comes to notice on an inscription at Athens, plausibly supplemented to show him *quaestor Augusti*.[5] The post may fall in 22, or 21—or even 20,

---

[1] PIR², F 46.

[2] Seneca, *De clem.* I. 9. 10: 'cedo, si spes tuas solus impedio, Paulusne et Fabius Maximus et Cossi et Servilii ferent?'

[3] M. Grant, *From Imperium to Auctoritas* (1946), 224; 228; B. E. Thomasson, *Die Statthalter der r. Provinzen Nordafrikas von Augustus bis Diocletianus* II (1960), 15 f.

[4] PIR², F 47. One may still consult with profit Groag's earlier study, *RE* VI, 1780 ff.

[5] *IG* II², 4130. PIR² has 'fortasse'.

since a quaestor may go on for the next year as proquaestor without that title being specified. Towards the end of 22 the ruler departed from Rome, first to Sicily, then to visit Greece, Asia, and Syria, for three years of absence. Another *quaestor Augusti* belongs to this period, namely P. Quinctilius Varus (*cos.* 13):[1] like Fabius a favourite of the Princeps and destined soon to be brought into matrimonial arrangements.[2]

A dedication at Paphos honours Marcia, the wife of Fabius, styling her a cousin of Augustus.[3] It has sometimes been supposed that Fabius was proconsul of Cyprus after being praetor. That is most unlikely. To be governor of a province like Cyprus carried no appeal, it was miserable for a man of rank. Under Augustus and the successors no descendant of the old nobility can be detected among the governors of Cyprus—or, for that matter, of Crete and Cyrene.[4]

From 16 to 7, that is to say, from L. Domitius Ahenobarbus and P. Cornelius Scipio to Tiberius Claudius Nero (consul for the second time) and Cn. Calpurnius Piso, the *Fasti* exhibit a resplendent efflorescence of aristocratic names. The list repays inspection and analysis.[5] It yields some clear results: of the *ordinarii* (excluding three consulates of the stepsons of the Princeps) there are sixteen *nobiles* and one new man, P. Sulpicius Quirinius (*cos.* 12). Two years only admit consuls suffect. In 16 'militaris industria' secures admittance for L. Tarius Rufus; and in 12, an unhealthy season, an *ordinarius* perished and also a *suffectus*.[6]

Of some among the aristocrats it can be affirmed that they reach the *fasces* in the earliest permissible year. Thus L. Piso (*cos.* 15), born in 48;[7] and Iullus Antonius was praetor in 13, consul in 10.[8] But nature cannot be expected to come out with a perfect sequence in

---

[1] *ILS* 8812 (Tenos).

[2] In 12 B.C. the wife of Varus was a daughter of M. Agrippa, as disclosed by *P. Colon.* inv. 4701, published and discussed by L. Koenen, *ZPE* V (1970), 217 ff. It may also be noted that his sister had married Sex. Appuleius (*cos.* 29 B.C.), a nephew of the Princeps, cf. *AE* 1966, 442 (Cyme). [3] *ILS* 8811.

[4] A Metellus Creticus universally held proconsul of Sardinia (*PIR*², C 62) should have been suspect, and can be thrown out. The shape of the inscription (*CIL* X. 7581) discountenances a second cognomen for this 'C]aecilius M. f. M['.

[5] See *The Augustan Aristocracy* (forthcoming).

[6] Viz. M. Valerius Messalla Barbatus Appianus and C. Caninius Rebilus. There were two other *suffecti*, C. Valgius Rufus and L. Volusius Saturninus. See further above, p. 111.

[7] Tacitus, *Ann.* VI. 10. 3. [8] Dio LIV. 26. 2.

a group of young *nobiles*, and a coincidence in age may entail a small delay. Fabius, it appears, acceded to his consulship in 11 late by one year, or perhaps by two. It was not grave; and no Fabius would now be content to be a *suffectus*, defrauding a Roman year of his name.

.   .   .

III. Rapid compensation accrued through special favour. Five years as the interval before the proconsulates in Asia and Africa was ordained by Caesar Augustus. From time to time perturbations ensued for various reasons, notably a shortage of ex-consuls when *suffecti* were still a rarity; and a man might miss the sortition through serving as legate in the *provincia* of Caesar.

The consular who went out to Asia in the summer of 12 had his tenure prolonged to a second year.[1] He may have been M. Vinicius (*suff.* 19).[2] Fabius followed, in 10/9. That was Mommsen's date, and it was accorded a wide acceptance.[3] It has recently been confirmed.[4]

Fabius indited a letter to the provincial assembly enjoining a change in the calendar of Asia: the natal day of Caesar Augustus should now open the official year. Large pieces of his letter (which is involved and verbose) and of the decree passed in concordance have been discovered in several cities; and a useful text can be put together.[5]

Asia hails the divine birthday with effusion and renders thanks to Providence, since that day brought glad tidings to the world, and so on. The documents are instructive, but need not detain. The worship paid to the Caesars (or rather the forms of homage) might be expected to engender tedium or distaste. By paradox, the subject has engaged to excess the zeal and energy of scholars in the recent time.[6]

Fabius in loyal devotion promoted honours for Augustus, and did

---

[1] Dio LIV. 30. 3.

[2] An inscription from Mylasa reveals a M. Vinicius honoured conjointly with Drusus. Therefore not the consul of A.D. 30, cf. L. Robert, *Rev. arch.* 1935, 152 ff.; G. W. Bowersock, *Augustus and the Greek World* (1965), 119. Not accepted by R. Hanslik, *RE* IXA, 116: 'das ist unmöglich.'   [3] *RE* VI 1782 f.; *PIR*², F 47 has 'probabiliter'.

[4] By U. Laffi in his thorough study *Le iscrizioni relative all'introduzione nel 9 a. c. del nuovo calendario della provincia d'Asia* (1967), 32; reprinted from *Studi classici ed orientali* XVI (1967), 5 ff.

[5] Ehrenberg-Jones, *Documents* (ed. 2, 1955), 98. See now the comprehensive edition of U. Laffi (above, n. 4).

[6] A reaction has set in; and healthy scepticism is expressed by a number of contributors in *Le Culte des souverains dans l'Empire romain* (Entretiens Hardt, 1973).

not miss them himself. Alexandria in the Troad instituted a festival, the *Pauleia*.[1] The next proconsul to receive that kind of commemoration, and the last, was C. Marcius Censorinus (*cos.* 8), some half-dozen years after Fabius.[2]

Fabius may well have had a second year in Asia.[3] An attractive notion, but it evades proof. That is unfortunate, the successor would be well worth knowing.[4] The sequence of proconsuls becomes a nexus of problems.[5]

There is a further incentive to study or debate. Cities in Asia and Africa now exhibit for a time the heads of proconsuls on their coinage.[6] The first of them is Fabius Maximus. Two other proconsuls of Asia receive that honour not long after; and similarly, three proconsuls of Africa.[7] They belong to a narrow range of time—and of cities: three in each province.

The significance of this innovation has not failed to excite curiosity and ingenious theories. One scholar discovers in these proconsuls a select group, to be defined as 'amici principis'.[8] Against which it will be observed that the selection is sporadic. No coins, for example, for L. Piso or for Iullus Antonius (the husband of a Marcella).

Furthermore, the theory is invalidated by the case of L. Passienus Rufus (*cos.* 4 B.C.), after an interval of some years.[9] As his consulship declares, this *novus homo* was a person of some consequence.[10] No evidence avails to show him a close friend of the Princeps. Passienus cannot be brought into the category of the Fabii and other aristocrats.

---

[1] *IGR* IV. 244.   [2] *SEG* II. 549. Cf. G. W. Bowersock, o.c. 119; 150 f.

[3] As suggested in *PIR²*, F 47. Coins of Hierapolis under Fabius carry the names of no fewer than seven local magistrates.

[4] Probably L. Piso (*cos.* 15), cf. Groag in *PIR²*, C 289: followed in *Rom. Rev.* (1939), 398. The evidence comes from Crinagoras, *Anth. Pal.* X. 25. 3 f.

[5] Lists have been drawn up by D. Magie, *Roman Rule in Asia Minor* II (1950), 1580 f.; K. M. T. Atkinson, *Historia* VII (1958), 324 ff. Both exclude L. Piso. The latter scholar is especially vulnerable (dates as well as assumptions); and Fabius Maximus is denied 10/9 B.C. (ibid. 326, cf. 328). Nor is Grant wholly acceptable in *FITA* (1946), 228 f.; 387. He argued that Fabius is best allocated to 6/5 B.C.

[6] M. Grant, *FITA* (1946), 139 f.; 224; 228 ff.; 387 f.

[7] Cf. also B. E. Thomasson, o.c. 13 ff.

[8] M. Grant, o.c. 228; *Aspects of the Principate of Tiberius* (1950), 51 ff.

[9] M. Grant, o.c. 139 f. Not, it is true, a city coinage. In Grant's second book (1950) Passienus makes a modest appearance, in a footnote only (55, n. 124).

[10] *PIR¹*, P 111. Son of a famous *rhetor*, on frequent show in the elder Seneca, Passienus gave his son in adoption to Sallustius Crispus.

Passienus counsels discretion and the avoidance of system. However that may be, the permission accorded to certain cities, while not to be over-estimated, is a compliment to proconsuls. The earliest is Fabius, and his governorship is firmly dated to 10/9 B.C.[1] Therefore a modest conjecture becomes admissible. The compliment can be interpreted as a kind of compensation (small enough in truth), granted in a season when the stepsons of the ruler acquired an enhancement of power and authority. That is, proconsular *imperium* conferred after the campaigns of 11 B.C.[2]

.   .   .

IV. For half a dozen years after his proconsulate Fabius Maximus lapses from record. In the middle of that period supervened an acute crisis in the government, the first since 23 B.C. In the year subsequent to his second consulship Claudius Nero broke with the ruler and went away to Rhodes, angry and obdurate.

The event brought no discomfort to certain aristocrats in the entourage. In the first place Domitius Ahenobarbus (*cos.* 16 B.C.), married to Antonia, a niece of the Princeps; next, Iullus Antonius (*cos.* 10 B.C.), who had taken over the elder Marcella when M. Agrippa divorced her (in 21 B.C.). In due course bright prospects might beckon to the young Aemilii, the sons of Paullus Aemilius Lepidus (*cos.* 34), with Scipionic ancestry through their mother: Marcus (*cos.* A.D. 6) and Lucius (*cos.* A.D. 1).[3]

In 3/2 B.C. Paullus Fabius Maximus is discovered in the north-west of Spain. Bracara sets up an altar with dedication to Caesar Augustus, on Fabius' own natal day; and he receives honour himself at Lucus Augusti, in Callaecia.[4]

The whole of Spain was included in the *provincia* of the ruler, and Spain was his first care. The conquest, a long matter, was carried

[1] The date demolishes, by the way, the hypothesis that the introduction of these coinages 'celebrates the second *decennalia* of the new régime, which fell in 7 B.C.', as the same scholar suggested in *Roman Anniversary Issues* (1950), 20.

[2] Above, p. 60.

[3] Lucius has always been regarded as the elder son. For the reverse, see the argument adduced (with appeal to Propertius IV. 11. 63) in 'The Crisis of 2 B.C.', *Bayerische S-B* 1974, Heft 7, 29. Lucius benefited by rapid advancement through his marriage to a princess, the younger Julia, *c.* 4 B.C. See further below, p. 208.

[4] *ILS* 8895; *CIL* II. 2581. The lower term for the Bracara inscription is given by the absence of the title 'pater patriae': it was conferred on February 5, 2 B.C.

out by the combined efforts of two armies, those of Citerior and
Ulterior.[1] For a time the region Asturia–Callaecia was attached to the
command of Caesar's legate in Ulterior. There has been some uncertainty about the position of Fabius: Citerior or Ulterior.[2]

Clarity can be elicited. Agrippa in 20 and 19 ended the wars by
dealing with the recalcitrant Cantabrians; and Augustus was again in
the peninsula during his second sojourn in the western lands (16–13).
The great wars of conquest designed now to ensue in Illyricum and
in Germany required a concentration of legions. The two armies in
Spain were fused, with Asturia–Callaecia transferred in consequence
from Ulterior to Citerior.[3]

Tarraconensis (as it may for convenience be styled) was a large and
important province, with four legions until A.D. 9.[4] The predecessor
of Fabius is not known. After Fabius the earliest governor on attestation is Cn. Calpurnius Piso (cos. 7 B.C.), in 9/10;[5] and the next after
Piso is M. Lepidus (cos. 6), in 14.[6]

The secession of Claudius Nero in 6 B.C. caused various changes in
government—though deficiency in the sources precludes a proper
estimate. M. Lollius emerged, his enemy, to be governor of Syria
when the prince C. Caesar went to the eastern lands.[7] More significant, some of the high aristocrats. Ahenobarbus held in succession the
commands in Illyricum and on the Rhine.[8] Away from Rome, he
missed the catastrophe in the dynasty that signalized the autumn of
2 B.C.: Iullus Antonius destroyed and the daughter of the Princeps
sent away to an island. Fabius Maximus may also have been absent.
There is no means of knowing the duration of his tenure in Tarraconensis, either before or after 3 B.C.[9]

.   .   .

[1] For the two armies, ignored in some accounts of Augustus' campaigns of 26 and 25 B.C.,
see *AJP* LV (1934), 298 ff.; *CAH* X (1934), 343.

[2] Instead of Caesar's legate in Ulterior the alternative was incorrectly stated as 'legatus
eiusdem Asturiae et Callaeciae' in *PIR*[2], F 47.

[3] As assumed in *Epigraphische Studien* VIII (1969), 126 = *RP* (1978), 733; G. Alföldy,
Fasti Hispanienses (1969), 10; 286.   [4] *JRS* XXIII (1933), 23.

[5] For his name to fill the erasure on the inscription from Cabo Torres near Gijón (*CIL* II.
2703), see *Epigraphische Studien* VIII (1969), 129 f. = *RP* (1978), 736 f.

[6] Velleius II. 125. 5.   [7] Above, p. 12.

[8] Dio LV. 10a. 2 f. (under A.D. 1, with reference to Germany).

[9] Alföldy suggests the triennium 4–1 B.C. (o.c. 10). But Fabius might have had a distinctly
longer tenure.

V. Fabius was married to a cousin of Caesar Augustus. Otherwise he hardly seems marked out for one of the high commands, although, like Claudius Nero, he may have seen warfare as a tribune when Augustus was in Spain (the campaigns of 26 and 25 B.C.). Eloquent testimony declares him endowed with manifold social gifts, a patron of poets, an orator,

> et pro sollicitis non tacitus reis
> et centum puer artium.[1]

A similar tribute recurs,

> vox, precor, Augustas pro me tua molliat aures,
> auxilio trepidis quae solet esse reis.[2]

If Fabius is on acclaim as a ready succour for anxious clients (the phrase is conventional), no names can be adduced. His talents might have found suitable employ when Nonius Asprenas, a friend of the Princeps, stood trial for poisoning, with Cassius Severus for prosecutor.[3]

The sole piece of evidence shows him attacking. Fabius took on the formidable Cassius Severus.[4] This man, of powerful voice and physique (he looked like a gladiator), was biting and aggressive. It was his habit to go against birth and rank. Hence many enemies, and exile in the end.[5]

The historian Tacitus conveys strong disapprobation in two passages.[6] Yet Cassius was remembered as a performer of classic quality, equal perhaps to Corvinus and Pollio, the much praised paladins of Augustan eloquence. One of the speakers in the *Dialogus*, an innovator himself, offers a warm and judicious appraisal: Cassius disliked

---

[1] Horace, *Odes* IV. 1. 14 f.

[2] *Ex Ponto* I. 2. 115 f. The adjective 'trepidus' is applied to the clients of an advocate in three other places: *AA* I. 460; *Fasti* I. 22; *Ex P.* II. 2. 50.

[3] Pliny, *NH* XXXV. 164; Suetonius, *Divus Aug.* 56. 3, etc. Cf. *PIR*[1], N 93. But the person is probably not that man (the consul of A.D. 6), rather his father, cf. Groag in *RE* XVII, 866 f. The case is generally assigned to 9 B.C. because of Dio LV. 4. 3 (an episode without names).

[4] Seneca, *Controv.* II. 4. 11: the only occasion on which Cassius Severus spoke for the defence (ibid. III, praef. 5).

[5] Below, p. 213. Seneca has a long appreciation, beginning with Gallio's verdict: 'cum diceret rerum potiebatur, adeo omnes imperata faciebant' (*Controv.* III, praef. 2).

[6] *Ann.* I. 72. 3 (his libellous pamphlets); IV. 21. 3: 'sordidae originis, maleficae vitae, sed orandi validus'.

long and verbose speeches, he saw that the changing times demanded a new style, vigorous and concentrated.[1]

Cassius (quoted by Seneca) defined for all time the multiple talents of Fabius Maximus: 'quasi disertus es, quasi formosus es, quasi dives es; unum tantum es non quasi, vappa.' Cassius, it appears, was parodying the manner of Fabius, of which Seneca goes on to produce a specimen, and damns it as deleterious.[2] Otherwise the only reference to Fabius in the work is his approval of a certain *rhetor*.[3]

Another passage, it is true, is cited in standard manuals.[4] Inspection will suffice. Seneca happens to mention some mediocre practitioners: 'hos minus nobiles sinite in partem abire, Paternum et Moderatum, Fabium, et si quis est nec clari nominis nec ignoti.' It is hardly to be conceived that Seneca would style this 'nobilissimus vir' by the bare *gentilicium* (he elsewhere calls him 'Fabius Maximus' and 'Maximus'), still less lump him together with persons called Paternus and Moderatus. The *cognomina* advertise an obscure origin, perhaps from the western provinces; and Spain has numerous Fabii.[5]

.　　.　　.

VI. A later age recalled Fabius as a patron of literature.[6] Two names only attest. First, Horace in the famous ode (IV. 1).[7] The poet begins with deprecation. No longer what he was in the days of kind Cinara, he entreats Venus to spare one who is now aged about fifty (1. 6). The goddess should turn to young Maximus, who will perform admirably in the fields of love: 'late signa feret militiae tuae' (16); victorious one day over a rival, Maximus will erect a shrine near the lakes of the Alban Hills (19 f.); and there will be a festival

---

[1] *Dial*. 19. 2 (the speaker is M. Aper).

[2] Seneca, *Controv*. II. 4. 12: 'hanc controversiam cum declamaret Maximus dixit quasi tricolum tale qualia sunt quae basilicam infectant.'

[3] *Controv*. II. 4. 9.

[4] *Controv*. X, praef. 13. Assigned to the consular in *RE* VI, 1787 and in *PIR*[2], F 47; likewise in the Index to the Loeb Seneca (ed. M. Winterbottom, 1974).

[5] For 'Paternus', of 381 specimens 239 occur in *CIL* II, XII, and XIII, cf. I. Kajanto, *The Latin Cognomina* (1965), 304. 'Moderatus' is not so common or so useful. The only persons of any interest to bear it are from Gades, viz. Columella (*PIR*[2], J 779) and the Pythagorean (*PIR*[1], M 467), probably related.

[6] Juvenal VII. 95.

[7] On which see the alert and sympathetic appreciation of E. Fraenkel, *Horace* (1957), 410 ff.

(21 ff.). Horace then reverts to vanished youth, 'me nec femina nec puer' (29). No wine, no gaiety any more, and it is only in dreams that he will pursue Ligurinus (37–40).

As elsewhere, Horace affords instruction and delight to the student of social life at Rome. Not, however, through Cinara, though grave enquirers find her 'more real' than the other girls. And not Ligurinus, who by exception carries a Roman *cognomen*: attested once, so it happens, and guaranteed by 'Ligurius', which is not a rarity.[1] These are questions not above antiquarism. But the poem declares a noteworthy fact that has failed to stimulate the curiosity of most critics and commentators. It is the age and condition of Fabius Maximus. He is still a bachelor.[2]

The dating of the poem therefore matters. Presumably between 17 and 15. To transfer the poem to 12 or 11, as a compliment to Fabius on his consulship, makes the thing worse—and may be held to conflict with what Horace says about his own age.[3]

Fabius was born in 46 or 45.[4] For a *nobilis* to be thirty, or close on thirty, without having acquired a wife, is abnormal if not scandalous. A parallel in this age is not easy to discover. Some may be tempted to surmise a distaste for women as well as for matrimony. A milder and more decorous explanation avails. Fabius chose, or consented, to wait until the heiress of the Marcii became nubile.[5] Certain other aristocrats were more fortunate. Thus Ahenobarbus marrying Antonia (who was born in 39) probably about the year 24;[6] and Iullus Antonius was providentially available for matrimony with the elder Marcella in 21.[7]

When C. Octavius (*pr.* 61) died in 58, his widow, Atia, passed to L. Marcius Philippus (*cos.* 56); and in the sequel Philippus' son by an

---

[1] Schulze, *LE* 191. For 'Ligurinus', PIR², C 497.

[2] No comment in E. Fraenkel; and L. P. Wilkinson, who quotes the whole poem, merely says 'one Fabius Maximus' (*Horace and his Lyric Poetry* (1945), 41).

[3] The dating is that suggested by G. Williams, *Horace* (*Greece & Rome*), New Surveys in the Classics No. 6, 1972, 44. For late datings of other odes in Book IV, below, p. 170.

[4] Above, p. 135.

[5] The marriage did not take place until 11 B.C., according to Carcopino, *Rencontres de l'histoire et de la littérature romaines* (1963), 136. That scholar also asserted that Fabius' career stopped abruptly in 2 B.C. (ibid. 139). It is venial in comparison that Ovid's wife is styled 'Fabia' (ibid. 83).

[6] PIR², A 884.

[7] PIR², A 800.

earlier marriage (*suff.* 38) annexed a younger sister of Atia: whence Marcia, first cousin to Caesar Augustus.[1]

Marcia's father is last heard of celebrating a triumph in 33, and using the war booty to restore a temple (*Hercules Musarum*).[2] Philippus left no son, neither did C. Marcius Censorinus (*cos.* 8). With them end the Marcii, an ancient house claiming descent from one of the kings—and not far below the patriciate in prestige.

The peculiar ode may perhaps be interpreted as a frivolous valedictory to a man on the eve of abandoning celibacy—or as a kind of disguised epithalamium.[3] However it be, Ovid composed a wedding song for Fabius Maximus, so one learns many years later (in A.D. 12 or 13).[4] Not until then does it emerge that Ovid had been a guest at his table, that Fabius praised the poems of Ovid (except, to be sure, those that brought harm to their author), and recited his own writings. The wedding furnishes an unexpected point of contact between the two poets. Which of them the illustrious patron found more congenial is a question that may be resigned without regrets to the erudite or the frivolous.

. . . .

VII. The same poem reveals a small fact about Ovid's wife. When Ovid married her she had long been a close and even domestic friend of Marcia, as previously of her mother, the 'matertera Caesaris'.[5] Ovid can hardly have acquired this widow earlier than 4 B.C., given the presumed age of her daughter: she married Suillius Rufus about A.D. 12.[6] Ovid's first two ventures had not been very durable, so it seems.[7] He may have led an unconstrained existence for quite a long time.

To revert to Fabius and Marcia. Ovid had already paid handsome tribute in the *Fasti*. In Book I he retails a number of historic *cognomina*, accruing from victories won in Africa and Crete and so on.

---

[1] The son's marriage is put in close vicinity to that of the father, 'gewiss schon damals', by Münzer in *RE* XIV, 1568. Doubt will arise if the hypothesis is entertained that the daughter of the younger Atia did not become nubile until *c.* 16 B.C. There is also the chance to be reckoned with that Fabius was not in fact the first husband of Marcia.

[2] *PIR*[1], M 173.

[3] For the ode as a wedding song see the elegant paper of A. T. v. S. Bradshaw, *CQ* XX (1970), 142 ff. As he notes, the idea occurred to Kiessling in 1876.

[4] *Ex P.* I. 2. 131 f.   [5] *Ex P.* I. 2. 136 ff.   [6] Above, p. 79.
[7] *Tristia* IV. 10. 69 ff.

They lead by way of the 'Magnus' of Pompeius to 'Augustus'. In between is artfully inserted a distich:

> nec gradus est ultra Fabios cognominis ullus:
> illa domus meritis Maxima dicta suis.   (I. 605 f.)

Of aristocratic houses still extant no other is registered by name in the *Fasti*, though individual members may occur, belonging to legend or history. It would have been easy enough to bring in a reference to the fame of the Claudii, Aemilii, or Valerii. The legend of the Valerii would offer if Ovid had bothered to notice the Ludi Saeculares.[1]

An insertion might be suspected, made by Ovid when revising the work. But that revision did not go very far; and no motive remained for obtruding the Fabii in A.D. 16 or 17.

Next, the conclusion of Book VI. Philippus' temple was in fact dedicated on the last day of June.[2] That gave Ovid an opportunity to bring in Marcia (and also Caesar's aunt). She is not merely a name. Birth, beauty, and character are extolled (VI. 804 ff.).

Apart from members of the dynasty, no other person achieves a named entrance into the *Fasti*. An exaltation of the wife of Fabius Maximus would lack reason or motive if the passage was composed subsequent to the dramatic revolution in domestic politics that supervened in the summer of the year 4. When Claudius Nero became Ti. Caesar, many and various ambitions were blocked or postponed. Fabius Maximus, as will become clear, was not merely a rival of Claudius Nero, but the foremost among his enemies.

This argument (it will not escape notice) is adduced to reinforce the hypothesis that Ovid, beginning the *Fasti* in A.D. 1 or 2, decided at some time in 4 that he would not go on.

.   .   .

VIII. In *Tristia* Ovid did not venture an approach to Fabius Maximus, anonymous but transparent, such as he made to the sons of Messalla Corvinus. *Ex Ponto* makes good with the second letter of Book I: the first went to Ovid's close friend Brutus, who concludes the triad (III. 9). The next place in Book I is occupied by the mysterious Rufinus, while Cotta and Messallinus have I. 5 and 7.

---

[1] Valerius Maximus II. 4. 5 ; Zosimus II. 4.   [2] Above, p. 35.

Fabius gets a long epistle, the second longest in the collection. It registers the fourth winter (I. 2. 26): that of 12/13. But it is not in fact among the earliest in Book I, for another poem refers to the fourth autumn (8. 28). As has been observed more than once, no poem in this book alludes to the Pannonian triumph celebrated on October 23, A.D. 12. This is a criterion of prime utility. None the less, the epistle to Fabius might in fact have been composed after the news reached Tomis—and, Fabius Maximus now seeming accessible, the author inserted it in high prominence.[1]

Some might be inclined to detect a clue for dating in the phrase

> di faciant igitur, quorum iustissimus ipse est. (2. 97)

Now on January 8 of 13 a 'signum iustitiae Aug.' was in fact dedicated at Rome; and it is alluded to in Book III.[2] However, it might not be safe or expedient to put emphasis on this item.

The poem, it will be recalled, carries a reference to Marcia. For the rest, what might be expected: the appeal to birth, character, and eloquence, and the incitement to intercede with Caesar.

The second (and last) epistle to Fabius is a graceful and ingenious piece of work (III. 3). The virtues of the aristocrat are again on show. Thus towards the end, with appeal to the mythical ancestor of the Fabii,

> conveniens animo genus est tibi, nobile namque
> pectus et Herculeae simplicitatis habes. (3. 99 f.)

Fabius is praised for a frank and open nature.[3] The same word is applied by Velleius to Ahenobarbus (*cos.* 16 B.C.) and to his son (*cos.* A.D. 32). Each is a 'vir nobilissimae simplicitatis'.[4] In the Ahenobarbi a lack of subtlety and artifice was translated into behaviour of brazen arrogance and brutality, if credit be accorded to sundry anecdotes reported by the biographer of the last Ahenobarbus.[5]

However, what rightly commands attention is the structure and allusive skill of the poem, which was designed to recall to the reader

---

[1] In that case the author must have deliberately suppressed all mention of the triumph.

[2] *Ex P*. III. 6. 25, cf. above, p. 42.

[3] Ovid has the word 'simplicitas' in ten other places, one of them referring to himself (*Tr*. I. 5. 42). The interest of the Fabii in Hercules goes back at least as far as the Cunctator, cf. Pliny, *NH* XXXIV. 40.

[4] Velleius II. 10. 2; 72. 3.

[5] Suetonius, *Nero* 4 f.

the Horatian ode.[1] Cupid appears in a dream, and Ovid speaks to
Cupid as an innocent disciple (3. 23 ff.). The response is words of
encouragement to the poet: 'mitescet Caesaris ira' (3. 83). There is no
need to admit fear or delay, the season being now propitious: the
Pannonian triumph has filled with joy all members of the dynasty
(3. 85 ff.).

The poet transmits the message as a gentle admonition (3. 95 ff.).
In this poem, it will be noted, Ovid refers to Livia by name. She is
also prominent in the first poem of Book III, the long piece addressed
to Ovid's wife. This procedure would hardly be to the liking of
Caesar Augustus.[2]

Ovid urged his wife to recognize where duty leads and confirm
her devotion to Marcia:

> cuncta licet facias, nisi eris laudabilis uxor,
>   non poterit credi Marcia culta tibi.   (III. 1. 77 f.)

That duty is made explicit. It is to bring entreaty to bear upon Livia
(1. 114 f.). Caesar's consort is introduced as a paragon of chastity
that 'prisca vetustas' cannot excel. She alone has been found worthy,
by virtue and beauty, to share the sacred couch,

> quae Veneris formam, mores Iunonis habendo
>   sola est caelesti digna reperta toro.   (1. 117 f.)

Further, the right season for an approach has arrived,

> cum status urbis erit, qualem nunc auguror esse,
>   et nullus populi contrahet ora dolor.   (1. 133 f.)

Finally, when audience is vouchsafed, 'vultum Iunonis adire' (1. 145),
long and careful instructions are enjoined about suitable language
and deportment.

The mention of Marcia (1. 78) links this poem to the first epistle to
Fabius Maximus (I. 2). It may have been written not long after—and
in the vicinity of the second epistle (III. 3). Perhaps all three poems
belong to the spring of the year 13. Ovid, it appears, had gained confidence: his output is copious and rapid in these months.[3] Also confidence in and from Fabius Maximus. It was of no long duration. The

---

[1] See the subtle and convincing interpretation of E. J. Kenney, *Proc. Camb. Phil. Soc.* XI
(1965), 44 f.

[2] For Livia's name in the *Fasti*, above, p. 23.

[3] Above, p. 42. By contrast Book IV, with poems from 13 to 16.

attempt to exploit Marcia may have aroused resentment. Ovid soon turns to Sextus Pompeius (IV. 1), anticipating his consulship in 14 (IV. 4).

. . .

The sons of Messalla were favoured with no more missives. The last to Messallinus came in Book II, the last three to Cotta in Book III (2; 5; 8). Cotta was to earn a valedictory at the end (IV. 16. 41 ff.). Fabius Maximus is accorded a kind of necrology. Writing to Brutus in the autumn of 14, Ovid alludes to his decease,

> certus eras pro me, Fabiae laus, Maxime, gentis,
>   numen ad Augustum supplice voce loqui.
> occidis ante preces, causamque ego, Maxime, mortis
>   (nec fuero tanti) me reor esse tuae.
> iam timeo nostram cuiquam mandare salutem:
>   ipsum morte tua concidit auxilium.
> coeperat Augustus deceptae ignoscere culpae:
>   spem nostram terras deseruitque simul. (IV. 6. 9 ff.)

Advocacy of Ovid's cause brought bad luck, so it appears. If credence were given to this elegant tribute, only an untimely death forestalled a beneficent intervention from Fabius Maximus—and the ruler himself had begun to relent before he left the mortal shores.

. . .

IX. Preceding by a short interval the death of Augustus, the death of Fabius became a subject of scandalous inventions, being brought into connection with Agrippa Postumus, the exile on Planasia (who was to be executed as the 'primum facinus novi principatus'). Perhaps quite soon. The story is preserved in five versions, with noteworthy discrepancies (three of them carry the name of Fabius). A brief inspection will be useful, for various reasons.

First Pliny, in compressed statement, clearly deriving from something much more explicit. As follows: 'abdicatio Postumi Agrippae post adoptionem, desiderium post relegationem, inde suspicio in Fabium arcanorumque proditionem, hinc uxoris et Tiberii cogitationes, suprema eius cura' (NH VII. 150). The statement is enigmatic, but (it will be noted) it does not impute any kind of criminal action against Livia.

Next, for completeness (and for curiosity), it will be appropriate to cite the version of Pseudo-Victor in late Antiquity: Augustus perished 'dolo Liviae', so some writers report, because she had ascertained that Agrippa Postumus was going to be brought back from the island to which she had exiled him 'novercali odio' (*Epit.* 1. 27).[1]

Third, a highly aberrant account in Plutarch, *De garrulitate* (11, p. 508). Augustus intended to bring back his grandson. 'Fulvius' (i.e. Fabius) told his wife, she told Livia; and Livia assailed Augustus with bitter reproaches. 'Fulvius', from the hostile comportment of Augustus, understood what had happened, so he went home and committed suicide, his wife first turning the sword against herself.

Fourth, and utilizable, Cassius Dio. Augustus undertook a secret voyage to the island, and a reconciliation seemed certainly on the way. Therefore, so some say, Livia poisoned her husband (LVI. 30. 1 f.).

Finally, Tacitus. Augustus was verging towards the end, and 'quidam scelus uxoris suspectabant' (I. 5. 1). The historian goes on to report a rumour. Augustus had gone to the island Planasia a few months earlier, with Fabius Maximus for sole companion. There occurred a touching scene, and expectation arose that the youth would be restored to home and family. Fabius, however, revealed the matter to Marcia, and from her through Livia it came to the knowledge of Caesar Augustus. Fabius met his end soon after (whether by his own hand, it was in doubt); and at the funeral the widow was heard blaming herself for his death.

The variants are instructive, and the whole matter calls for delicate handling. There is an obvious temptation to take the simplest and shortest version to be the earliest, the rest being later accretions.[2] Caution is in place. Pliny's notice presupposes a fuller account; and Dio looks abbreviated. Dio's source may well have included Fabius Maximus: Dio has a marked tendency to neglect or excise the names of persons.[3]

---

[1] One may (or may not) quote 'novercalibus odiis' (*Ann.* I. 6. 2). The passage from Pseudo-Victor is not registered in *RE* X, 185 (Gardthausen), *PIR²*, J 214, or in the recent commentaries of E. Koestermann (1963) and F. R. D. Goodyear (1972).

[2] Thus F. R. D. Goodyear, ad loc.: 'this strange story appears to be a fairly late fabrication, based upon an earlier and more simple story, preserved in Plin. *N.H.* 7. 150 and Plut. *De Garr.* 11.'

[3] Goodyear's commentary ignores Dio LVI. 30. 1 f. (important for more reasons than one); and even the name of Marcia does not appear. She is also absent from *RE*.

However, the voyage of Augustus to Planasia (only in Dio and Tacitus) may have accrued later, being a specimen of that 'corroborative detail' which is all too apparent (and useful) in historical fictions. How much later, that is the question.

There are no valid reasons for denying the emergence of an explicit story not long subsequent to the decease of Caesar Augustus. The 'prudentes' might have been able to use it at the funeral. Items of this kind were not reserved for later inventiveness. As the historian affirms in another place, when demolishing a vulgar and persistent rumour, 'atrociore semper fama erga dominantium exitus'.[1]

A close parallel offers. When Augustus breathed his last at Nola, Livia had the house and the roads picketed so as not to let out the news until the necessary provisions had been made: 'provisis quae tempus monebat'. That is the showing of Tacitus.[2] He reports in a similar fashion what Agrippina did when Claudius Caesar was defunct.[3]

Hence a notion that has attracted critics and commentators: the statement about Livia is false, being a retrojection of Agrippina's action in October of the year 54.[4] To no purpose.[5] These things may happen in any age when a despot dies and the transmission of the power has to be managed without anxiety or disturbance.

.   .   .

X. The story about Fabius and Marcia is a fable.[6] Yet not without instruction. In the first instance, for the study of the various historical sources relating the death of Augustus and the accession of Tiberius. Next, as reflecting and confirming the belief that Paullus Fabius Maximus was deep, deeper than anyone else, in the counsels of Caesar Augustus. The favour he earned went back a long way.

Whereas the sons of Messalla stand by Tiberius Caesar, Fabius appears single-minded in his devotion to Augustus. He is an isolated figure. The tradition (such as it is) does not bring him into relation with other groups or persons in the *nobilitas*—and there is no trace of a *novus homo* whom his patronage brought to high office.

---

[1] *Ann.* IV. 11. 2.   [2] *Ann.* I. 5. 4.   [3] *Ann.* XII. 68. 3.

[4] Cf., at some length, F. R. D. Goodyear (o.c. 125 f.). Observe that most of Dio's sources had the statement about Livia (LVI. 31. 1).

[5] For brief scepticism, *Tacitus* (1958), 483.

[6] Some credit the visit to Planasia. Thus V. Gardthausen, *Augustus und seine Zeit* I (1904), 1252 f.; *RE* X, 185: B. Levick, *Tiberius the Politician* (1976), 64 f.

One link, however, can be discovered, with the Appulei. It is significant. The Appulei were near to Caesar Augustus. Sextus Appuleius married an Octavia, daughter of C. Octavius by his first marriage (to an Ancharia: Atia was his second wife). Not consul, but he was accorded the honour of a public funeral.[1]

Next, the son and the grandson.[2] Sex. Appuleius, consul in 29 B.C., is on scanty record, but happens to be attested as legate of Illyricum in 8 B.C., succeeding Claudius Nero. The grandson is Sex. Appuleius, holding the *fasces* in 14 with Sex. Pompeius as colleague.

Fabia Numantina supplies the evidence, a daughter or perhaps a niece of Maximus. When in 24 the praetor M. Plautius Silvanus threw his wife out of the window, Numantina was incriminated, with allegations of sorcery.[3] She is styled the 'prior uxor' of Silvanus (without any indication in the text of a present husband).

At some time or other Numantina was married to Sex. Appuleius (*cos.* 14), as an inscription reveals.[4] In the general belief, Appuleius married Numantina after her divorce from Silvanus.[5] But there happens to be no evidence for the survival of Appuleius after his consulate, and he may have died quite soon. Better, Appuleius was the first husband of Numantina. It would be permissible to conjecture that young Silvanus married the widow and heiress about the year 18, and did not retain her affections for long.[6]

． ． ．

XI. As with other aristocrats of the time, the evidence is capricious and fragmentary. Estimates of Fabius will exhibit variation. The ode of Horace tends to encourage a benevolent appraisal. Ovid permits more than a glimpse of the other aspect: the opportunism of the *nobiles*, their pliancy and their subservience.

The ode stands in prominence, announcing the poet's return to the writing of lyrics. It is a notable, and a curious, performance. The second piece introduces, though only as a poet in the Pindaric vein, another member of the dynastic group: namely Iullus Antonius.

One does not have to wait long for the two Claudii (IV. 4). But, a surprise. It is the glory of the younger Claudius that comes first

---

[1] *PIR*[2], A 960. For the funeral, *ILS* 8963 (Carthage).   [2] *PIR*[2], A 961 f.

[3] *Ann.* IV. 22. 3.   [4] *ILS* 935 (Luna).

[5] *PIR*[2], A 962; F 78.   [6] Below, p. 159.

(4. 17 f.). Tiberius is subsumed in the young Nerones (28), in the laudation of the Claudian house in ancient history (37 ff.), in the confident prediction about their present actions: 'nil Claudiae non perficient manus' (73). In the other poem devoted to the Alpine campaign of 15 B.C., Drusus again precedes (14. 9 ff.). But Tiberius is now accorded generous space for martial exploits against the Raeti, introduced by 'maior Neronum mox grave proelium / commisit' (14 f.).

'Fortes creantur fortibus et bonis' (4. 29). Thus the Claudii. Introduced by Fabius and Iullus, the book is largely engrossed with aristocracy (Marcius Censorinus also has an ode). The name of Marcus Lollius might seem to strike a false note. The anomaly is ostensibly redeemed by the praise of what might be deemed true nobility: that is, civic virtue and personal integrity (9. 30 ff.).[1]

Lollius in 17 suffered a mishap at the hands of raiding Sugambri.[2] It was Tiberius who took his place the year after. Though praetor, he set out in the company of Augustus and governed Gallia Comata for about a year.[3] There arose ill feeling manifested in the sequel— or rather a feud.

These poems look as though they were produced to command, or through gentle persuasion, the author being in no way recalcitrant.[4] The priority accorded to Drusus reflects the propensities of Caesar Augustus; and Marcus Lollius stood in need of some rehabilitation. Horace was not impercipient. Neither was Claudius Nero.[5]

Seven years previously Horace knew how to be alert and tactful. Amicable enquiry about the journey of Claudius Nero to the East, and about his companions, was directed to Julius Florus (*Epp.* I. 3).[6] Horace also wrote to the secretary, Albinovanus Celsus; and he commended a certain Septimius (8; 9).[7] Finally, an extravagant compliment enhances a mission never intended to be military:

> Cantaber Agrippae, Claudi virtute Neronis
> Armenius cecidit. (12. 26 f.)

---

[1] For a friendly view of this ode see E. Fraenkel, o.c. 425 f. Groag conjectured that Lollius was endowed with literary tastes and that Maecenas suggested to Horace the writing of the ode (*RE* XIII, 1383 f.).   [2] Above, p. 3.

[3] Suetonius, *Tib.* 9. 1; Dio LIV. 19. 6.   [4] Below, p. 172.

[5] His friendship with another poet, Julius Montanus, terminated in a notable 'frigus' (Seneca, *Epp.* 122. 11).   [6] For Florus, above, p. 106.

[7] Septimius (*PIR*[1], S 306) was also a friend of Augustus. The two epistles (8 and 9) are not cited in *PIR*[2], C 941.

Book IV was published in the course of 13 B.C. Tiberius held the *fasces*, with a benefit of four years on the standard age. His colleague was Quinctilius Varus, like him a son-in-law of Marcus Agrippa.[1] Nobody would expect that the robust Agrippa would disappear— and Tiberius was only the stepson of Augustus. The husband of Marcia was perhaps not far from parity. Two deaths in the following year (Agrippa and Barbatus Appianus, the husband of the younger Marcella) may have lent some encouragement.

. . .

XII. By Marcia Fabius left a son, Persicus.[2] One son only surviving to reach consular years, that is less a surprise among *nobiles* than one wife. Born about 1 B.C., Persicus was co-opted among the Arvales in May of 15 and he became consul in 34.[3] Under Claudius he held the proconsulate of Asia: a large portion of his verbose edict is preserved.[4] But birth was not enough to secure Fabius Persicus a place in the run of iterated consulships from 43 to 46. A *novus homo* was among those benefiting from the abnormal honour: L. Vitellius, his colleague a decade earlier.

Seneca transmits an evil report of Persicus, who was notorious for the cynical depravity of his life. When Persicus, along with Caninius Rebilus, offered to the virtuous Julius Graecinus a contribution to the cost of games, he refused.[5] In another place Seneca explains why it is that vile aristocrats gain honour and priority before the active energy of new men. Not without reason, he says, since 'sacra est magnarum virtutum memoria'. The prime and recent specimen is Fabius Persicus, 'cuius osculum etiam impudici devitabant'.[6]

The *Annales* as extant fail to exhibit Fabius Persicus. The lost portion no doubt contained suitable revelations. The author was waiting for Persicus. He had a domestic incentive: Julius Graecinus was the grandfather of his wife.[7]

. . .

[1] *P. Colon.* inv. 4701, cf. above, p. 137.   [2] *PIR²*, F 51.   [3] *AE* 1947, 52.
[4] *SEG* IV. 516A (Ephesus). For full text and discussion, F. K. Dörner, *Der Erlass des Statthalters von Asia Paullus Fabius Persicus* (Diss. Greifswald, 1935).
[5] *De ben.* II. 21. 5.   [6] *De ben.* IV. 30. 2.
[7] *PIR²*, J 344. Recording the death by suicide of Caninius Rebilus (*suff.* 37), Tacitus condemns his 'libidines muliebriter infamis' (XIII. 30. 2).

The Fabii show no more consuls. Like the descendants of Messalla, Persicus illustrates the decline of the *nobilitas*. 'Saeva pax' claimed many victims, ancestry or excellence being perilous. Likewise involvement with the dynasty, as the Aemilii show. It was not the suspicions or the hostility of the Caesars that brought down the Valerii and the Fabii.

IX

SEXTUS POMPEIUS

I. ALLUSION has already been made to certain changes manifest in Book IV of *Ex Ponto* on comparison with the preceding triad. Old friends are in eclipse, apart from Graecinus and Brutus. There is no hint of Pompeius Macer, Ovid's companion on foreign travels in the days of his youth. In this instance a ready explanation avails. Macer, as Strabo attests, was a close friend of Tiberius Caesar.[1] By the same token, Pomponius Flaccus: recipient of I. 10, but in Book IV only approached through the letter to his brother Graecinus.[2]

By contrast, the poet's aim is now directed more and more towards the entourage of Germanicus, with Carus the tutor of his sons, with Suillius his quaestor.

The sons of Messalla Corvinus fade out, but a new patron comes in, suddenly: Sextus Pompeius, the consul of 14, with no fewer than four poems. In fact, the book is dedicated to Pompeius. He has the first poem, and the penultimate, before the catalogue of poets.[3]

Germanicus is a clue. In the last poem of the four the reference is discreet and unobtrusive, perhaps embracing the whole imperial family,

> quod quoniam in dis est, tempta lenire precando
> numina, perpetua quae pietate colis. (15. 23 f.)

But observe the language used when Ovid acclaims and describes the functions of the consul. In the first place, homage to Augustus and Tiberius, but next to them Germanicus engrosses everything,

> tempus ab his vacuum Caesar Germanicus omne
> auferet: a magnis hunc colit ille deis. (5. 25 f.)

---

[1] Above, p. 73. [2] *Ex P.* IV. 9. 55 ff.; 75 ff.; 119 f.

[3] Therefore Ovid survived to publish Book IV—or perhaps at least to arrange it. The contrary view is sometimes expressed. Thus W. Kraus, *RE* XVIII, 1966: 'kein Zweifel'. And, indeed, the length of the book might be relevant: longer by nearly a quarter than the other three.

That recalls the loyal devotion of Suillius Rufus, 'di tibi sunt Caesar iuvenis' (8. 23).

It may be observed in passing that Ovid's eager preoccupation would not be to the liking of Tiberius Caesar. His son Drusus had been named only once in these books (II. 2. 72). Apart from that he came in only three times, in general references along with Germanicus, as a member of the family.[1] Ovid's attitude reflected all too clearly the predilections manifested by Caesar Augustus in his dynastic policy.

To be sure, Ovid at the outset expresses personal gratitude towards Sextus Pompeius,

> debitor est vitae qui tibi, Sexte, suae. (1. 2)

At the same time, he must proffer excuses for not having written earlier (1. 5 ff.). Pompeius had given financial aid,

> nec mihi munificas arca negavit opes. (1. 24, cf. 5. 37 f.)

Indeed, Pompeius had secured him a safe journey across Thrace,

> barbariae tutas exhibuisse vias. (5. 34)

That was when, coming from Samothrace, Ovid landed on the coast at Tempyra, a small place near Doriscus (*Tr.* I. 10. 21).

Sex. Pompeius, it is generally held, was proconsul of Macedonia for the tenure 8/9.[2] A double impediment was ignored. It is not altogether likely that a person of this rank held a praetorian proconsulate, still less so that, if he did, he had to wait five years before becoming *consul ordinarius*.[3] There is a better reason for Ovid's gratitude. Pompeius owned great estates in Macedonia as well as in Campania and in Sicily (15. 15 ff.). He could have furnished help of various kinds from a distance.[4]

.   .   .

II. Sex. Pompeius Sex. f.: this person remains enigmatic in more ways than one. First of all, his extraction. The line goes back to

---

[1] *Ex P.* II. 2. 81 ff.; IV. 9. 109; 13. 31 f. Cf. above, p. 45.

[2] R. Hanslik, *RE* XXI, 2265. He uses the word 'muss'.

[3] Cf. above, p. 137 (on Cyprus). But it may be conceded that Macedonia was better than Cyprus.

[4] As suggested by Dessau in *PIR*[1], P 450.

Sex. Pompeius, the brother of Pompeius Strabo, who made a brief entrance into history during the Bellum Italicum. An episode shows him present in Strabo's camp in 89 B.C.[1] He acquired renown as a scholar, a lawyer, an adept of Stoic doctrines, but held aloof, so it appears, from the rewards and hazards of public life.[2]

A stray anecdote discloses his son as a boy when Sulla was dictator.[3] This person next turns up many years later as consul in 35 B.C. To adorn the *Fasti* the Triumvirs had room for historical relics as well as eager partisans of any rank.[4] The obscure old man was a first cousin of Pompeius Magnus. Seneca was alert to Sextus Pompeius, and to his descendants. They owed honour and their consulships to the memory of Magnus.[5]

Between the consuls of 35 B.C. and A.D. 14 an intermediate generation should be allowed for, as happens in the stemmata of other noble families. Hence a Sex. Pompeius who leaves no trace, save in the filiation of his consular son.

At this stage a word of warning may be interpolated. A standard work of reference comes up with 'Sex. Pompeius Cn. f.' as consul suffect in 5 B.C.[6] He never existed.

Like his colleague Sex. Appuleius, the consul of 14 had a connection with the dynasty, so Cassius Dio states.[7] A fact of some interest, since the reigning group tended to keep descendants or kinsfolk of Magnus at a distance. The link would be worth knowing. Derivative erudition produces a Marcia for his mother, a daughter of L. Marcius Philippus (*suff.* 38 B.C.) and Atia, hence, like the wife of Paullus Fabius Maximus, a first cousin of Caesar Augustus.[8] The notion goes back to Borghesi: the inscriptions he relied on were forgeries.[9]

---

[1] Cicero, *Phil.* XII. 27: 'doctum virum atque sapientem'. The occasion was a parley with Vettius Scato, the Marsian leader. Cicero was there.

[2] For the evidence, Drumann–Groebe, *Geschichte Roms* IV² (1908), 324; R. Hanslik, *RE* XXI, 2059 f.

[3] Plutarch, *Cato* 3. His existence is elsewhere certified by two authors: Seneca, *De ben.* IV. 30. 2; Dio XLIX. 18. 6.

[4] Cf. above, p. 100.　　　　　　　　　　　　　　　　[5] Seneca, *De ben.* IV. 30. 2.

[6] He gets a double entry: *RE* XXI, 2060 and 2265. Also referred to at 2055 under Cn. Pompeius (*suff.* 31 B.C.), and at 2265, under Sex. Pompeius (*cos.* 14). The creature derives from Borghesi by way of *PIR¹*, P 449 (where the judicious Dessau expressed doubts).

[7] Dio LVI. 29. 5.

[8] R. Hanslik, *RE* XXI, 2265 (on the alleged consul of 5 B.C.).

[9] *CIL* VI*. 977ᵃ⁻ᶜ. Cf. *JRS* XXXIX (1949), 9 = *Ten Studies in Tacitus* (1970), 63.

However that may be, other options are open. For example, she might be an Appuleia, daughter of Sex. Appuleius (*cos.* 29 B.C.), who, being the son of an Octavia, was a nephew of Caesar Augustus.[1] Or, for that matter, daughter of M. Appuleius (*cos.* 20), who can, and should, be regarded as his younger brother.[2]

Ovid in two poems furnished a lavish prediction of the loyal comportment and public actions of the consul Sextus Pompeius (IV. 4 f.). History records that he broke his leg through impetuosity when hurrying to join the funeral procession.[3]

As for public honours, Pompeius may be the 'Sex[' who was co-opted among the Arvales in the year 21.[4] Some prefer Sex. Appuleius.[5] That person, however, may have been already dead for several years: his widow Fabia Numantina was taken over by M. Plautius Silvanus (*pr.* 24).[6]

In 20, when Cn. Piso was to stand trial, he approached five eminent 'patroni', all of whom declined. Pompeius was of their number.[7] He could have alleged 'pietas' towards the memory of Germanicus.

The next year shows him in an unfavourable light. When pro-consulates were being discussed in the Senate, he seized the opportunity to launch a savage attack on M'. Aemilius Lepidus (*cos.* 11), a descendant of Sulla and Pompeius. He derided Manius Lepidus as slothful, impoverished, a disgrace to his ancestry; and he urged that Manius be debarred from Asia.[8] Senators came out in defence of Manius (a mild and innocuous character), the attempt failed, and he went out to Asia.

Contemptuous language could not have been used about the other Lepidus, namely Marcus, the consul of 6. He won fame during the war in Illyricum and in 14 was holding Tarraconensis, with an army of

---

[1] Above, p. 152. He married a Quinctilia, a sister of Varus, cf. *AE* 1966, 442 (Cyme): set up when he was proconsul.

[2] Not heard of after his consulate. In *PIR*², A 959 he was identified with the M. Appuleius attested as quaestor in 45.

[3] Dio LVI. 29. 5.

[4] *CIL* VI. 2023b.

[5] Thus J. Scheid, *Les Frères arvales* (1975), 128 ff. Nothing was said in *PIR*², A 962.

[6] As suggested above, p. 152.

[7] *Ann.* III. 11. 2.

[8] *Ann.* III. 32. 2.

three legions. In fact, the man whom a notorious anecdote designates as 'capax imperii'.[1]

Pompeius, it is clear, was trying to disencumber the field of competitors and ensure or accelerate his own proconsulate. Which in fact ensued before long.

.   .   .

III. In the middle epoch of the previous reign the five-year interval for Asia and Africa had been disturbed by various factors, notably a shortage of ex-consuls.[2] When *suffecti* became the normal practice, the contrary phenomenon intruded, extending the interval. There were also prorogations of tenure in a season of emergency, military or political. Tiberius Caesar was able for a time to keep to a decennial norm. Thus C. Junius Silanus, proconsul in 20/1, and succumbing to prosecution the year after.[3]

Though the warfare in Africa (from 17 to 24) caused prorogations, the prospects of Sex. Pompeius in the year 21 were not at all bad; and without extreme personal annoyance Caesar or the friends of Caesar might induce a man to withdraw from the sortition.[4] Nor were many available to compete among the immediate predecessors of Pompeius, as a brief glance at the *Fasti* of 11–13 will show.

M'. Lepidus (*cos.* 11) secured Asia. Of his colleague T. Statilius Taurus and the *suffectus* L. Cassius Longinus there is no trace subsequent to their consulships: perhaps no longer among the living.[5] C. Fonteius Capito (*cos.* 12) went to Asia, it is true, either in 22 or in 23: he was prosecuted in 25 (but not condemned).[6] Next, C. Visellius Varro (*suff.* 12) and C. Silius (*cos.* 13), both absent in 21 with the armies of the Rhine.[7] There remains L. Munatius Plancus (*cos.* 13).[8]

---

[1] *Ann.* I. 13. 2. For the distinction between the two Lepidi see *JRS* XLV (1955), 22 ff. = *Ten Studies in Tacitus* (1970), 30 ff. The references being redistributed, Manius is left with two, viz. III. 22. 1; 32. 2. Accepted by E. Koestermann in his Teubner text (ed. 2, 1965).

[2] Above, p. 138.   [3] *Ann.* III. 66 ff., cf. *PIR²*, J 825.

[4] For the technique, Tacitus, *Agr.* 42. 1 f.

[5] Cassius would be an old man if the son of L. Cassius who fell at Philippi (Appian, *BC* IV. 135. 571), as suggested in *PIR²*, C 502.

[6] *Ann.* IV. 36. 3. *PIR²*, F 470 suggests the tenure 23/4.   [7] *Ann.* III. 42. 2.

[8] For the theory that Plancus was legate of Pannonia, see (discussing *CIL* VI. 1743), J. Morris, *Bonner Jahrbücher* CLXV (1965), 88 ff. It will be convenient to reserve judgement about the enigmatic ']cus' who appears to be registered as *suffectus* on the *Fasti Arvalium* (*Inscr. It.* XIII, 1, p. 297): admitted by Degrassi in *I fasti consolari* (1952). Doubts are expressed by S. Panciera, *Bull. Comm.* LXXIX (1963-4), 97.

After Fonteius Capito on record (conveniently to be put in 23/4), the next proconsul is M. Aemilius Lepidus (*cos.* 6).[1] That a consular of such great seniority was admitted to the sortition is abnormal, but not lacking parallel or a ready explanation:[2] the favour of Ti. Caesar —and Marcus Lepidus had missed his year previously, when legate of Tarraconensis.[3] Further, an inscription reveals his tenure as a biennium.[4] That is, 26–8. Therefore Sex. Pompeius may be assigned without discomfort to 24/5.[5]

It may be of use to present these results in the form of a table: proconsuls from 20 to 28. Certain lists, and likewise studies of individual proconsuls, are obsolete or erroneous. One of the reasons (but not the only reason) was the failure to distinguish Marcus Lepidus from Manius or take into account the biennium of Marcus.[6]

C. Junius Silanus (*cos.* 10)	20/1
M'. Aemilius Lepidus (11)	21/2
———	22/3
C. Fonteius Capito (12)	?23/4
Sex. Pompeius (14)	?24/5
———	25/6
M. Aemilius Lepidus (6)	26/8

.   .   .

IV. The proconsulate of Sex. Pompeius (and his survival) is bound up with problems concerning the use of literary evidence. Valerius Maximus, the compiler of ethical *exempla*, accompanied Pompeius, his friend and patron, to Asia, so he states (II. 6. 8). Not long after, this loyal client indulges in sad reflections prompted by

[1] *Ann.* IV. 56. 3.

[2] Cn. Lentulus (*cos.* 14 B.C.) was proconsul of Asia in 2/1 B.C. (*SIG*[3], 781). His command in the Balkans may belong *c.* 9–6 B.C., cf. *Rom. Rev.* (1939), 401 (briefly), and, a fuller statement, *Danubian Papers* (1971), 70.

[3] Velleius II. 125. 5.

[4] *AE* 1934, 87 (Cos). Too late for *PIR*[2], A 369, but registered by Groag in an addendum (vol. III, p. ix).

[5] It will be recalled in passing that neither 23/4 nor a biennial tenure is excluded by any known fact.

[6] Thus the list in D. Magie, *Roman Rule in Asia Minor* II (1950), 1581.

the decease of Pompeius: 'optimi amici iactura' (IV. 7, Ext. 2).[1] That must fall before the beginning of 29, for Valerius Maximus speaks of Livia as still among the living (VI. 1. 1).[2] Estimates that put the proconsulate 'later than 27' therefore run into trouble—not only because Marcus Lepidus occupies the biennium 26–8.[3]

That is not all. Another author now comes in. Seneca holds disquisition on the vicissitudes and the fragility of wealth and power.[4] Who was richer than Pompeius? His domains embraced the sources of rivers and their mouths, yet he thirsted for a drop of water. Caligula, 'vetus cognatus, hospes novus', took Pompeius into the Palace and starved him to death. At the same time Caligula made arrangements for a public funeral for his victim—'dum illi heres publicum funus esurienti locat'.

The passage has generally been referred to the consul of 14—with interesting (or rather intolerable) consequences for the chronology of Valerius Maximus.[5] Rather, surely, a son.[6] Hence a new item for classical encyclopedias, a brief entry. The public funeral might be taken to imply consular rank. But who can tell with Caligula? And Pompeius was kin to the dynasty, albeit now remote. Thus perished miserably the last in this line of paradoxical Pompeii. The Appuleii had already terminated.[7] The son born to Sex. Appuleius, the consul of 14, and Fabia Numantina, was carried off young, before acceding to the career of honours.[8]

·　　　·　　　·

[1] The point was not taken in *PIR*[1], V 82, or by R. Helm, *RE* VIIIA, 90.

[2] The next indication of time is Seianus, denounced at some length in IX. 11, Ext. 4.

[3] *PIR*[1], P 450 had '*c*. 27–30', *RE* XXI, 2267 'nach dem J. 27'. Similarly R. Helm, VIIIA, 90, 'etwa 27'; and *OCD*[2] (1970), 1106 (on Valerius Maximus). Magie's list (o.c. 1581) puts Pompeius after Cotta Messallinus (*cos*. 20). That placing of Cotta was in no way plausible. Cotta should probably go in 35/6, cf. above, p. 131.

[4] Seneca, *De tranq*. 11. 10.

[5] Thus *PIR*[1], P 450 and elsewhere. A unique and peculiar notion has been promulgated by Hanslik, *RE* XXI, 2267. Namely that Pompeius was starved to death in 33, or shortly after. At that time (so he supposes) Caligula, no longer living in the house of Antonia, had a residence of his own in the Palace. Hanslik thus interprets the phrase of Seneca: 'cum Gaius, vetus cognatus, hospes novus aperuisset Caesaris domum ut suam clauderet'.

[6] Cf. the curt hint in *AJP* LXXIX (1958), 21 = *Ten Studies in Tacitus* (1970), 82.

[7] The ancestor of the Appuleii (*PIR*[1], A 960) had a public funeral (*ILS* 8963). Perhaps also the two consuls, of 29 B.C. and A.D. 14. The date of the latter's decease being uncertain, it is perhaps relevant to point out that Tacitus has no public funerals (and consequent obituary notices) before the year 20 (*Ann*. III. 30. 1).

[8] *ILS* 935 (Luna), set up by Fabia Numantina, 'ultimo gentis suae'.

V. Under the spell of Ovid's other writings, notably the *Ars Amatoria* (predilection for which is venial, respectable, and even laudable), or the *Metamorphoses*, coming to high and even extravagant laudation in the recent age, the *Epistulae Ex Ponto* incur dispraisal, or simply neglect. This is not the place to document the virtuosity not abating of language, style, and structure. When extolling his *Heroides* Ovid put out a proud claim of original genius,

ignotum hoc aliis ille novavit opus. (*AA* III. 346)

Critics endorse the claim. By paradox, something better was yet to be, the product of ill fortune.

Advancing in dexterity as well as confidence, Ovid in Book IV achieves novel affects in a variety of tones and modes. At his touch the elegiac couplet renders a brisk military narration when he tells how Aegissus was recaptured (7. 19 ff.). The long catalogue of rivers, ending with great Danube which refuses to concede primacy to Nile, passes on to describe how the fresh water debilitates the Pontus and robs it of taste and colour,

quin etiam, stagno similis pigraeque paludi,
caeruleus vix est diluiturque color. (10. 61 f.)

Again, imagination calls up the imperial city and the induction o a consul (4. 23 ff.), first the procession to the Capitol and the solemn prayers, next the Curia and the speech of thanksgiving, 'meritas superis cum Caesare grates' (4. 39).[1] The next poem goes on to recount the consular functions of Sextus Pompeius (5. 17 ff.). The same theme recurs for Pomponius Graecinus in 16, at some length (9. 17–50), but without tedium or monotony.

Finally, Rome and the Pontus combine neatly. Ovid's poem in the Getic language celebrates Tiberius Caesar, the new deity, the dynasty. It impressed the audience; and one of the natives duly concludes

Caesaris imperio restituendus eras. (12. 38)

.   .   .

[1] The earliest attestation, so it happens, of a practice that was to have dire results. It was presented by a *senatus consultum* (Pliny, *Pan.* 4. 1). The next comes in *Laus Pisonis* 68 ff.

VI. Ovid's lot was cast, as he says and says again, among tribes of wild barbarians,

> Sauromatae cingunt, fera gens, Bessique Getaeque.   (*Tr.* III. 10. 5)

Distinctions should be drawn. About Getae, no problem. Getae inhabited both banks of the lower Danube. There were Getae either subject to the rulers of Thrace or living obscurely in villages in Dobrogea on the territories of the Greek colonies; and also Getae in Wallachia and southern Moldavia, who made incursions across the river. Ovid specifies as Getae the raiders who harried the towns of Aegissus and Troesmis.[1] As for his Bessi, they were inhabitants of Dobrogea: a portion of that proverbially savage nation which the Romans had transferred from their homeland in inner Thrace.[2]

The Sarmatians are another matter. Beyond the Danube delta in Bessarabia and in south Russia, as Ovid indicates,

> hactenus Euxini pars est Romana sinistri:
> proxima Bastarnae Sauromataeque tenent.   (*Tr.* II. 197 f.)

That is, nowhere near the 'regio Tomitana'. Not but that the poet had acquired fluency in their tongue as well as in Getic, after a fairly short time, so one learns (and some believe).[3]

To Ovid both Sarmatians and Getae are horsemen equipped with bows and arrows. In fact, they parade the streets of Tomis,

> Sarmaticae maior Geticaeque frequentia gentis
>   per medias in equis itque reditque vias.
> in quibus est nemo, qui non coryton et arcum
>   telaque vipereo lurida felle gerat.   (*Tr.* V. 7. 13 ff.).

It will not with safety be believed that any of the Greek cities on the shore of Pontus tolerated the presence of armed natives within their walls.[4]

Bastarnae are named by Ovid in the one place. The word 'Sarmaticus' had a convenient and metrical appeal for the poet. He uses it at least fourteen times. Genuine Sarmatians are not so easy to certify.

---

[1] *Ex P.* I. 8. 16; IV. 9. 78.

[2] For Thracians, R. Vulpe, *Histoire ancienne de la Dobroudja* (1938), 108 f.; 186 f.

[3] Above, p. 17.

[4] Native elements or features in Tomis tend to be exaggerated. Thus R. Vulpe, *Studi Ovidiani* (1959), 39 ff. For the population of the city and its territorium in the early Roman period see C. Danoff, *RE*, Supp. IX, 1406 ff.; D. M. Pippidi, *Athenaeum* LV (1977), 250 ff.

'Sarmatia' and 'Sarmatae' began as vague and comprehensive appellations. Sarmatians duly inherit the features familiar for ages as Scythian: nomadic peoples of the far cold lands, formidable with horse and bow.

Accurate information took a long time to percolate. The first author to supply it was Posidonius, so it has been asserted.[1] But the equipment reported for the Rhoxolani is Scythian, not Sarmatian, and they were easily dealt with by generals of Mithridates.[2]

The authentic Sarmatians had no use for bows and arrows. They were mailed cavalry, their peculiar weapon being the long heavy lance called a 'contus'. The earliest testimony, clear and vivid, comes in the *Argonautica* of Valerius Flaccus.[3] Next, Tacitus, who describes an invasion of the Rhoxolani in the winter of 68/9.[4]

Ovid may delight the reader in any age with portrayal of the frozen Danube, with waggons on the ice, drawn by Sarmatian oxen, and the like. He can also furnish precise and precious details. Ovid is the first Latin writer to mention another Sarmatian people, the Iazyges.[5] His notice indicates that at this time the Iazyges were located not far from the mouth of the Danube. When next on record (in A.D. 50) they are discovered on the other side of the Carpathians, on the Hungarian plain. They are clients of the Roman power, usefully separating the Dacians from the Germans of Bohemia and Moravia.[6]

Again, albeit only a curiosity, Ovid mentions the Coralli, situating them in Dobrogea.[7] Which appears correct.[8] The next attestation of the Coralli is in Valerius Flaccus, where they are numbered among the motley nations of Scythia.[9] Ovid describes the Coralli as 'yellow-haired'; and since, according to the other poet, the Coralli went into

---

[1] K. Kretschmer, *RE* I A, 2545.

[2] Strabo VII, p. 306 (from Posidonius). These natives wore jerkins and caps of leather.

[3] Valerius Flaccus VI. 161; 231 ff. Cf. R. Syme, *CQ* XXIII (1929), 129 ff. The 'contus' is also specified as Sarmatian by Silius, *Punica* XV. 683 ff., and by Statius, *Achill.* II. 132. The item in the three poets (it is argued) reflects the campaigns of Domitian against the Iazyges in 89 and in 92.

[4] Tacitus, *Hist.* I. 79 (with full and vivid detail).

[5] *Ex P.* I. 2. 77; IV. 7. 9; *Ibis* 133.

[6] *Ann.* XII. 29. 3, cf. *Hist.* III. 5. 1. They may have been encouraged to migrate by the Romans.

[7] *Ex P.* IV. 2. 37; 8. 83.

[8] Strabo VII, p. 318. In Appian, however, they appear among Scythians and Sarmatians (*Mithr.* 69. 293).   [9] Valerius Flaccus VI. 89 ff.

battle chanting heroic lays, somebody no doubt has claimed them Germanic. This enigmatic people left no traces in Dobrogea.[1]

More to the point, Ovid supplies precise information about the Getic raid in the year 12: names of towns and of Roman officers. Otherwise Danubian history in the time of Augustus can show nothing comparable. The 'triumphalia de Getis' won by Cn. Lentulus (*cos.* 14 B.C.) defy both time and place.[2]

The operations disclose Pomponius Flaccus and P. Vitellius. That is welcome. Some will discover greater value in Vestalis, of the princely house that ruled the Cottian Alps: he served as *primus pilus* in a Roman legion, and was then promoted to a post of authority.[3] The 'principes' of Tres Galliae, his peers, normally command regiments of native cavalry.

·   ·   ·

VII. The names in the four books *Ex Ponto* convey varied and precious detail illuminating Roman society and government. For example, the first emergence of P. Suillius Rufus and (C. Vibius) Rufinus, rendered attractive through either success or delay in their subsequent careers.

In the broader sphere, the poems show how polite studies informed and embellished relations between men of worth from the towns of Italy and the high aristocracy. Thus Ovid claims a young *nobilis* like Cotta as one of his 'sodales'. At the same time, due deference to rank and station. And nobility of character is inevitably consonant with high birth in the sons of Messalla. Velleius indeed can go one better. Of Messallinus he affirms 'vir animo etiam quam gente nobilior'.[4] Hence an entertaining contrast when in the sequel the behaviour of noblemen like Cotta or Sex. Pompeius is shown up by Cornelius Tacitus.

One stage further, the language invoked when the ruler is praised, or his consort.[5] To catalogue or analyse would be tedious.[6] One specimen may suffice. 'Aeternitas' had been predicated of Rome, and

[1] They are not in Mela or Pliny—or in *RE*.
[2] *Ann.* IV. 44. 1; Florus II. 28 f. See above, p. 68.
[3] *Ex P.* IV. 7. 13 f., cf. above, p. 81.   [4] Velleius II. 112. 1.
[5] For Livia, above, p. 148.
[6] For a catalogue, K. Scott, *TAPA* LXI (1930), 43 ff.

it was now being annexed by the Caesars.[1] Ovid applies 'aeternus' to the Princeps, as the object of passionate devotion on the part of Messallinus.[2]

Ovid himself had set up a domestic cult at Tomis (that city now reconciled and conferring honours), and all the Pontic shore can know and gladly testify:

> nec pietas ignota mea est: videt hospita terra
>   in nostra sacrum Caesaris esse domo.
> stant pariter natusque pius coniunxque sacerdos,
>   numina iam facto non leviora deo.
> neu desit pars ulla domus, stat uterque nepotum
>   hic aviae lateri proximus, ille patris.   (IV. 9. 105 ff.)

Cotta, it will be recalled, sent statuettes for that shrine.[3] To put the matter briefly, Ovid permits the language and comportment to be divined which Roman aristocrats were ready to adopt towards Caesar Augustus and the dynasty. The other name is 'adulatio'.

In general terms, the cult of the Caesars is worship of power, a requital for benefits or a token of hopeful expectations. Even in the lower classes it cannot have had much emotional content. For the upper order (that is, knights as well as senators), homage developed out of social deference and patronage, extending into public life. Beyond order and decency, it is true. In the political vocabulary 'obsequium' can be employed without distaste, and for praise.[4] But the Caesars reduced honourable men to the position of clients. Hence 'deforme obsequium'.[5] And before long treason can be styled 'impietas'.[6]

On one count objections could be evaded, the harm extenuated. Forms and words had nothing to do with inner beliefs.[7] That is to say, the traditional religion is comparable. Neither inspired fervour,

---

[1] Cf. A. D. Nock, *Essays on Religion and the Ancient World* I (ed. Z. Stewart, 1972), 384. The Roman state as eternal comes up first in Cicero, *Pro C. Rabirio* 33; Livy IV. 4. 4.

[2] *Ex P.* II. 2. 48 (quoted above, p. 128). Observe already Augustus as Pontifex Maximus, *Fasti* III. 421 f.: 'ignibus aeternis aeterni numina praesunt / Caesaris.' Also 'deus aeternus' along with Apollo and Vesta on the Palatine (IV. 954).

[3] *Ex P.* II. 8. 1 ff.   [4] *Tacitus* (1958), 58.

[5] *Ann.* IV. 20. 3.

[6] *Ann.* VI. 47. 2: the case of 'multorum amoribus famosa Albucilla'.

[7] The poet's cult of Augustus has sometimes been taken seriously. Thus T. F. Higham, *CR* XLVIII (1934), 107 f. Indeed, 'he had even become a missionary of his strange faith.'

neither deserved anger or protest. Hypocrisy, to be sure, needs an outlet. At Rome it is discovered in devotion to the 'res publica'.

.   .   .

For the enquirer in these late days, the *Epistulae Ex Ponto* contribute powerfully to an understanding of life and letters in the time of Caesar Augustus, especially valuable because of the dearth of contemporary evidence for the last epoch of the reign. It is not merely the useful details about persons and events, permitting close dates and references. Ovid illustrates the language in current use for homage towards ruler and dynasty. In general and above all, he is a necessary counterpart to the poets whom the government liked and rewarded.

X

POETRY AND GOVERNMENT

I. NOTHING is more easy to decry than the fashion of dividing literary history by epochs or periods. The line drawn may be either too sharp or not sharp enough; and a political definition may not go well with developments in polite letters. Common usage operates with the categories of 'Ciceronian' and 'Augustan'. The consequences are sometimes perilous, as happens when standard manuals deposit the historian Sallust in the former period. He is better regarded as proto-imperial.

And the term 'Augustan' needs careful handling. To take the shining glories of Augustan Rome: Virgil was born in 70 B.C., Horace in 65, Livy in 64.[1] All three had come to manhood in the years of tribulation.

Periodization cannot be avoided, and it has plain advantages. Something might be said in favour of a new and novel period, from the institution of the Triumvirate in 43 B.C. to the return of normal government in 28 B.C. The latter year advertised a visible sign when the victor of Actium passed the twelve *fasces* to his colleague in the consulship by monthly rotation;[2] and Cornelius Tacitus assigns to 28 the end of the age of misrule, through the ordinances now to obtain under the dispensation of 'Pax et Princeps'.[3]

Political and literary history can thus be persuaded to concur. The fifteen years of rapid change saw a rich and variegated effervescence: Virgil with the *Georgics* after the *Eclogues*, all the early Horace (and several odes already to his credit), while Book I of Propertius appeared in 28 (it is probable), and Tibullus was writing. Furthermore,

---

[1] For Livy the year 64 is preferable to 59, cf. above, p. 109.

[2] Dio LII. 1. 1: a good beginning for a book—and a passage often misunderstood, as in *CAH* X (1934), 123. Dio's words do not indicate a dividing of twenty-four *fasces* with Agrippa.

[3] *Ann.* III. 28. 2.

Roman history. Sallust, whose first monograph was composed in the year of Philippi, was cut off in 35, his *Historiae* not finishing their fifth book. But Asinius Pollio who took up the theme of decline and fall was narrating the hazardous years of the Civil Wars; and Livy (so it may be conjectured) embarked on his vast enterprise as early as 30 or 29.[1]

A second segment of fifteen years also acquires clarity and definition through the *Aeneid* and through Horace: *Odes* I–III (in 23) being completed by Book IV in 13.[2] The word 'Augustan' may be attached with strict propriety to writers who through their themes and ideals reflect the policy of the new dispensation—and who, by allegiance, stand in close and even personal relation to the ruler.[3]

To make the next cut in 13 B.C. concords with the movement of imperial history. After an absence of three years in Gaul and Spain, Caesar Augustus came back to Rome. The western provinces had been pacified, ordered, and organized; and his return was celebrated by the dedication of the Ara Pacis. The occasion called for a third closing of Janus, so some at the time may have fancied. Others, of deeper understanding, the 'prudentes', knew that 'Pax' can announce renewed efforts of warfare.

Horace in the Fourth Book of the *Odes*, so it happens, when summarizing at the end the achievements of the Princeps, registers the closing of Janus, 'vacuum duellis / Ianum Quirini clausit.'[4] The reference is of a general nature. None the less, with this item for encouragement, several scholars in the recent age argue that Augustus' third and last closure of the Gates of War occurred precisely in 13.[5]

[1] The standard notion has him begin between 27 and 25 B.C. Rather, several years earlier: thus J. Bayet in vol. I of the Budé edition (1940), xvii ff.; R. Syme, *Harvard Studies* LXIV (1959), 41 ff. = *RP* (1978), 416 ff.; T. J. Luce, *TAPA* XCVI (1965), 209 ff.

[2] The standard date. That Book IV was not in fact published until 9/8 B.C., the last year of Horace's life, is the ingenious thesis recently promulgated by G. Williams, *Horace* (*Greece & Rome*, New Surveys in the Classics, No. 6, 1972), 44 ff. He suggests, *inter alia*, that the poems dedicated to Fabius Maximus and Marcius Censorinus (IV. 1 and 8) may be compliments to their consulates (11 and 8).

[3] Livy is in a special case. The patriotic and moral ideals may already have been present in this man from Patavium (in the old-fashioned zone of the 'frontier'), or in some of his sources.

[4] IV. 15. 8 f.: preceded by a reference to the Roman military standards, 'derepta Partho-rum superbis / postibus' (7 f.). Cf. *Epp.* II. 1. 255 f.

[5] I. S. Ryberg, *Mem. Am. Ac. Rome* XIX (1949), 93; S. Weinstock, *JRS* L (1960), 48 (citing the passages noted in the previous footnote); N. Reed, *Latomus* XXXII (1973), 782.

The case is feeble. If closed in 13, Janus must have been opened at once, since the Senate voted its closing at the end of 11, in the sequel of notable conquests in the North, but the ceremony had to be postponed.[1]

In fact, the year 13 gave a clear sign to the contrary: the campaign waged by Marcus Agrippa against the Pannonians.[2] That declared the inception of the conquest of Illyricum and the winning of the land route from Italy to the Balkans. In short, the necessary task and the prime achievement, valid for ever despite miscalculations elsewhere in the zone of the northern frontiers.[3] On a sober estimate the invasions of Germany may be seen as subsidiary.

.   .   .

II. The same year marks a cleavage in literary history. That is, the publication of Book IV of the *Odes*.[4] The collection includes the two panegyrical pieces that celebrate the exploits of Tiberius and Drusus in 15, in the subjugation of the Alpine lands (4 and 14). But Horace also, devolving on Iullus Antonius a Pindaric theme, is able to suggest and amplify a victory of Augustus over the Sugambri (2. 53 ff.), with the joyous prospect of a triumph (2. 49 ff.).[5] Further, another poem acclaims or anticipates the return of Caesar Augustus, after conquests and in peace with no hint of a German triumph: 'lucem redde tuae, dux bone, patriae' (5. 5). Finally, in the concluding ode is celebrated

> imperi
> porrecta maiestas ad ortus
>   solis ab Hesperio cubili.   (15. 14 ff.)

That, so one scholar avers, is 'possibly the latest of all his poems'.[6] In any event, the end of an epoch.

---

[1] Dio LIV. 35. 2. The third closing can be assigned to 8 or 7 B.C., for various reasons (above, p. 25).

[2] Velleius II. 96. 2; Dio LIV. 28. 1 f.

[3] As argued in *CAH* X (1934), 351 ff., and elsewhere. Cf. above, p. 52.

[4] Above, p. 170.

[5] For the Sugambri, above, p. 5. In fact, no campaign in 16 B.C.: they came to terms (Dio LIV. 20. 6). The poem is assigned to that year by E. Fraenkel, *Horace* (1954), 433. Which is highly plausible. The Sugambri are quiescent in *Odes* IV. 14. 51 f. (subsequent to 15 B.C.). G. Williams, however, regards a date in 13 B.C. as 'much more likely' (*Horace* (1972), 47). He also states that Augustus returned in 13 'from a successful campaign in Germany' (ibid. 48).   [6] E. Fraenkel, o.c. 449.

According to Suetonius, Augustus instructed Horace to honour the Alpine victories of his stepsons and thus compelled him to produce after a long interval a fourth book of odes. Furthermore, having read some 'sermones' void of any mention of his name, the ruler raised complaint and extorted the piece beginning with 'cum tot sustineas'.[1] The notion of compulsion will be suitably played down, or even discounted.[2] None the less, the wishes of Caesar and the poet's response are in concordance.

Likewise the relation in time between his *Epistula ad Augustum* (*Ep.* II. 1) and *Odes* IV. Towards the end Horace deprecates his capacity to render the achievements of Caesar Augustus and the high themes of peace and war. Not for him

> terrarumque situs et flumina dicere, et arces
> montibus impositas.   (II. 1. 252 f.)

The reference seems clear enough to the Alpine War of 15, to the 'arces / Alpibus impositas tremendis' (*Odes* IV. 14. 11 f.).

Furthermore, the same context carries a reference to Janus linked (though illicitly) to the humbling of the Parthians,

> claustraque custodem pacis cohibentia Ianum,
> et formidatam Parthis te principe Romam.   (255 f.)

Similarly in *Odes* IV. 15. 8 f. That ode is assigned with some confidence to 13 B.C.

Hence a fairly close dating for the *Epistula* in standard works. For example, *c.* 14, or 14/13.[3] Two recent surveys, of some amplitude, eschew any indication of date.[4] Which comes as a surprise. And there is another surprise. A recent enquiry inclines to take the *Epistula* several years back, putting it in near sequel to the *Carmen Saeculare* (of 17 B.C.).[5]

---

[1] Suetonius, ed. Roth, p. 298.

[2] E. Fraenkel, o.c. 383, cf. 364. For Fraenkel 'it is obvious' that the 'sermones quosdam' cannot refer to *Epp.* I, but only to *Epp.* II. 2 (to Florus) and the *Ars Poetica*. *Contra*, G. Williams, o.c. 39.

[3] e.g. Schanz–Hosius, *Gesch. der r. Lit.* II⁴ (1935), 133; C. Becker, *Das Spätwerk des Horaz* (1962), 194; C. O. Brink, *Horace on Poetry* (1963), 191.

[4] E. Fraenkel, *Horace* (1954), 383 ff.; G. Williams, *Tradition and Originality in Roman Poetry* (1968), 72 ff., cf. 160 ff.

[5] G. Williams, *Horace* (1972), 39. He suggests that the subject matter puts it earlier than odes such as IV. 4 and 14.

The dedication to Augustus stands in sharp relief and emphasis.

> Cum tot sustineas et tanta negotia solus,
> res Italas armis tuteris, moribus ornes,
> legibus emendes, in publica commoda peccem,
> si longo sermone morer tua tempora, Caesar.

These four lines contain a clue, and also a problem that not all have seen. Augustus carries the burden of empire. The phrase 'tanta negotia' represents good prose usage, indeed of the best, for Sallust, meditating upon the crisis of the Roman state, had been impelled to ask 'quae res maxume tanta negotia sustinuisset'.[1]

The line ends with the emphatic 'solus'. A question arises. Caesar Augustus did not stand alone as supreme arbiter of war and peace. What of Marcus Agrippa? The husband of Julia was not only the father of the two boy princes whom the ruler had taken as his sons. Agrippa held the *tribunicia potestas*, that potent 'summi fastigii vocabulum'. Moreover in 13, so it might be conjectured, his *imperium* over armies and provinces was made equal with that of Caesar Augustus.[2] That is, a position to which Tiberius Caesar acceded in A.D. 13.[3]

Hence a dilemma, which not all will perhaps concede.[4] After an arduous winter campaign in Pannonia Marcus Agrippa died in 12 B.C., in the month of March. The *Epistula* should be subsequent. If so, it acquires sharp relevance. The solitude of Augustus is enhanced, although he is not yet 'senex et solus'.[5] Augustus was now fifty, and the year was unhealthy, two consuls having perished in office.[6]

Otherwise, if 13 B.C. be retained for the date, the poet's testimony is misleading. Now Horace, so weighty authority avers, 'never lies'.[7]

---

[1] Sallust, *Cat.* 53. 2. Fraenkel (o.c. 384) quotes *Pro Roscio Amerino* 22 on the position of Sulla: 'solus' with 'tot tantisque negotiis distentus'. Ovid, it may be observed, has a more stylish term for the burden of rule, *Tr.* II. 221: 'moles Romani nominis'; *Met.* XV. 1 f.: 'quis tantae pondera molis / sustineat'.

[2] Cf. Dio LIV. 28. 1. The question has been elucidated, and made more complex, by the papyrus fragment of Augustus' funeral oration, *P. Colon.* inv. 4701, published by L. Koenen, *ZPE* V (1970), 226. See also E. W. Gray, ibid. VI, 227 ff. An *imperium* such as that conferred on Tiberius might have been mentioned later in the oration.

[3] Velleius II. 121. 1; Suetonius, *Tib.* 21. 1. Cf. above, p. 56.

[4] As assumed in *Rom. Rev.* (1939), 392.

[5] As his successor said of himself in the despatch from Capreae (Suetonius, *Tib.* 65. 1).

[6] Above, p. 111.

[7] An entry in Fraenkel's General Index (o.c. 456).

Quite so, he is too crafty for that. And this epistle will be found to disclose craft of a high calibre, in both senses of the term.

. . .

III. The *Letter to Augustus* is a marvellous exhibit of structural skill. Starting with the ruler, the argument evokes literary fashions and the repute of ancient writings, passes to a comparison of Greece and Rome (how their literature arose) and through poetry comes back to Augustus towards the end.

After the initial four lines, Horace at once introduces his theme with Romulus and certain Greek demi-gods. They missed fame when alive, it accrued only after death. By contrast Caesar Augustus had already earned due recognition (15 ff.). He is unique, 'nil oriturum alias, nil ortum tale'. But the Roman People, 'sapiens et iustus' in according primacy over all 'duces' Roman or Greek, does not show judgement in other matters.

The Romans loathe and despise all that is not defunct, they are possessed by a passion for the ancients,

> sic fautor veterum, ut tabulas peccare vetantis
> quas bis quinque viri sanxerunt, foedera regum
> vel Gabiis vel cum rigidis aequata Sabinis,
> pontificum libros, annosa volumina vatum
> dictitet Albano Musas in monte locutas.   (23 ff.)

The pronouncement is firm and vivid, duly equipped with choice examples. It needs to be interpreted, and toned down.

The study of Roman antiquities benefited enormously from the years of tribulation, being one form of escape from the evil present, and more congenial (to some, at least) than Arcadia, the Age of Gold and the Fortunate Isles. Like the writing of history, old documents and sacerdotal law were a suitable refuge and consolation for the statesman deprived of action or public eloquence.[1] Furthermore, to maintain their despotic rule the Triumvirs enlisted support not only from the mandate of the heavenly powers, from alien superstitions and from astral science. They made use of ancient cult and legend. That practice was at once reinforced and extended by the

---

[1] The noteworthy example is Messalla Rufus (*cos.* 53), who wrote a book *De auspiciis.*

victor of Actium. The year 29 exhibits sundry ritual operations enacted by the new Romulus.[1]

Acquiring favour and repute, antiquarian studies no doubt excited a Varronian enthusiasm for the archaic language of the Latin muses. Such predilections may have abated somewhat in the sequel (like other themes or attitudes on show in the first years after Actium). As transmitted (and diluted) in the early books of Livy, the appeal would not persist. Antiquarism can hardly have been predominant or pervasive when Horace was writing the *Epistula*. He exaggerates, in gentle but obvious humour. And with a purpose. The passage leads on to brisk logic which demolishes the distinction between ancient and modern (28 ff.).

Next, something more serious. The old poets, he alleges, are all the rage,

> Naevius in manibus non est et mentibus haeret
> paene recens? adeo sanctum est vetus omne poema.
> ambigitur quotiens, uter utro sit prior, aufert
> Pacuvius docti famam senis, Accius alti,
> dicitur Afrani toga convenisse Menandro,
> Plautus ad exemplar Siculi properare Epicharmi,
> vincere Caecilius gravitate, Terentius arte.
> hos ediscit et hos arto stipata theatro
> spectat Roma potens.   (53 ff.)

Again, a firm pronouncement. And no less firmly will it be doubted whether the poem of Naevius was often in the hands or much in the minds of the reading public. The old dramatists are another matter, be it conceded. Yet there is no means of knowing how popular their plays were in this age, or how often put on the stage. Augustus, who detested archaism in prose writing, had an affection for the 'vetus comoedia', so it happens to be recorded.[2] Which is easy to credit.

His liking for Roman comedy leaves no trace in Ovid's apologia addressed to the Princeps (*Tristia* II). Instead, the poet spreads himself on 'mimos obscena iocantes' (497 ff.), as indeed is more

---

[1] Thus the closing of Janus and the celebration of the *Augurium Salutis*.

[2] Suetonius, *Divus Aug*. 89. 1: 'delectabatur etiam comoedia veteri et saepe eam exhibuit spectaculis publicis.' For his dislike of archaism, ibid. 86.

closely pertinent to his defence. These exhibitions have cost a lot of money,

> inspice ludorum sumptus, Auguste, tuorum. (509)

They were numerous, the ruler himself was often present,

> luminibusque tuis, totus quibus utitur orbis,
> scaenica vidisti lentus adulteria. (513 f.)

.   .   .

IV. The Romans abode under the spell of old documents and the early poets, to the disallowance of modernity, so Horace alleges. The writer is subtle and humorous, outrageous and evasive. Valid suspicions obtruding, it is expedient to look for the purpose of his exposition.

Praise of the ruler, that was enjoined. It is direct in the exordium, confirmed at once by the equation with gods and heroes. And it is conveyed indirectly, when Caesar Augustus is linked to the efflorescence of Latin poetry in the present age—and to the capacity of his loyal friend. Horace would have wished to celebrate the high themes of history,

> res componere gestas,
> terrarumque situs et flumina dicere, et arces
> montibus impositas et barbara regna, tuisque
> auspiciis totum confecta duella per orbem,
> claustraque custodem pacis cohibentia Ianum,
> et formidatam Parthis te principe Romam. (251 ff.)

To those themes, however, the poet may not rise, he cannot be worthy of 'maiestas tua'. Which, to be sure, is a manifestation of 'manly independence' towards the exigencies of the Princeps. Yet there is no call to put a high estimate on the 'deprecatio' of Horace. No despot can compel a poet to compose an elogium in epic verse.

In fact, others can do it. Alexander had only an inferior poet, whereas for Augustus stand

> dilecti tibi Vergilius Variusque poetae. (247)

Those two poets happen to be conjoined in another place, in praise of the moderns against the ancients,

> quid autem
> Caecilio Plautoque dabit Romanus ademptum
> Vergilio Varioque? (Ars Poetica 53 ff.)

That is to say, the *Epistula* conveys a vindication of 'the better sort' of contemporary poets. It is firm and direct, with Virgil and Varius for the epic mode (and, through Varius, for drama also).[1]

But also, indirect: Horace himself. Horace did not write in the epic vein (who expected or demanded?), but he had made in his own fashion a powerful contribution, exalting the ruler and commending the policy of the government. Splendid pieces stood as a monument, notably the 'Roman Odes' (III. 1–6). After an interval came the *Carmen Saeculare*, to reinforce which were added the august themes of war and peace in the last book of the Odes.

The *Letter to Augustus* parades the excellence of the poets whom the ruler cherished. The present is vindicated against the over-valued past. The poet issues a manifesto. Against whom, in truth? Where are the real enemies?

.   .   .

V. The time has come to put a pertinent question about the condition of polite letters in this season. What manner of poetry was in fashion with the reading public? The answer cannot be deferred or evaded: love poetry in the elegiac measure.

In the first place, the great originator, Cornelius Gallus. They may still have been reading his poems. Of Gallus, however, no word anywhere in the works of Horace. Not even in *Satires* I. 10, written in 35 or 34 B.C. That piece registers a number of poets and their patrons, not all of them by any means in close relationship to the young Caesar or to Maecenas. The consular Asinius Pollio is mentioned, now writing tragedies, and Messalla Corvinus. Also Valgius Rufus, and even a certain Fundanius, who wrote comedies.[2]

Next in the line after Gallus comes Albius Tibullus, the period of whose writing falls between 30 and 19. Horace favoured him with an ode (I. 33). It says nothing about Delia, or about Nemesis, the other 'inamorata'. Instead, Albius is urged not to grieve about the

---

[1] Varius had written a *Thyestes*: a theme, like that of Atreus, which appealed to Romans in more ages than one. In Horace it is only the epic poet who earns praise (*Sat.* I. 10. 43 f.; *Odes* I. 5. 1). Which is not without significance. For the testimonia about L. Varius Rufus (much confused with scholiasts' erudition), see *PIR*[1], V. 194; Schanz–Hosius, o.c. 163 f. He hardly finds a mention save in relation to either Virgil or Horace.

[2] Horace, *Sat.* I. 10. 42 ff.; 81 ff. Fundanius is elsewhere not on record except in *Sat.* II. 8. 19. For Valgius Rufus (*suff.* 12 B.C.), above, p. 111.

asperity of Glycera, 'neu miserabilis / decantes elegos'. All in all, a trivial or evasive piece. Tibullus has also an epistle (I. 4). His grace of form is praised, his ease of life and his riches. And it is surmised that he may be active in composing,

scribere quod Cassi Parmensis opuscula vincat.   (4. 3)

The reference to that Cassius carries no compliment: one of the assassins of the Dictator, he had written among other things a libel about his heir, styling him grandson not only of a banker but of a baker.[1] Therefore, a specimen, to be sure, of the poet's 'playful humour', or 'friendly irony'.

Finally, Propertius. Not deigned with a mention, even for valediction.[2] Soon after the laudation on Cornelia, the wife of Paullus Aemilius Lepidus (in 16), Propertius died—or perhaps reverted to family and patrimony.

There remains a potent and damaging name, that of Ovid. His precocious genius took and captivated the town. By 13 B.C., when he celebrated his thirtieth birthday, his *Amores* were no doubt on the lips of young and old; and the first edition (in five books) was surely on the market by now.[3] Further, he was going on to a kindred work, the *Heroides*.

Another product of Ovid's youthful prime was the famous dramatic piece, the *Medea*. It may also have seen the light about this time. An item, by the way, which suggests some relevance to Horace, but cannot encourage any conclusions. That is, the disquisition on drama, commonly styled *Ars Poetica*. The date of that work is of notorious dispute. Recent estimates verge towards 18 B.C., after Book I of the *Epistulae* and the *Letter to Florus* (*Epp.* II. 2).[4] A late date is not excluded, about 10 B.C.[5] On that hypothesis, the

---

[1] Suetonius, *Divus Aug.* 4. 2. For Cassius see further F. Skutsch, *RE* III, 1743 f. His end was miserable: executed at Athens soon after an ominous dream (Valerius Maximus I. 7. 7).

[2] For their mutual hostility see now J. P. Sullivan, *Propertius* (1976) 12 ff.

[3] Above, p. 8.

[4] Thus C. Becker, *Das Spätwerk des Horaz* (1963), 68 f.; 111; G. Williams, *Horace* (1972), 38 f. Also, apparently, Fraenkel, though his references are curiously indirect, viz. 383 (on 'sermones quosdam'); 388 f., 'the advice he had given to the young sons of Piso', cf. 389, 'the epistle to the sons of Piso'. Absent from the General Index, the *AP* occurs once only in the index of poems and passages discussed.

[5] C. O. Brink inclines to a dating 'after the years 14–13 B.C.' (o.c. 217). It is put *c.* 15 by P. Grimal, *Essai sur l'Art Poétique d'Horace* (1968), 27.

Medea might have furnished the incentive to a piece of writing which, instructive on several counts, lacks verve and exhilaration.[1]

. . .

VI. Apart from themes and metre, the elegiac poets of Augustan Rome have certain features in common. First, the question of patrons, which does not permit a single answer. Tibullus enjoyed the protection of the illustrious Messalla Corvinus: a relationship that seems to have been exclusive. The Cornutus whom he honours with two poems (II. 2. 9; 3. 1) belongs to a senatorial family, but is not a person of high consequence;[2] Macer (II. 6. 1) is Aemilius Macer, a poet from Verona;[3] and there is a certain Titius (I. 4. 73), who remains enigmatic.[4]

As for Propertius, the Tullus to whom Book I is dedicated (he has the first poem and the last) was not quite a patron, although the nephew of a consul (L. Volcacius Tullus, *cos.* 33 B.C.). Rather a friend attached by congeniality of age and tastes. Likewise in that book the two poets (Ponticus and Bassus) along with the unidentified Gallus.[5]

Tullus went to Asia with his uncle, either in 30 or in 29: perhaps the latter year is preferable.[6] If a *legatus* of the proconsul (cf. I. 6. 19 f.), he need not have been a senator at the time; and in fact he renounced the career of public honours. A number of years later Tullus is found residing at Cyzicus (III. 22. 1), a graceful city of

---

[1] Williams asks 'what then was he doing from the age of 52 to 57' (o.c. 46)? If that scholar's late dating of *Odes* IV is rejected (it is highly vulnerable), the 'argument of the unemployed bard' can be put to good employ.

The 'Pisones', by the way, are defined as 'pater et iuvenes patre digni' (*AP* 24). For the baffling problem of identity, cf. (briefly), *JRS* L (1960), 19 f. = *RP* (1978) 508 f. Further, above, p. 115.

[2] Presumably M. Caecilius Cornutus (*PIR*[2], C 34), cf. C. Cichorius, *Römische Studien* (1922), 264. This man is, however, highly enigmatic, since he occurs among the earliest Arvales, attested in 21 B.C. (*CIL* VI. 32338).

[3] *PIR*[2], A 378. According to Jerome, he died in Asia in 16 B.C. An early friend of Ovid (*Tr.* IV. 10. 44).

[4] For a presumed Titius Rufus, above, p. 79.

[5] Above, pp. 98 ff.

[6] His proconsulate was not registered in D. Magie, *Roman Rule in Asia Minor* (1950), 1580; cf. remarks in *JRS* XLV (1955), 159 = *RP* (1978), 267. Nor in *RE* IXA (1961), 757. The tenure 26/5 was suggested by K. M. T. Atkinson, *Historia* VII (1958), 312 ff. Not plausible, and based upon error about Propertius I. 22. 7 f.

varied and ample seductions—and obdurate against the appeal of duty and the family as expounded by his friend,

> hic tibi pro digna gente petendus honos,
> hic tibi ad eloquium cives, hic ampla nepotum
> spes et venturae coniugis aptus amor. (III. 22. 40 ff.)

Patrons are likewise not to be discovered in the *Amores*. Ovid dedicates a poem each to Atticus, to Pompeius Macer, to Pomponius Graecinus.[1] Atticus remains enigmatic, but Macer was Ovid's coeval and his companion in travel abroad. Graecinus, belonging to a new family from Iguvium in Umbria, was probably Ovid's junior by a number of years.

For Ovid as for Propertius, 'sodales' are disclosed, of about the same age and class. Each is independent from the outset, he does not need to seek support from the powerful and illustrious. The reader only comes upon the 'magna nomina' many years later in the poems of exile: Ovid in youth had entry to the mansion of Messalla Corvinus, and in the sequel he became a close friend of the younger son, Cotta Maximus.[2] Furthermore, Paullus Fabius Maximus.[3]

Cyzicus had already been elected for domicile by a certain Erucius who wrote Greek poems; and it attracted more illustrious residents later on.[4] The most potent allurements came from the cities of Ionia and from the adjacent islands, from Lesbos down to Rhodes. Confined within a sombre and impoverished Italy during the years of tribulation, men longed for the shores of light. The advent of peace liberated a pack of tourists from the educated class or from the newly enriched, impelled by the higher thought or by the appetite for low living.[5] It was the counterpart to the wave of Greek intellectuals that now invaded the capital of the world. The old habits resumed.[6]

Marcus Antonius was defeated, but not the 'externi mores ac vitia

---

[1] Ch. V. [2] Ch. VII. [3] Ch. VIII.

[4] For Erucius, Cichorius, *Römische Studien* (1922), 304 ff.: perhaps from Spoletium, cf. T. P. Wiseman, *New Men in the Roman Senate* (1971), 230. The princess Antonia Tryphaena (*PIR*², A 900) was the widow of Cotys, the ruler of Thrace (C 1554), to whom Ovid addressed *Ex P.* II. 9.

[5] G. W. Bowersock, *Augustus and the Greek World* (1965), 75 ff. As an obscure specimen may be cited the Bullatius to whom Horace sent *Ep.* I. 12. The name is rare, but not prepossessing, cf. Schulze, *LE* 350; and he has been left out of *PIR*².

[6] Above, p. 107.

non Romana' which condemned him.[1] Benefiting from a prosperous epoch, dissipation and gaiety revived at Rome, with no heed for exhortations to Sabine frugality (and the monitors were all too equivocal).[2]

In the previous age the doctrines of Epicurus permeated society, decried by eloquent expositors of lofty ideals, but not shunned by senators and men of action like the austere Cassius.[3] The civic and military programme of the New State discountenanced that creed. It was no longer professed, merely practised. Aversion from politics did not diminish. A number of ancient families regain a place on the *Fasti* through loyal adherence to Caesar Augustus. Others held aloof, like the last of the patrician Manlii.[4] Nor were the better sort in the towns of Italy easily reconciled to the tedium and the cost of a senatorial existence.

The circle of a poet can offer manifold instruction. Young Propertius is in amicable converse with men of his own age, not courting the favour of consular notables.

· · ·

VII. Next, the question of status and origins. It requires delicacy of assessment, with firm distrust in the face of the normal language of social disparagement. Persons against whom obscure birth is alleged often turn out to belong to the class of 'domi nobiles', the men of substance and repute in the towns of Italy.

Virgil, it is true, came from a region that was still a 'provincia'. But Mantua was an ancient city, and the poet's family should not be put low on the scale: it could afford him the best education. Horace, however, was the son of a freedman, a profiteer perhaps in war as in peace. Venusia enjoyed no good fame—the sole Latin colony to defect when Italy rose against Rome in 91 B.C.[5]

---

[1] Seneca, *Epp.* 83. 25 (drink was the cause, 'nec minor vino Cleopatrae amor').

[2] For the persistence of 'Antonian habits' see J. Griffin, *JRS* LXVII (1977), 17 ff.

[3] Cf. *Sallust* (1964), 242 f.; 271 f.

[4] Horace, *Epp.* I. 5; *Odes* IV. 7. By a strange aberration, *PIR*[1], M 122 expressed strong doubts about the extraction of Torquatus. It is proved by the poet's language. See also Münzer, *RE* XIV, 1193; 1181 f. (the stemma). Between 164 and 65 B.C. the Manlii had shown no consul. The eclipse of the Valerii Messallae (161 to 61) is comparable, cf. above, p. 135.

[5] Appian, *BC* I. 39. 188.

By contrast, the three elegiac poets.[1] All equestrian. Tibullus was a knight from old Latium.[2] This placid friend of peace and of rural pursuits may have served as *tribunus militum* under Messalla.[3] The Propertii were an old aristocratic family of Asisium, as an inscription attests.[4] A near relative of the poet perished in the War of Perusia (I. 21. 7) and the family estates suffered diminution in the confiscations (IV. 1. 129 f.).

Ovid's rank as an *eques* was not the product of luck or warfare, so he affirms more than once.[5] The family was already eminent when the Paeligni fought for liberty and honour in the Bellum Italicum.[6] Whatever their vicissitudes in the sequel, the Ovidii emerged without damage from the civil wars, loyal no doubt to Caesar's heir when 'tota Italia' took the oath of allegiance in 32 B.C. An inscription at Sulmo honours L. Ovidius Ventrio as the first citizen to be accorded a public funeral;[7] and Ovid's father possessed the means to launch two sons on the senatorial career.[8]

In this instance the policy of Caesar Augustus was frustrated. And Sextus Propertius did not give any sign of response to calls of civic duty. His friend Volcacius Tullus soon gave up. There was another Propertius, however, who became a senator, C. Propertius Postumus, enrolled in the tribe 'Fabia':[9] Asisium has 'Sergia'. He is generally held identical with Postumus who married an Aelia Galla (III. 12. 1).[10]

---

[1] The importance of their social rank is properly brought out by M. Hubbard, *Propertius* (1974), 96 ff.

[2] See the scrappy *Vita* attached to the manuscripts. Tibullus had an estate 'in regione Pedana' (Horace, *Epp.* I. 4. 2). Pedum was an ancient town, and obsolete, its territory having been assigned to Gabii: or, more probably, to Praeneste.

[3] Cf. I. 7. 9 ff. The *Vita* states that he earned military decorations.

[4] *CIL* XI. 5389 (in the Umbrian dialect). Of sixteen Propertii in *CIL* XI, all but two are at Asisium. One of those two, at Ameria (4443), is patently bogus.

[5] *Am.* III. 15. 5 ff.; *Tr.* II. 110 ff.; IV. 10. 7 f.; *Ex P.* IV. 8. 17 f.; 'equites ab origine prima / usque per innumeros inveniemur avos.' For the type of 'sanguine factus eques' (*Am.* III. 8. 10), where the Oxford text (1961) prefers 'pastus', and 'militiae turbine factus eques' (15. 6), observe the tribune with whom Ovid had converse at the games (*Fasti* IV. 381 ff.).

[6] *Am.* III. 15. 9: 'quam sua libertas ad honesta coegerat arma'.

[7] *CIL* IX. 3082. He had held military posts.

[8] *Tr.* IV. 10. 27 ff. His brother, born on March 20, 44 B.C., died at the age of twenty. Before resigning the *latus clavus* Ovid had served in the vigintivirate, in two posts (ibid. 34; *Fasti* IV. 384), as could happen at that time, cf. *ILS* 914 (C. Propertius Postumus).

[9] His ancestors might have acquired the citizenship before the Bellum Italicum. An eminent knight, C. Tettius Africanus (*PIR*[1], T 100) has the 'Oufentina' (*CIL* XI. 5382).

[10] Above, p. 102.

Nor, since the name is so rare, should Propertius Celer be omitted, in danger of forfeiting his status through 'paternae angustiae'.[1]

The elegiac poets also made a poor contribution to the governmental programme of encouraging marriage and procreation among the better sort. No offspring of Albius Tibullus is discoverable, no wife. Of Propertius a descendant is on record in the time of Trajan, a certain Passennus Paullus of equestrian rank.[2] Yet not perhaps a descendant deriving from an actual marriage of the poet: testamentary adoption may account for the transmission of the name. As for Ovid, divorce terminated the first two marriages, the second producing a daughter who was twice wedded.[3]

· · ·

VIII. Ruler and government are not on high show in these poets. They feel no affection for the new name 'Augustus', which conveyed veneration as well as power. It is absent from Tibullus and from the *Amores*; and in the more varied repertoire of Propertius it occurs in four poems only.[4] The ruler himself is mentioned, in the *Amores*: twice as 'Caesar', once subsumed under 'Caesares'.[5] Indeed, the pages of Tibullus ignore him totally.[6]

The first book of Propertius betrays no hint that the Civil Wars have ended, that Rome and Italy have been rescued from the menace of Antonius and the foreign woman. The book concludes with a piece that evoked the tragic fate of Perusia,

> Italiae duris funera temporibus. (I. 22. 4)

The next poem, however, shows that Propertius has been approached by Maecenas. But not to great advantage either way, it should seem. After retailing several epic themes Propertius affirms that, if only heroic verse were within his reach, he would be eager to celebrate 'bellaque resque' of 'Caesar tuus'. He then enumerates several

---

[1] *Ann.* I. 75. 3. Tiberius helped him with a subsidy. Perhaps a close relative of the poet.

[2] Pliny, *Epp.* VI. 15. 1; *ILS* 2925 (Asisium).

[3] *Tr.* IV. 10. 69 ff. The daughter had a child from each husband (ibid. 75 f.). In the autumn of 8 she was absent, in Africa (*Tr.* I. 3. 19). One of Ovid's wives came from Falerii (*Am.* III. 13. 1).

[4] Namely in II. 10; III. 11 and 12; IV. 6.   [5] *Am.* I. 2. 51; II. 14. 18; III. 12. 15.

[6] A mention might have been expected in I. 7 (Messalla's exploits in the East). On this poem see now R. J. Ball, *Latomus* XXXIV (1975), 729 ff.

episodes. The selection and the language would not be to the liking of the ruler. The great victory of the Caesarian cause is designated 'civilia busta Philippos' (II. 1. 27).[1] Perusia was better forgotten.[2] Perusia had been named in the previous poem, and it now comes in again by melancholy allusion,

eversosque focos antiquae gentis Etruscae.   (1. 29)

Actium and the triumph would have been the culmination. But Propertius, who announces in the first line his vocation as the poet of love, must decline. At a subsequent stage, Actium comes in for cursory and unheroic mention in two successive poems. First, the erotic life is warmly and vividly commended. If men chose to adopt it, there would be no weapons or ships of war, no Roman dead:

nec nostra Actiacum verteret ossa mare.   (II. 15. 44)

Next, enslavement to luxury and riches is castigated, in women in the first instance; and the descent to folly is illustrated by Antonius as the conspicuous example of dishonour (16. 37 ff.).

After an interval (how long, it is not clear) Maecenas receives one more poem (III. 9). It conveys a neat and artful 'recusatio'. The poet has learned 'vitae praecepta' from Maecenas, who abstained from public honours (9. 21). Therefore, only with aid and guidance from Maecenas would he be able to embark on the lofty themes.

Those themes, Greek and Roman, are duly specified. They lead naturally to the victory of Caesar's heir (9. 55 f.). Almost at once, Propertius supplies a piece which, starting from servitude to women, is devoted in the main to Cleopatra (III. 11). Then finally the long poem describing the Battle of Actium (IV. 6). In various ways peculiar, it does not look like a serious effort—and some critics apply heavy censure.[3] The poem is dated to 16 B.C. by the reference to the Sugambri (6. 77).

The laurels of Actium, ambiguous or distasteful to many in the educated class, had faded long since. Young Ovid came too late to

---

[1] Cf. Lucan VII. 862: 'Romani bustum populi'. Worth a citation in commentaries.

[2] There is no 'Perusina cohors' among the Etruscan allies of Aeneas in Virgil.

[3] Frivolous and incompetent in the opinion of G. Williams, *Tradition and Originality in Roman Poetry* (1968), 51 ff.; 130 ff.; 653 ff. That the poem is subversive, and hostile to the patriotic myth, is argued by W. R. Johnston, *Cal. Studies in class. Ant.* VI (1974), 151 ff. See also K. Galinsky, *Wiener Studien* LXXXII (1969), 86 f.; J. P. Sullivan, o.c. 145 ff.

bother, one way or the other. His elegiac poems eschew the name of the 'Actiaca victoria' although at a late stage he could not omit a reference.[1]

The signal success that accrued during the first fifteen years of stability under the new dispensation was the conquest of north-western Spain, completing the work of two centuries: terminated, according to the official version, in two campaigns and celebrated by the second closing of Janus, though not by a triumph (superfluous, and indeed an anticlimax after 29 B.C.). The Spanish War was advertised as the personal exploit of Caesar Augustus, who in fact had taken the field against the Cantabri in 26 B.C.[2]

Horace has the Cantabri no fewer than six times. But never Astures or Callaeci. On the contrary, he brings in a peculiar item: the Concani, an obscure tribe in Cantabria. Horace introduces the Concani between the Britanni and the Geloni (the latter a traditional people of Scythia), and he asserts that they drank the blood of horses.[3] A novelty for the Roman reader, if not an enigma; and scholiasts need not be censured for opining that the Concani were either Scythian or Spanish. Nowhere else in prose or verse do the Concani appear, save in a scholarly poet, who knew his Horace—and who assigned them the Massagetae for ancestors, naturally enough.[4]

Propertius and Ovid are devoid of allusions to the conquest of Spain. Not even a sporadic occurrence of 'Cantaber' (a word with some outline and resonance). By paradox, the Sugambri made a conspicuous entrance.[5] The earliest emergences of certain ethnic names in Latin poetry are sometimes instructive—in diverse fashions. And Ovid contributes.[6]

---

[1] *Met.* XV. 826 ff. Otherwise only 'Actiacus Apollo' in XIII. 715. Tacitus in his exordium was able to avoid the name until 'iuniores post Actiacam victoriam' (I. 3. 7).

[2] Above, p. 51.

[3] *Odes* III. 4. 34. Nisbet and Hubbard wish to date this poem 'about 28/7' (o.c. xxxi).

[4] Silius Italicus III. 360. Ptolemy registers Concana, a town in Cantabria (II. 6. 50). Otherwise, nothing. The source of Horace's information is a question. Persons he knew had served in Spain. Thus a certain Lollius, *Epp.* I. 18. 55: 'militiam puer et Cantabrica bella tulisti.' That is, as military tribune. Presumably the same as Lollius Maximus (*Epp.* I. 2. 1), cf. *PIR²*, L 317. Nothing suggests identification with a son of M. Lollius (*cos.* 21 B.C.). On which question, cf. *JRS* LVI (1966), 59 (discussing a non-existent consul).

[5] Above, p. 3.

[6] Above, p. 165. The Concani are a close parallel to the Coralli named by Ovid—and by Valerius Flaccus.

Topics of this kind will attract the curious and the erudite. They concern literary problems rather than issues in history. The same holds for most of what the poets have to say about the Orient. Like Horace, Propertius proclaims revenge against the Parthians, warfare in the eastern lands, and the near prospect of conquests; and nations will be evoked that dwell on the horizon of the world or survive only in obsolete ethnography.[1] Propertius, however, setting for once a limit to his fancy, contemplates the creation of a Roman province at the expense of the nearer Parthian dominions.

> Tigris et Euphrates sub tua iura fluent;
> sera, sed Ausoniis veniet provincia virgis.   (III. 4. 4 f.)

The poem leads off with fancies about India. And an earlier piece proceeds from Parthia to India (II. 10. 13 ff.). One end of the world at once evokes the other, so there is a hint of Britain, not named (10. 17). Similarly, in the second poem to Maecenas a triumph is envisaged, from both shores of Ocean: 'currus utroque ab litore ovantis' (III. 9. 53).

A tedious topic. As has been shown, Spain not Britain was the goal when Caesar Augustus went away to the western provinces in 27 B.C.[2] His journey from Asia to Syria seven years later might arouse martial expectations; and in fact a Roman army entered Armenia, conducted by the young Claudius Nero.

Poets had been advertising a Parthian war for several years, not without encouragement from the government, so it would appear. Public opinion, that is something more easy to invoke than assess. In this instance, the ruler had his own policy. Negotiation induced the Parthians to surrender the Roman standards. Peace this time, not war. That was the second imperial success in the course of those fifteen years. Up till now, Propertius had been lavish and exuberant. He loses interest. In the sequel he mentions the return of the standards, only once, however: in one of the latest poems of all, in 16 B.C. That poem still looks forward to Parthian triumphs—perhaps to be

---

[1] The Scythian Geloni are mentioned by Virgil and by Horace, three times each. Not in Propertius—or even in Ovid. It is strange that they should be absent from Strabo. The erudite but incautious Kiessling opined that the Geloni lived close to the Roman frontier in the time of Augustus (*RE* VII, 1017 f.). Sallust in his famous description of the Pontus may have helped the Geloni to survive.

[2] Above, p. 51.

reserved for the sons of Caesar Augustus. The prediction was fulfilled, at least in the manner it deserved, by the expedition of C. Caesar; and Ovid portrayed the triumph to ensue.[1]

Why did Propertius insist on the Parthian theme? One reason is clear: he took delight in names, the remote and exotic no less than the recondite products of mythological erudition. Spain afforded no scope or exhilaration, but the matter of Parthia opened up the whole Orient, extending to Bactra, to India and the Seres, to the world's end.

A pair of poems offers instruction and a contrast. Propertius blames Postumus for going to the wars and abandoning his wife Aelia Galla. Local detail is added. Postumus will use his helmet to drink from the water of the Araxes, there is peril lest arrows kill him or the mailed horseman,

> ferreus aurato neu cataphractus equo. (III. 12. 12)[2]

The poem has relevance to 20 B.C. Nothing Armenian had been mentioned hitherto by Propertius, except tigers (I. 9. 19).[3] No other Latin poet exhibits the word 'cataphractus'.

The rebuke which Propertius administered to Postumus inspired him to a notable essay in fiction. A lady called Arethusa sends a letter to Lycotas, lamenting his obdurate absence on far campaigns,

> te modo viderunt iteratos Bactra per ortus,
>   te modo munito Sericus hostis equo,
> hibernique Getae, pictoque Britannia curru,
>   ustus et Eoa decolor Indus aqua. (IV. 3. 7 ff.)

The opulent variety of names and lands has been a source of trouble to earnest commentators.[4] It is pure ornamentation. Of the two details that stand out in the earlier poem (the objurgation of Postumus), the

---

[1] Above, p. 9.

[2] The first occurrence of 'cataphractus' in Latin is Sisenna, IV. 81. Armenian cataphracts had been seen at the Battle of Tigranocerta in 69 B.C. They are named and described by Sallust, *Hist.* IV. 64–6. See J. W. Eadie, *JRS* LVII (1967), 164. The commentary of Butler and Barber (1933) neglects the word.

[3] The Araxes had been introduced into Roman poetry by Virgil, *Aen.* VIII. 728.

[4] Especially 'Britannia' and 'Sericus', which have provoked emendation. And also speculation: 'Lycotas had perhaps served in the N W. of Gallia Belgica, and may even have visited Britain', according to the normally sober Butler and Barber in their commentary (1933). They also suggest that the references to 'campaigns in the East' would have more point before the settlement with the Parthians in 20 B.C. (o.c. 26).

river Araxes recurs (3. 35), but the cataphract recedes from reality and becomes a 'Sericus hostis' riding on an armour-clad horse (3. 8).[1]

However that may be, warfare in far lands of legend and romance has a deeper meaning for Propertius. From the outset he proclaims that no son of his shall be a soldier or contribute to any Parthian triumph (II. 7. 13 f.); and a poem that heralds designs of Caesar Augustus against Indians and Parthians is followed by 'pacis Amor deus est' (III. 5. 1).

In short, Propertius speaks for the primacy of love and poetry. Warfare and glory are to be deprecated and dismissed. That lesson is spelled out in the address to a real person, his friend Postumus. Further, Caesar had his eyes on the wealth of India, and the Romans are invited to go forth to war: 'magna, viri, merces' (III. 4. 3). The fate of Paetus, who perished on a voyage to Egypt, is used for a sermon to denounce travel and the search for profit (III. 7).[2]

Conforming to a current fashion, and ostensibly responsive to imperial themes, this poet turns out to be insidious and subversive.

.   .   .

IX. In sharp contrast to Virgil and Horace, the writers of elegiac verse eschew national and patriotic attitudes; they are averse from extolling governmental achievements in war and peace; and they are not moved by official ceremonies or pageants. Not for them the *Ludi Saeculares*, or Janus closed more than once.[3] And, although Propertius towards the end worked up some interest in legend and antiquities, the four poems which he produced on that matter are not closely relevant to Augustan programmes or aspirations.[4]

The comportment of the elegiac poets is fairly uniform. Various explanations are canvassed. One is the theory of 'two generations' in

[1] The two items are enough to prove the derivation; and the two poems may be close in time. For the belief that 'Lycotas' is a pseudonym, i.e. for Postumus, see Butler and Barber, ad loc. *PIR*[2], L 460, reports the notion that he is a Lupercus, i.e. Q. Gallius Lupercus (G 45). Nothing precludes total fiction.

[2] It need not be assumed that Paetus was in fact on a commercial mission. For (?Aelius) Paetus, Aelia Galla, and (?Propertius) Postumus, see further above, p. 102.

[3] It is strange that Ovid's *Fasti* should omit the third closing (or any closing) of Janus; above, p. 24.

[4] Propertius IV. 2 (Vertumnus); 4 (Tarpeia); 9 (Cacus); 10 (the *spolia opima* and the stories of Romulus, Cornelius Cossus, and Claudius Marcellus).

Latin literature.[1] The first, represented by Virgil and Horace, was seasoned through warfare and hardships, it learned civic responsibility, and it wished to encourage the propagation of high ideals. By contrast, the young *epigoni*, coming to manhood in the years of peace: empty and frivolous and lovers of pleasure.

As concerns the ages of the writers in question, the theory fits Ovid, but Tibullus may have been born as early as 55 B.C., Propertius about 52.[2] Nor, for that matter, will everyone be prepared to concede moral amelioration and good citizenship as products of civil strife and social change.

Instead, it is expedient to bear in mind literary genres. The three poets inherit and continue the Neoterics; they are allergic to Caesar Augustus (and to the poets he protected).[3] In one sense retarded, they recall the Republic by their tastes. One compares Tiberius Caesar (the close coeval of Ovid), with his predilection for Hellenistic poetry.[4]

Finally, a plain crude fact. Roman Elegy is personal and private, it is love poetry by predominance. Ovid, the great 'praeceptor amoris', carries on from Gallus, Tibullus, and the 'blandi praecepta Properti' (*Tr.* II. 465). Why obtrude official policy, current affairs, or contemporary allusions?[5] That would be a divagation, and most inartistic.

·   ·   ·

X. In the writers of elegy a 'concealed opposition to Augustus' has been detected.[6] And some might be tempted to adduce the 'Republicanism' of Messalla Corvinus as helping to explain Tibullus. But the attitudes of the illustrious patron can be denied a political purpose.[7] Nor is any kind of opposition to Caesar Augustus to be expected from Messalla's sons or from Paullus Fabius Maximus.

---

[1] E. Martini, *Einleitung zu Ovid* (Prague, 1933), 1 ff.

[2] Jerome has not transmitted dates for those two: perhaps just as well.

[3] B. Otis, *TAPA* LXXVI (1945), 177 ff. See now J. P. Sullivan, o.c. 12 ff.; 116 ff.

[4] Above, p. 107.

[5] If the Parthian allusions in Propertius appear an exception, they serve an ornamental and negative purpose.

[6] B. Otis, o.c. 190: 'a concentrated opposition to Augustus'. Later defined as a non-political anti-Augustanism (*Ovid as an Epic Poet* (1966), 339).

[7] Above, p. 133.

One should speak rather of indifference towards the government, its aspirations—and the chief promoters of its policy. Something more than that, however, might be discovered in Ovid: malicious frivolity or even muted defiance. Though reluctant to have Augustus obtrude in the *Amores*, he admits him—as a 'cognatus' of Cupid by the descent of the Julian line from Venus (I. 2. 51). The trick is used again, at a much later date (*Ex P.* III. 3. 62). The ruler would not be amused.

Nor is it clear that the prince of peace would derive pleasure from being so often styled 'dux' (no fewer than eleven times), even when it conveyed a compliment like 'pacificumque ducem' (*Fasti* IV. 408) or 'sacrati provida cura ducis' (II. 60). One of the instances betrays irreverence. When urging husbands to keep sharp watch on their wives the preceptor composes a triple injunction,

hoc leges duxque pudorque iubent.   (*AA* III. 614)[1]

There is a lack of tact that looks wilful. Three instances can be brought up. First, lavish praise for the exploits of Julius Caesar, proconsul and dictator, at the climax of the *Metamorphoses* (XV. 745 ff.). To be sure, the poet had an unexceptionable reason—the supreme achievement of Caesar the Dictator is the parentage of Augustus, 'quod pater exstitit huius' (XV. 751), and his deification was a necessity,

ne foret hic igitur mortali semine cretus
ille deus faciendus erat.   (760 f.)

After alluding to the assassination through a speech from the ancestral goddess and a catalogue of the dire omens, Ovid in the sequel duly expatiates on the achievements of the ruler in war and peace (819 ff.), eschewing the word 'Augustus', with one exception (860). The poem concludes with the poet's panegyric upon himself,

iamque opus exegi quod nec Iovis ira nec ignis
nec poterit ferrum nec edax abolere vetustas.   (871 f.)[2]

There is something else, noteworthy, but not perhaps in itself of great value, allusions to Julius Caesar in the *Fasti*—supplemented (that could not be avoided) by compliments to the son and avenger.

[1] Observe, however, the emendation 'iusque' presented by G. P. Goold, *Harvard Studies* LXIX (1965), 93.

[2] For hostility to Augustus detected in the *Met.*, C. Segal, *AJP* XC (1969), 257 ff.

Namely Caesar's work on the Roman calendar (III. 155 ff.), and the assassination, with Vesta expressing horror at the fate of the Pontifex Maximus (III. 699 ff.). But Ovid also records the games celebrated in honour of Caesar's African victory (April 9), with, as though to justify, the anecdote about his then meeting one of Caesar's officers (IV. 377 ff.).

Any mention of Julius Caesar comes as a surprise in this age. In sharp contrast stand the 'Augustan' writers, Virgil, Horace, and Livy. For them, a delicate topic, since 'Divi filius' after the return of 'normal government' soon abated the advertisement of that parentage. Their different techniques will be found instructive.[1]

Second, another person better forgotten. Ovid mentions by name Cornelius Gallus, no fewer than seven times.[2] Already in the *Amores* he allowed himself to doubt whether Gallus had been disloyal or guilty of treason,

> si falsum est temerati crimen amici.   (III. 9. 63)

Augustus, it will be recalled, had formally renounced the 'amicitia' of Cornelius Gallus, which left him vulnerable to prosecution. Many years later, in his apologia to Augustus, Ovid makes a bold statement, and implies clearly that the offence of Gallus had not been very serious,

> non fuit opprobrio celebrasse Lycorida Gallo,
> sed linguam nimio non tenuisse mero.   (*Tr.* II. 445 f.)

Third, the *Ars Amatoria*. In the autumn of 2 B.C. the daughter of the Princeps came to grief through political intrigue, with flagrant immorality alleged by the angry parent. In the course of the next year the 'praeceptor amoris' gave his masterpiece to the world. Not for the first time but for the second, so it can be argued.[3] The second edition made the provocation more open and deliberate. Nor was it palliated by the insertion of a panegyric on Gaius Caesar, going out to martial exploits in the Orient.[4]

The first two books of the *Ars* expounded the techniques to be adopted by the roving male: how to find his prey, how to capture

---

[1] *Rom. Rev.* (1939), 317 ff.; *Tacitus* (1958), 432 f. The discreet silence of Horace in the *Odes* is not impaired by 'Iulium sidus' (I. 12. 47) or 'Caesaris ultor' (2. 44).

[2] *Am.* I. 15. 29; III. 9. 64; *AA* III. 334; *Rem.* 765; *Tr.* II. 445; IV. 10. 53; V. 1. 17.

[3] Ch. I.   [4] *AA* I. 177–228.

and keep her. The friend of the fair sex now adds a third book. Advancing from precepts for 'puellae' to tuition, the master furnished practical guidance in culmination. That was requisite, since 'non omnes una figura decet.'[1] In short, a specimen of that 'Romana simplicitas' which was not disdained by persons of rank.[2]

Next, with no delay, *Remedia Amoris*. Only by its title a recantation, the book is a wilful anticlimax, and may be regarded as the epilogue to Ovid's erotic verse. Reaching the age of forty-two (early in 1 B.C.), he had been very active, completing and revising the whole corpus, to rebut any reproach of wasted years.[3]

Remedia carries a retort to those who now condemn the 'Musa proterva'. The poet takes a high line and establishes his claim to lasting renown.[4] Ovid may well have been assailed by the malevolent or opportunistic in a season when the defence of morality was heavily advertised. In the aftermath of the great scandal, the delinquents being punished, a number of women were in fact prosecuted for adultery.[5]

Ovid, to be sure, professed at the outset that the *Ars* was innocuous. Nothing to do with virgins or matrons, only 'Venerem tutam concessaque furta'.[6] The cover was not adequate. The didactic treatise merely confirmed *Amores*. Ovid's writings portrayed the normal habits of high society in everything that was distasteful to Caesar Augustus.

.   .   .

XI. Taking the consulship in 2 B.C. and inducting Lucius Caesar into public life, the Princeps proposed to set his mark on the year. On February 5 the Senate conferred the title 'pater patriae'. August had stood as the ruler's memorable month. On its first day was dedicated the Forum Augusti, along with the temple of Mars Ultor; and martial pageantry ensued, notably the naval battle between Athenians and Persians.[7] Mars Ultor, vowed forty years before on the field of

---

[1] *AA* III. 772. The poet is 'more frank than we could wish in matters of sex', according to H. Fränkel, *Ovid* (1945), 3.

[2] Martial uses the term when quoting from 'lascivi versus' composed by Octavian against Antonius (XI. 20. 10).

[3] *Am.* I. 15. 1 ff. (above, p. 20).   [4] *Rem.* 361 ff. (above, p. 14).

[5] Dio LV. 10. 16 f.   [6] *AA* I. 33.

[7] *AA* I. 271–6 (above, p. 8).

Philippi, had gradually been diverted into a proclamation of vengeance in prospect for the Parthians.[1] It could now advertise civic harmony as well as pride of empire.

Now sixty years old and a 'senex' by the standard definition, Caesar Augustus might feel or even express a longing for release, but he knew that he could not step aside from his 'statio' or give up the power.[2] None the less, the season had arrived to put his accounts in order and prepare for his demise. To this year precisely (the conjecture is painless) belongs the all but ultimate version of the *Res Gestae*. The document rises to its climax and proper termination with 'pater patriae'.[3]

Fortuna whose caprice governs the nations now intervened. The Princeps was impelled to denounce his daughter, and she was banished to an island. The fullest account of her evil conduct is furnished by Seneca. It is ornate and dramatic: packs of lovers, and wanton frolics in the Forum and on the Rostra.[4] Cassius Dio goes back to the same source, and a brief notice in Pliny confirms.[5] Suetonius, however, eschews detail about the episode. His chapter takes in two other delinquent members of the family, he goes on to describe how Augustus treated the exiled Julia, how he refused more than once to let her come back.[6]

The accounts of Seneca and Dio convey a sudden discovery of transgressions and a savage reaction. Both put emphasis on the parent's anger.[7] According to Seneca, Augustus felt shame and remorse in the sequel and lamented the absence of good counsellors.

In the sources so far registered, interest is engrossed by the Princeps, his daughter, her immoral conduct. Against Julia numerous adulteries were alleged. Only one of those four writers discloses a name: Dio mentions Iullus Antonius.[8]

---

[1] As comes out clearly in *Fasti* V. 569 ff.

[2] Seneca quotes Augustus' words from a despatch to the Senate (*De brevitate vitae* 4. 3).

[3] *Res Gestae* 35. [4] Seneca, *De ben.* VI. 32. 1.

[5] Dio LV. 10. 12, cf. Pliny, *NH* XXI. 9: 'filia divi Augusti cuius luxuria noctibus coronatum Marsuam litterae illius dei gemunt'. He may even have asserted that his life was in danger, ibid. VII. 149: 'adulterium filiae et consilia parricidae palam facta'.

[6] Suetonius, *Divus Aug.* 65.

[7] Seneca, *De ben.* VI. 32. 2: 'parum potens irae'; Dio LV. 10. 12; 14 (with two expressions denoting anger).

[8] Dio LV. 10. 15.

Clarity emerges, though obscure and equivocal, with Velleius Paterculus: 'horrenda in ipsius domo tempestas erupit.'[1] For Velleius the event is a scandal in the household and the guilty men, despite the enormity of their offence, merely paid the penalty that any act of adultery comported: 'quasi cuiuslibet uxore violata, cum Caesaris filiam et Neronis uxorem violassent'.[2]

More to the point, Velleius names five aristocrats, and states that there were other guilty men, both senators and knights. In the forefront stands Iullus Antonius, basely ungrateful to Caesar ('violator eius domus'), and the husband of his niece.[3] Next, another consular, austere to outward view but a monster of depravity: T. Quinctius Crispinus Sulpicianus (cos. 9 B.C.). There follow an Appius Claudius, a Scipio, a Sempronius Gracchus.[4] According to Velleius, Antonius took his own life. The others, so it is here implied, suffered only the penalty of relegation.[5]

It is premature and impercipient to acquiesce in the notion of scandal in the family. Were it only that, no need for publicity and a missive read out by Caesar's quaestor to the Roman Senate. The names so usefully supplied by Velleius confirm the suspicion that high politics are in cause, and deep designs.[6]

In any age offences against morality aggravate—and cover up— the graver charges. In fact, Cassius Dio states that Iullus perished for treasonable ambitions.[7] And a passage from another treatise of Seneca can be adduced. He speaks of an aged ruler, vainly aspiring to

---

[1] Velleius II. 100. 2.　　　　[2] Velleius II. 100. 5.　　　　[3] Velleius II. 100. 4.

[4] The Appius Claudius is probably a son or nephew of the consul of 38 B.C. (PIR², C 985, cf. 982). As for Scipio, he may well be a son of P. Cornelius Scipio, cos. 16 B.C. (PIR², C 1438): for another presumed son see now AE 1967, 458 (Messene): P. Cornelius Scipio, quaestor of Achaia in A.D. 1/2. For Sempronius Gracchus, below, p. 196.

[5] Along with Antonius other men of rank were put to death (Dio LV. 10. 15).

[6] E. Groag, Wiener Studien XLI (1919), 74 ff.; H. Dessau, Gesch. der r. Kaiserzeit I (1924), 466 f.; R. Syme, Rom. Rev. (1939), 425 ff.; P. Sattler, in Studien aus dem Gebiet der alten Geschichte (Wiesbaden, 1962), 1 ff., reprinted in Augustus (Wege der Forschung CXXVIII, 1969), 486 ff.; E. Meise, Untersuchungen zur Geschichte der julisch-claudischen Dynastie (1969), 17 ff.; R. Syme, 'The Crisis of 2 B.C.', Bayerische S-B, 1974, Heft 7. The book of Meise has a doxology of close on fifty names (o.c. 4).

[7] Dio LIV. 10. 15: Ἀντώνιος ὡς καὶ ἐπὶ τῇ μοναρχίᾳ τοῦτο πράξας ἀπέθανε μετ' ἄλλων τινῶν ἐπιφανῶν ἀνδρῶν.

After the first three words what follows is from Xiphilinus. The passage contradicts Velleius' allegation about the nature of the punishment meted out (II. 100. 5). Observe also Ann. III. 24. 2: 'adulterosque earum morte aut fuga punivit.'

ease and tranquillity: a band of young *nobiles* terrifies him, pledged through adultery like a kind of oath—and 'iterum timenda cum Antonio mulier'.[1]

Conspiracy or treason may elude definition no less than proof. However, in this instance the situation is perhaps more easily intelligible than the evidence. A glance at the Roman government will discover guidance.

The autocrat was approaching the sixty-third year: the 'grand climacteric', which threatened hazard, calamity, or decease, so it was believed.[2] For the succession, two boy princes: one aged eighteen, the other fifteen. It was plain duty for Julia and for others to make provision against an emergency. Hence the need for something like a council of regency.[3] In due course the operation might entail divorce for Julia, and a fourth husband. The role of the Triumvir's son takes shape—and the five *nobiles* are a faction, not a society coterie that enjoyed the favours of a princess.

They would have to take into account other members of the dynastic group, such as Domitius Ahenobarbus, at the time in charge of Illyricum; and Fabius Maximus may still have been in Tarraconensis.[4] A younger man, L. Aemilius Paullus, should not be allowed to recede from view. He was close kin to Julia, since his mother Cornelia was like her a daughter of Scribonia.[5] Further, in 5 or 4 B.C. Paullus married the elder daughter of Agrippa and Julia;[6] and he was perhaps already intended, or even designated, to share the *fasces* with C. Caesar, his wife's brother, in A.D. 1.[7]

Apprised of intrigue in his entourage, the autocrat had every incentive to vindicate injured morality. Prosecutions were set on foot

---

[1] *De brevitate vitae* 4. 6.

[2] By Augustus himself: observe the letter he wrote to Gaius and Lucius on his sixty-third birthday (Gellius XV. 7. 3).

[3] The thesis developed in *Bayerische S-B*, 1974, Heft 7, 25 ff. It is certain that Julia would not have stopped short of murdering her father—according to Carcopino, *Passion et politique chez les Césars* (1958), 141.   [4] Above, p. 141.

[5] *PIR*², C 1475: the Cornelia of Propertius IV. 11, sister of P. Cornelius Scipio (*cos.* 16 B.C.). The latter may (or may not) have been still alive in 2 B.C.

[6] As deduced from two facts: Julia was born in 19 or 18 B.C., and her daughter Aemilia Lepida gave birth to a son in A.D. 14, viz. M. Junius Silanus (*cos.* 46).

[7] Paullus was probably the younger of the two brothers, cf. *Bayerische S-B*, 1974, Heft 7, 29; and his marriage to a princess (it may be assumed) secured abnormally rapid access to the consulship.

against a number of women.[1] The world of fashion received a sharp
admonition. In the verdict of Velleius, Julia knew no limits to
'luxuria' and 'libido'. More indulgent testimony shows her a wit and
an intellectual.[2] She may have found the verses of Iullus Antonius no
less congenial than his person. Further, Sempronius Gracchus, to
whom Tacitus applied the label 'sollers ingenio et prave facundus',
may be none other than the tragic poet in Ovid's catalogue.[3]

Men of the time would not be deceived, but an official version
may prevail with posterity. The tradition kept its concentration on
Julia, Iullus being neglected and all but forgotten.[4] Moreover, men's
judgement is impaired by benevolence towards governments or
preoccupation with sexual morality. A good historian may thus fall
victim to inadvertence.[5]

.   .   .

XII. The isolated references in Tacitus have been kept apart and
postponed. When examined in order, without prepossessions deriving from the rest of the testimony, they will be found instructive on
several counts.

First, Julia. Tacitus relates her demise at the end of 14. He states
that her arrogance was the real motive behind Tiberius' departure to
Rhodes.[6] Immoral conduct is not brought up in this context, but it is
documented in the subjoined and cognate notice about the killing of
Sempronius Gracchus, already lover of Julia while she was the wife
of Agrippa—and proving a 'pervicax adulter'.[7]

Next, in allusion to Julia (and to her daughter), the author puts on
show the domestic ill fortune that befell Caesar Augustus: 'domi
improspera fuit ob impudicitiam filiae ac neptis.' Indeed, the ruler
punished adultery as though it were an offence against the state and
against religion. In so doing he went against Roman tradition and

---

[1] Dio LV. 10. 15 f.   [2] For specimens of her wit, Macrobius II. 5. 5 ff.

[3] Ex P. IV. 16. 31: 'cum Varius Gracchusque darent fera dicta tyrannis'; Tacitus, Ann. I.
53. 3. For Gracchus see especially Groag, RE II A, 1371 ff. Some doubt identity, supposing
Ovid anxiously discreet.

[4] Iullus does not figure in Suetonius' list of conspirators (Divus Aug. 19. 1).

[5] Thus in CAH X (1934), 156: 'the domestic catastrophe which befell Augustus'. The
frequent use of 'domus' in this context by two Latin writers is evident: Julia may have
occupied her husband's house, 'in Carinis' (Suetonius, Tib. 15. 1).

[6] Ann. I. 53. 1: 'nec alia tam intima Tiberio causa'.   [7] Ann. I. 53. 3.

exceeded the terms of his own legislation.[1] Tacitus, so it appears, confines his argument to the punishment of adultery, mere adultery, as he gently styles it.

Finally, in the summing up on Tiberius, there is a reference to the failure of his marriage. A rapid, compressed, and enigmatic phrase conveys at the same time both Julia's misbehaviour and the departure of Tiberius: 'impudicitiam uxoris tolerans aut declinans'.[2] Again the word is 'impudicitia', with no hint anywhere of Iullus or of political involvements.

Second, Iullus Antonius, likewise with three references. At the funeral of Caesar Augustus the 'prudentes' curtly evoke the victims of the peaceful years: 'interfectos Romae Varrones Egnatios Iullos'.[3]

Next, in epilogue on Cn. Piso it is stated that on the *Fasti* the name had not been erased of Iullus Antonius 'qui domum Augusti violasset'.[4] Both the language and the conception recall Velleius, a phenomenon hardly to be expected.[5]

Third, when the decease of L. Antonius is related, the passage carries an allusion to the parent; 'patre eius Iullo Antonio ob adulterium Iuliae morte punito'.[6] As before, only adultery.

What Tacitus has to say about Iullus and Julia leads towards a paradox. The separate items show the historian preoccupied with adultery, not with dynastic politics. He fails to bring out anywhere the significance of the son of M. Antonius.

A reason for the inadvertence of Tacitus is not far to seek. Signs can be detected early in the *Annales* indicating that he set about his task without having devoted enough study to the previous reign.[7] Before long, certain particulars excited his attention and made him cast his eyes backwards, as is shown by the close linkage in Book III: the prosecution of an Aemilia Lepida, once betrothed to L. Caesar

---

[1] *Ann.* III. 24. 2: 'adulterosque earum morte aut fuga punivit. nam culpam inter viros ac feminas vulgatam gravi nomine laesarum religionum ac violatae maiestatis appellando clementiam maiorum suasque ipse leges egrediebatur.'

[2] *Ann.* VI. 51. 2.   [3] *Ann.* I. 10. 5.   [4] *Ann.* III. 18. 1.

[5] The verb is not elsewhere applied by him to adultery. Velleius has it twice in the one passage, also 'violator' (II. 100. 4 f.). Tacitus also uses another highly emotional word: 'eandem Iuliam in matrimonio M. Agrippae temeraverat' (I. 53. 3).

[6] *Ann.* IV. 44. 3.

[7] Cf. *Tacitus* (1958), 370 ff.. For a full statement see 'How Tacitus wrote *Ann.* I–III' (*Historiographia Antiqua*, Louvain, 1977), 231 ff.

(III. 22 f.); the return to Rome of D. Junius Silanus (24); the *Lex Papia Poppaea* (25). Cornelius Tacitus is now prompted to make a firm declaration: if life be vouchsafed he will turn back and narrate that history.[1]

Perhaps the suspicion was now nascent in the mind of the historian that he had not chosen well his point of inception: indeed, for continuity, the year 4 would have been better, with the last decade of Caesar Augustus as an appeal to his subversive talent.[2] The foreign wars dominated the tradition, obscuring sundry domestic transactions: above all, renewed discord in the dynasty and the estrangement of the government from educated opinion.

[1] *Ann.* III. 24. 2.   [2] As argued in *Tacitus* (1958), 369 ff., cf. 374.

XI

LEGISLATION AND MORALS

I. LIKE the verses, the whole attitude of Ovid was congenial to many members of the upper order. For some the splendour of national and patriotic transactions, made manifest in Virgil and Horace after their different fashions, had faded long before the last book of the Odes appeared. While others had always kept their fancy for Hellenistic poetry old or recent. By the year 13 B.C. Ovid shone forth as the bright star of modernity. This man, not ancient poetry, there stood the enemy evident and annoying to Horace. Ovid mocked the laudation of old days, the enthusiasm advertised for robust peasant soldiers and unkempt women coming out of the Sabine country.

Of authentic opposition to the new order, no sign or prospect. The government grew in strength all the time, through legal prerogatives, the aura of authority, the efflux of time. While the brave and the bold had perished, the *nobiles* now renascent through support and subsidy from Caesar were arrogant and pretentious—and also subservient. Malcontents might exist, late survivors of lost causes or discouraged from seeking high honours, but they lacked resources of power with provinces and armies; and the 'domus regnatrix' annexed their *clientelae* at Rome and throughout Italy.

When danger menaced the government it arose, not from any rival aristocrats, but from intrigue and dissension within the dynastic group. That was demonstrated by the crisis of 2 B.C. It is also confirmed, in a negative fashion, by a conspiracy that never was: the plot of Cn. Cornelius Cinna, a grandson of Pompeius Magnus on the maternal side.[1]

Criticism, however, could not always be evaded or stifled. Something more than murmurs might be heard in the high assembly when

---

[1] For this literary figment see *Rom. Rev.* (1939), 414.

moral or social reforms were promulgated; and malicious talk about
the ruler, his family, and his friends (some of them vulnerable in
various ways) was rampant as ever in clubs and salons. The comportment of Messalla Corvinus has been noted and discounted. There
were more genuine forms of protest. Some of the 'principes viri'
made a point of staying away from the funeral of Marcus Agrippa,
an enemy of the aristocracy.[1]

Above all, the legislation of 18 B.C. provoked resistance.[2] Designed
to encourage and protect matrimony, the *Lex Iulia de maritandis
ordinibus* laid down penalties for the celibate and the childless. More
drastic the *Lex de adulteriis*. Marital misconduct was now elevated
into a crime. The guilty parties were open to prosecution, the
penalty being relegation and loss of much property. State regulation
and any inquisition into private morality was held objectionable by
an aristocrat such as Tiberius Caesar.[3] As the historian Tacitus, perhaps taking his cue from that Princeps, was careful to declare, the
new dogma about adultery contravened Roman tradition: it was an
affront to the 'clementia maiorum'.[4]

.   .   .

II. The elegiac poets in the time of Augustus are alien to the 'res
publica', indifferent to marriage, the family, procreation. They
declare the primacy of love and the individual. A question therefore
arises—or rather has been conjured up. How does their behaviour
stand in relation to the *Leges Iuliae*?

It turns largely on the civil and social condition of the ladies whose
charms or caprice they celebrate.[5] The mistress of the great predecessor, Cornelius Gallus, is a convenient point of departure. His
Lycoris was Cytheris, the freedwoman of a Volumnius, so the
scholiast Servius affirms.[6] The seductive graces of the actress Volumnia Cytheris are on abundant show: she was openly paraded for a

---

[1] Dio LIV. 29. 6.
[2] On the Augustan legislation see especially H. M. Last, *CAH* X (1934), 441 ff.; P. A.
Brunt, *Italian Manpower 225 B.C.–A.D. 14* (1971), 558 ff.
[3] *Ann.* III. 69. 2 f. (rebutting in firm language the proposal of an obsequious consular).
[4] *Ann.* III. 24. 2.
[5] G. Williams, *Tradition and Originality in Roman Poetry* (1968), 525 ff.
[6] Servius on *Ecl.* X. 1.

time by Marcus Antonius, and the milieu of P. Volumnius Eutrapelus, bringing together high society, lax living, and literary pastimes, does not baffle enquiry or parallel.[1]

Cytheris as Lycoris, the notion is highly plausible. Yet gentle dubitation intrudes. The scholiasts in late Antiquity are capable of any fantasy or folly. And, even if some of the items they transmit go back a long way, that is no help. Inventions or deductions about the lives of classical poets had an early origin. Rigorous scepticism is in place.[2]

A late compilation, the *Epitome de viris illustribus*, carries useful facts not elsewhere on clear record, such as the quaestorship of Marcus Brutus; and Brutus, the treatise states, was along with Antonius and Gallus a fancier of Cytheris.[3] All in all, the temptation is strong to concede the identity of Lycoris.

Still, there is a disturbing parallel. According to a scholiast, the Licymnia whose charms captivate Maecenas in an ode of Horace is none other than his wife Terentia (the half-sister of Varro Murena).[4] Modern scholarship concurs. Only recently has doubt emerged, and a strong denial: this Licymnia is not a wife (albeit a sportive and decorative wife) but 'a crafty puella'.[5] If that is correct, eminent interpreters of the language and the manner of the poet have gone sadly astray.

As concerns the other ladies celebrated in Roman elegy, scholars have set up a dichotomy and relied upon antithesis: the ladies are either imaginary (like the light loves old or recent of Horace) or libertine by status: cultivated and expensive *hetaerae* in the line of Volumnia Cytheris.

A learned writer in the middle of the second century brings up two positive statements: the Delia of Tibullus was called Plania (which corresponds by etymology as well as metrically), whereas Propertius' Cynthia was a Hostia.[6] There might be something in these

---

[1] For the lady, W. Kroll, *RE* XII, 218 f.; H. Gundel, IXA, 883; for the milieu, *JRS* LI (1961), 23 ff. = *RP* (1978), 518 ff. (on Vedius Pollio).

[2] Observe the warning words of Kroll, o.c. 218. Still valid, for credulities persist.

[3] *De vir. ill.* 82. 2. Brutus as quaestor declined to go to Gaul but joined Ap. Claudius Pulcher. His quaestorship belongs presumably in 54 B.C.

[4] Pseudo-Acro on *Odes* II. 12. 9; *Sat.* I. 2. 64.

[5] G. Davis, *Philol.* CXIX (1975), 70 ff.   [6] Apuleius, *Apol.* 10.

notions, for all the distrust normally aroused by traditions of the schools or biographies of poets. Hostia at least may not be out of reach. One poem (which may, or may not, be addressed to Cynthia) alludes to her 'doctus avus'.[1] An epic poet, a certain Hostius, happens to be on record, perhaps about a century earlier.[2]

Furthermore, there is the woman styled Nemesis who in the second book of Tibullus takes over the role of Delia, less amiably. The poet is able to equip her with a deceased sister, who fell out of a window.[3]

Finally, Corinna. Although Ovid's presentation is equivocal, the source of his inspiration is defined at the end as

nomine non vero dicta Corinna mihi.

That statement comes in the long, careful, and patently honest piece of autobiography that concludes Book IV of the *Tristia*.[4] On the other hand, in his apologia to Caesar Ovid strenuously denied any adulterous pursuits.

So far on short statement the facts, if they are all facts. There is no point in registering and assessing the various opinions which scholars derive from interpreting the poems. However, a recent study attempts to transcend the traditional antithesis. The ladies, it is suggested, not only existed: some of them may in fact be Roman matrons. Hence the crime of adultery, or at least the praise and condonation of adultery—and peril emanating from the *Lex Iulia*.[5]

A short disquisition may suffice. Not enough field work (it appears) has been done along the borderlands of society in a post-war world. Useful specimens of flora and fauna flourish in that country. Warfare brings a crop of widows; and divorce ensues in the sequel, enjoined for reasons of high politics. After Sulla's victory M. Pupius Piso gave up Annia, Cinna's widow, whom he had recently married; the young Pompeius surrendered his wife Antistia to acquire Aemilia, the stepdaughter of Sulla; and the fifth wife of the Dictator was an aristocratic young Valeria, recently separated from her husband.[6]

By sad misfortune the aftermath of Actium happens to exhibit no such paradigms in the senatorial order. Analogy or rational surmise

[1] Propertius III. 20. 8.   [2] W. Kroll, *RE* VIII, 2516.   [3] Tibullus II. 6. 39.
[4] *Tristia* IV. 10. 60.
[5] G. Williams, o.c. 540.
[6] Velleius II. 41. 2; Plutarch, *Pompeius* 4; *Sulla* 35.

may assume without discomfort a number of women reduced to a marginal existence through calamity or the love of pleasure: women of ruined houses who had lost husbands by death or divorce, girls from distressed families in the *municipia* that had chosen the wrong side in the recent disturbances, perhaps more than once. They might be on show at games, at the theatre, and in the various haunts of the fashionable world as specified in Ovid's manual, potent rivals of the superior *hetaerae*. They possessed education, and graceful talents to ensnare young poets or senior government officials.[1]

If Tibullus' Delia was a Plania, she may have belonged to a Campanian family of some note in foreign commerce.[2] As for Hostia, the name occurs in several inscriptions at Capua of the late Republican period;[3] and, for what it is worth, to illustrate Hostia may be mentioned the conjecture that Capito, registered by the elder Seneca, is perhaps the *rhetor* Q. Hostius Capito known from an inscription.[4]

. . .

III. No call therefore to invoke matrons and tampering with matrimony. And a large question subsists. Horace in forced or frivolous hyperbole pronounced the enactments of Caesar Augustus valid and inviolate among far and foreign nations to the ends of the world,

> non qui profundum Danuvium bibunt
> edicta rumpent Iulia, non Getae,
>   non Seres infidive Persae,
>   non Tanain prope flumen orti. (IV. 15. 21 ff.)

In narrower scope and vision, it must be asked how far the moral and social legislation modified the behaviour of men and women. Grave authority concludes that 'it is impossible to say that it failed'.[5] Quite so. What can be known?

Like the praises of frugality, moral attitudes were equivocal and suspect in this prosperous season; and the commerce of the sexes

---

[1] For those topics see now J. Griffin, *JRS* LXVI (1976), 87 ff.
[2] F. Münzer, *RE* XX, 2186.   [3] *ILS* 3609; 5641; 6303.
[4] *PIR²*, C 407, adducing *CIL* XIV. 4201 (Nemus Dianae). The nasty fellow Hostius Quadra whose habits Seneca describes was a *libertus* (*NQ* I. 16).
[5] H. M. Last, *CAH* X (1934), 456.

defies regulation in any age. The conduct of the Princeps himself might be impugned. Some of his allies and associates were far from edifying in their way of life; and malice was not slow to point out that neither of the consuls who introduced the law of the year 9 (a Papius and a Poppaeus) had wife or child.[1] Strong doubts will be conceived about an amelioration in the habits of the upper order at Rome.[2] Casual facts help.

Thus marriage might become popular and frequent, though not at all in the sense that the Princeps intended, as was demonstrated by Vistilia, who ran through six husbands. If extenuation be deemed appropriate, she also produced a string of children.[3] The other Vistilia, her niece, is also paradigmatic. She tried to register as a prostitute.[4] Perhaps as a reflection on her aunt. Better, a way of avoiding prosecution for adultery.[5]

More serious the evidence to be gleaned from Tacitus. Speaking in his own person, the historian denies the success of the *Lex Papia Poppaea*.[6] Further, sumptuary laws offer a useful parallel, for their results (if any) are visible and easily assessed. Tiberius Caesar, when evading a proposal that he should take on the task of curbing conspicuous expenditure, declared in his despatch to the Senate that the measures of his predecessor had been a failure.[7] Encouraged by that document the historian came out with a notable digression, and a diagnosis. He set out from the axiom that luxury had flourished unabated for a whole century after the War of Actium.[8]

None the less, it has recently been affirmed that the Augustan code bore heavily on poetry, that it helps to explain 'the curious fact that love elegy more or less died with Ovid'.[9]

The term 'more or less', often a harmless enclitic, or mere evasion, ought not to be attached to asseverations deemed important. Brief reflection suggests factors of another order.

---

[1] Dio LVI. 10. 3.

[2] P. A. Brunt comes to a firm and negative conclusion (o.c. 566).

[3] Pliny, *NH* VII. 39 (on her irregular pregnancies). For the children (a notable collection) see C. Cichorius, *Römische Studien* (1922), 429 ff. and (with some different solutions), *JRS* LX (1970), 27 ff. = *RP* (1978), 805 ff.　　　　　[4] *Ann.* II. 85. 2.

[5] Suetonius, *Tib.* 35. 2; *Dig.* XLVIII. 5. 10. 2: 'mulier quae evitandae poenae adulterii gratia lenocinium fecerit'.

[6] *Ann.* III. 25. 1.　　　　　[7] *Ann.* III. 54 f.　　　　　[8] *Ann.* III. 55.

[9] G. Williams, o.c. 540.

Roman epic had attained its acme, which was not far below Homer: as the orator Domitius Afer said, 'secundus est Vergilius, propior tamen primo quam tertio.'[1] And the lyric perfection of Horace was not likely to find a rival. Likewise elegy. The canon of the three poets accepted by Quintilian was already forming (it is an easy assumption) when Ovid about A.D. 1 revised and rounded off his erotic corpus.[2]

Each of these poets acquired the rank of classic in his own lifetime. They had exhausted the best themes, it might appear. That would not deter other authors. There was a plethora, as Ovid testifies in the last of his letters from Pontus; and he alludes to young men coming on who have not yet published.[3] The excellence that Ovid achieved would not avail to kill the genre.

If in fact love poetry lost favour and abated its productivity, there is no call to impugn the *Leges Iuliae* of 18 B.C. A reason is not far to seek: the atmosphere of gloom and repression that clouded the last decade of the reign.

.   .   .

IV. Fortuna made a mock of Caesar Augustus before 2 B.C. ended, the year he designated for solemn and joyous pageantry, but, after various disappointments, secure prospects seemed to open when the dynastic succession was defined in June of A.D. 4. A panegyrist writing some twenty-five years later duly hailed the dawn of a happy epoch.[4] The facts confute, with disaster and distress supervening everywhere: 'iuncta deinde tot mala'.[5]

In A.D. 5 great earthquakes and a flooding of the Tiber were heralds and portents (with a conflagration at Rome in the next year). Famine for four years now ensued, and there was pestilence in the train of famine. Discontent pervaded the army, money was short, and novel taxation had to be imposed. Further, grave disturbances in many of the provinces, and even warfare, notably against nomadic or mountain peoples: the Gaetulians and the Isaurians.[6] Enough,

---

[1] Quintilian X. 1. 86.   [2] Quintilian X. 1. 93.   [3] *Ex P.* IV. 16. 39.

[4] Velleius II. 103. 5.

[5] Pliny, *NH* VII. 149. The main details come from Dio. For the difficulties of the government between 5 and 9 see now T. Wiedemann, *CQ* XXV (1975), 264 ff. (discussing *Tristia* II).

[6] Above, p. 66.

without the military disasters: all Illyricum insurgent in 6, with the catastrophe in Germany ensuing three years later.

Nor was the dynasty exempt from strain and discord. Augustus had insisted on adopting, along with Tiberius, the last son of Marcus Agrippa. The experiment went wrong. Agrippa Postumus assumed the 'toga virilis' in A.D. 5.[1] In that year, or in the next, he was consigned to seclusion at Surrentum.[2] Then, in 7, a decree of the Senate banished Postumus to the island of Planasia; and his property was confiscated for the benefit of the newly established military treasury.[3]

Velleius Paterculus, an alert and often cautious writer, might have been tempted to keep off the fate of Agrippa Postumus altogether. He chose to insert an apologia. It will be found instructive, for more purposes than one.[4]

A boy lacking grace or promise such as Claudius, the brother of Germanicus, might be held back and kept out of public life. Of Postumus it is alleged that he was brutish and recalcitrant.[5] Postumus could be discarded and sent away without inordinate scandal, the Princeps no doubt being ready to declare to the Senate his devotion to the public weal; and preoccupation with the foreign wars would divert attention for the moment.

·   ·   ·

V. In the next year a catastrophe shook palace and dynasty. Julia, the sister of Postumus and wife of L. Aemilius Paullus, was banished to an island. That happens which might be expected. Not the

---

[1] Dio LV. 22. 4. A year later than normal: he was born in 12 B.C.

[2] Suetonius, *Divus Aug.* 65. 1 (not in Dio). It is not easy to refuse the supplement in the *Fasti Ostienses* under A.D. 6: 'Agrippa Caesar [abdicatus est]': *Inscr. It.* XIII. 1, p. 183.

[3] Dio LV. 32. 2 (under A.D. 7); Suetonius, *Divus Aug.* 65. 4. The *senatus consultum* is noted by Suetonius and by Tacitus, *Ann.* I. 6. 1.

[4] Velleius II. 112. 7: 'hoc fere tempore Agrippa, qui eodem die quo Tiberius adoptatus ab avo suo naturali erat et iam ante biennium, qualis esset, apparere coeperat, mira pravitate animi atque ingenii in praecipitia conversus patris atque eiusdem avi sui animum alienavit sibi, moxque crescentibus in dies vitiis dignum furore suo habuit exitum.' Velleius enters the notice under the year 7, and the verb 'alienavit' clearly pertains to that year. The phrase beginning 'moxque' therefore alludes to the subsequent fate of Postumus (that is, in 14). For a different interpretation, see now A. J. Woodman, *CQ* XXV (1975), 305. That scholar's truncated quotation omits 'moxque'. He argues that the 'exitus' of Postumus referred to in that phrase means his banishment in 7, not his ultimate fate. For the normal interpretation, and for the two stages in the removal of Postumus, see now B. Levick, *Tiberius the Politician* (1976), 57 f.

[5] Tacitus, *Ann.* I. 3. 4: 'robore corporis stolide ferocem'.

consequence of loose habits or an evil heredity but something liable to be falsified by the government.

The evidence is fragmentary and defective. It will be expedient to set forth the matter in a certain order. Clarity may thus emerge, but imperfect, obscurity clouding the greater part.

First, Tacitus. After recording the prosecution of an Aemilia Lepida, who, he notes, had once been betrothed to Lucius Caesar, the historian came upon another transaction concerning the great houses.[1] M. Junius Silanus (*suff.* 15) asked that his brother be permitted to return to Rome. Tiberius Caesar concurred. His response before the Senate was dignified and tinged with gentle irony. He too, he said, was gratified that D. Silanus had come back from a 'peregrinatio longinqua'. Nothing impeded, neither a law nor a decree of the Senate; but Tiberius Caesar could not pass over an affront to his predecessor.

Silanus had been guilty of adultery with the younger Julia. The historian adds annotation about the 'impudicitia' of mother and daughter and the punishment meted out to their accomplices: 'morte aut fuga punivit'.[2] It is therefore with some surprise that the reader learns what had happened to D. Junius Silanus. The ruler breaking off 'amicitia', Silanus saw that he had to leave.[3]

Cornelius Tacitus was growing curious about the previous reign. With good reason. And he did not miss the death of Julia after twenty years of exile on an island: condemned and punished for adultery, so he states.[4]

Second, Cassius Dio. In the narration of A.D. 8 a large piece (four folia) has fallen out of the manuscript, taking with it, among other things, the great victory over the Pannonians at the river Bathinus (probably on August 3).[5] The scandal of Julia could not have been hushed up and totally forgotten. The historians whom Cassius Dio followed were writing within forty years of the event. If nothing else, the oral tradition was still alive.[6]

---

[1] *Ann.* III. 24. [2] Ibid. 24. 2.

[3] Ibid. 24. 3: 'exilium sibi demonstrari intellexit.'

[4] *Ann.* IV. 74. 4, cf. Pliny, *NH* VII. 149: 'aliud in nepte adulterium'.

[5] Assumed to be indicated by the *Fasti Antiates*: 'Ti. Aug ⟨in⟩ Inlyrico vic.'

[6] Dio's sources produced anecdotal material. Thus concerning C. Vibius Rufus (*suff.* 16), cf. above, p. 84.

Third, Suetonius. The biographer furnishes no indication of date. He did not need to specify any crime, since he describes mother and daughter as 'omnibus probris contaminatas'.[1] But Suetonius illustrates the resentment of the ruler. Augustus pulled down Julia's sumptuous villa; he refused to let an infant she bore go on living; and her ashes would be denied entrance to the Mausoleum.[2]

Julia's transgression was adultery. Whatever value may be assigned to 'impudicitia', adultery is a precise term—and Cornelius Tacitus was an accurate author. Therefore L. Aemilius Paullus (*cos.* A.D. 1) was still among the living in the year 8. Which at once demolishes several theories.[3]

So far, silence about Paullus in the context of Julia's misdemeanours. A passage from another biography now comes in. Young Claudius had to forfeit his bride, 'Aemiliam Lepidam, Augusti proneptem': her parents had given offence to Augustus.[4] Claudius is there described as 'admodum adulescens', and in fact his seventeenth birthday fell on August 1, A.D. 8. This small item is of some value, for it discountenances theories that have Paullus predecease Julia's exile.[5]

.   .   .

VI. The husband of Julia is all but lost to knowledge. Paullus was still a boy when on exhibit in the poem of Propertius, written in 16 B.C.[6] Otherwise only two writers mention him by name, Suetonius and a Juvenalian scholiast. Velleius, it should seem, could have used him; but Velleius was deterred by the eminence of Marcus, the brother (*cos.* 6), who enjoyed the esteem of Tiberius Caesar. However, it is strange that Paullus should be absent from the pages of Seneca.[7]

---

[1] Suetonius, *Divus Aug.* 65. 1.   [2] Ibid. 72. 3; 65. 4; 101. 3.

[3] Thus E. Hohl, *Klio* XXX (1937), 323 ff. (A.D. 1); F. Norwood, *CP* LVIII (1963), 150 ff. (A.D. 6). Paullus' death in 8 was assumed in *Rom. Rev.* (1939), 434; *Tacitus* (1958), 403 f. Paullus is absent from *CAH* X (1934), and from R. Seager (*Tiberius*, 1972).

[4] Suetonius, *Divus Claudius* 26. 1: not registered in *Rom. Rev.* (1939), 434.

[5] Paullus' death is put in 8, or perhaps at the end of 7, by E. Meise, *Untersuchungen zur Geschichte der julisch-claudischen Dynastie* (1969), 45; 233.

[6] Cornelia there exhorts the widower to act as a mother: 'fungere maternis vicibus pater' (IV. 11. 75): unseemly and 'not Roman' after the assumption of the *toga virilis*. For the age of Paullus, above, p. 140; *Bayerische S-B*, 1974, Heft 7, 30.

[7] A number of modern texts print 'Paullusque' (Rubenius) in *De brevitate vitae* 4. 6, where 'Iullusque' (R. Waltz) is patently the remedy.

Paullus is registered in Suetonius' list of those who conspired against Augustus; and in another place he has a neutral notice about the marriage of Julia.[1] The *scholium* on Juvenal, a peculiar product, purports to elucidate the gold ring which Berenice, the Jewish princess, gave to her brother, King Agrippa (VI. 158). As follows:

Iuliam neptem Augusti significat quae nupta Aemilio Paulo cum is maiestatis crimine perisset ab avo relegata est, post revocata, cum semet vitiis addixisset, perpetui exilii damnata est supplicio. huius frater Agrippa propter morum feritatem in Siciliam ab Augusto relegatus est.

This piece of erudition carries errors or patent absurdities. For the Princeps to allow Julia to return after he had consigned her to relegation, for reasons ostensibly adequate, would impair his credit and prestige, confute his policy. Nor does any other source betray a hint that the wife (or widow) of Paullus suffered two separate banishments. Not but that notion has been accorded wide acceptance.[2] It is time to discard it.[3] The scholiast, it appears, amalgamated Julia and her mother.[4]

The sources, it might be said, are so meagre as to deter argument. Yet something can be established. Julia was punished for adultery, Paullus for conspiracy. Separate charges, but perhaps a shared transgression. Disjunction may have served the contrivances of Caesar Augustus. In any event, Paullus could not have been indicted for adultery with Julia.[5]

Modern accounts of these transactions duly disclose preoccupation with Julia. Paullus tends to be disjoined. Indeed, the husband can even be left out altogether.[6]

Husband and wife are linked by a common fate. The date is clear, the year 8, but not the nature and extent of their guilt. When public

[1] Suetonius, *Divus Aug.* 19. 1; 'Plauti Rufi Lucique Pauli progeneri sui' (for Plautius Rufus, below, p. 212); 64. 1 (the marriage).

[2] Registered and accepted without comment in PIR², J 635. Further, after some initial doubts, accepted by B. Levick, *Latomus* XXXV (1976), 331. In the view of that scholar, 'by mid-7 L. Paullus was dead.' Cf. also *Tiberius the Politician* (1976), 59 (late in 6 or early in 7); 151 (in 7).   [3] Thus E. Meise, o.c. 40 ff.

[4] As suggested, when discussing scholiastic erudition, in *Ammianus and the Historia Augusta* (1968), 86. That explanation is dismissed because it would show 'incredible ineptitude' by B. Levick, *Latomus* XXXV (1976), 309. Modern writers can offer parallels in error, cf. below, p. 216.

[5] Thus, briefly, *Rom. Rev.* (1939), 434.

[6] Not in H. Dessau, *Gesch. der r. Kaiserzeit* I (1924) or in *CAH* X (1934).

emphasis is put on moral transgressions, a political motive will be suspected. Yet treason is a term of generous interpretation, and it is easier to suppress a conspiracy than to prove its existence. The plots against Augustus were detected and denounced before they had gone very far.[1]

Paullus and Julia had grievances, whatever their feelings about Agrippa Postumus, who had been put under rigorous custody in 7. Paullus, so far as known, had not been allowed to see an army, whereas his brother Marcus was holding a high command in 8, if not earlier.[2] Germanicus went into the field the year before, when quaestor, at the age of twenty.[3] Germanicus was the husband of Agrippina. For Aemilius Paullus, marriage to her elder sister lost promise and splendour three years previously when the ruler ordained the succession.

The slow progress of warfare in Illyricum aroused comment at Rome, with disparagement of the high command. It was not yet evident that Tiberius was the 'dux invictus'. Paullus had something to talk about; and the pair may have gone in for conspicuous luxury or unseemly levity, as protest and defence, in that sombre atmosphere. By the same token, war and the pestilence excited ambition again, through the hope and prospect of some deaths in the family.

In the event, it was Paullus who perished. Death, not banishment, such is the persuasion that has prevailed, all too natural and not requiring support from the scholiast on Juvenal—which happens to be the sole explicit testimony to his fate.

Yet doubt obtrudes, and more than a doubt. A stray piece of documentation has failed to be interpreted as it permits and deserves. Early in 14 (or perhaps late in 13) one of the *Fratres arvales* died, being replaced in May of 14: namely L. (Aemilius) Paullus.[4]

Hence pertinent surmise about identity. Perhaps a son of Paullus and Julia.[5] Given the age of Julia, he would be very young on entry

---

[1] Suetonius, *Divus Aug.* 19. 1.

[2] Velleius II. 114. 5. Marcus might also have been a praetorian legate under Tiberius in 4 and 5.

[3] Dio LV. 31. 1 (with the allegation that Tiberius was unduly prolonging the war).

[4] *ILS* 5026. Neither he nor Paullus Aemilius Regillus (*ILS* 949) was mentioned in the study concerning M. Lepidus (*JRS* XLV (1955), 22 ff. = *Ten Studies in Tacitus* (1970), 30 ff.).

[5] Thus *PIR²*, A 392.

into the confraternity. A member of the dynastic group can secure admission when assuming the *toga virilis*, it is true.[1] But this putative son could not reach the age for co-optation by the year 8. Nor is it likely that in the near sequel Augustus would confer the honour on a son of the disgraced pair: L. Antonius, an 'adulescentulus' at the time of his father's catastrophe, was sent into exile at Massilia.[2]

Against that objection an older youth has been conjured up: a son of Aemilius Paullus by a supposed earlier marriage.[3] That device, however, becomes implausible. Untenable rather, if it be held that Paullus himself was a youthful husband (aged about twenty-two) when he married the princess in 5 or 4 B.C.[4]

A solution therefore emerges without discomfort. The *arvalis* is none other than L. Aemilius Paullus, the consul of A.D. 1.[5] A casual statement in the elder Pliny helps: only death can deprive an *arvalis* of his status, even if he be an exile.[6] Paullus, it follows, was banished in 8, not executed.[7]

Paullus succumbed unnoticed on a penal island or in some secluded city during the last months when Caesar Augustus was verging towards the end. The demise of the ruler overshadowed the scene— and a scandal that could not, however, be suppressed, namely the execution of Agrippa Postumus, to stand as the 'primum facinus novi principatus'.[8]

.   .   .

VII. So far the catastrophe of the year 8. Cumulated discomforts issued in public discontent. The historian Cassius Dio furnishes some indications, not all of them clear and adequate. In A.D. 6 subversive pamphlets were going about, products of a certain Publius Rufus.

---

[1] Cf. above, p. 154 (the son of Paullus Fabius Maximus).

[2] *Ann.* IV. 44. 3.

[3] A marriage to the younger Marcella (*PIR*², C 1103), after the decease of her husband Barbatus Appianus (*cos.* 12 B.C.), was suggested by E. Bayer, *Historia* XVII (1968), 118 ff.; for the stemma, ibid. 123. There was certainly a 'Marcella Pauli' (*CIL* VI. 9000; X. 5981). It had previously been assumed that Marcella enjoyed brief matrimony with Paullus Aemilius Lepidus (*cos.* 34 B.C.) after he lost Cornelia in 16.

[4] Above, p. 140.

[5] As now argued firmly by J. Scheid, *Les Frères Arvales* (1975), 91 f.

[6] Pliny, *NH* XVIII. 6.

[7] See further 'The End of L. Paullus' in *The Augustan Aristocracy* (forthcoming). The chapter, among the earliest, was composed in 1972.

[8] *Ann.* I. 6. 1.

Not to much effect (Dio says), but others were circulated under his name, leading to official enquiry and denunciations.[1] The name of 'Publius Rufus' has excited due curiosity, with recourse to the emendation 'Plautius Rufus'.[2] That notion received wide acceptance because it could be linked, so it seemed, with an item in Suetonius' list of conspiracies against Augustus, which names a Plautius Rufus in conjunction with Aemilius Paullus.[3] However, even were it to be argued that Paullus was banished in A.D. 6, he was still alive, still the husband of Julia two years later: but that argument would be wrecked by a piece of testimony that cannot be discarded.[4]

For the year 8, account must be taken of missing transactions since there is a gap in Cassius Dio. Next, in the following year the knights raised protest. They objected to the penalties incurred by the celibate and the childless.[5] The Lex Papia Poppaea was passed, affording some relaxations. There may have been a resumption of moral and sumptuary legislation a few years earlier, excused and commended by the military crisis.

Finally, the year 12. Dio mentions writings that defamed certain individuals: the noxious pamphlets were consigned to public conflagration, some of the authors being punished.[6]

Names and details would be welcome. Some remedy comes from other sources, with startling revelations, showing how the government had grown estranged from educated opinion in the course of this decade.

There was a certain T. Labienus whose very name declared the vicissitudes of a family, allegiance to the Pompeian cause, and detestation of the present order. An orator of vigour and violence, combining the virtues of the old style and the new, Labienus won notoriety by an excess of 'libertas' that spared no rank or person.

---

[1] Dio LV. 27. 2.

[2] Cf. *PIR*[1], P 360. Yet he might have been a Publilius or a Publicius. The 'Publius Gallus' of *Ann.* XVI. 12. 1 (cf. *PIR*[2], G 66) seems so far to have escaped incrimination.

[3] Suetonius, *Divus Aug.* 19. 1: 'Plauti Rufi Lucique Pauli progeneri sui.' There was a C. Plautius Rufus a good generation earlier (*ILS* 926: Auximum). Also the *monetalis* C. Plotius Rufus (*PIR*[1], P 923) about 23 B.C.: not possibly identical with the preceding.

[4] The offence of Paullus and Julia deprived Claudius of his bride when he was 'admodum adulescens' (Suetonius, *Divus Claudius* 26. 1).

[5] Dio LVI. 1. 2, cf. Suetonius, *Divus Aug.* 34. 2.

[6] Dio LVI. 27. 1: pamphlets ἐφ' ὕβρει τινῶν.

He was also the author of a history, parts of which he ostentatiously left out when reciting.

Labienus succumbed to a prosecution, and all his writings were burned by decree of the Senate. No matter, said one of his enemies, Cassius Severus, who had them by heart.[1]

Thus the elder Seneca, who expatiates on the savage eloquence of Cassius Severus. The judicious Quintilian even put him on a level with the greatest orators of the age, namely Pollio and Messalla.[2] Seneca, quoting Cassius' derisive assessment of Paullus Fabius Maximus, records his prosecution by that illustrious person; and he has an analogous (but not enigmatic) reference to the fate of Cassius' own writings.[3]

Clarity comes from Tacitus. Early in the annalistic record of 15, when the praetor Pompeius Macer asked Tiberius Caesar whether prosecutions for *maiestas* were admissible, the historian carefully prefixes a brief digression on that important matter, being alert not only to *maiestas* but to notable names and incidents in the history of Roman eloquence.[4] It was Caesar Augustus (so Tacitus affirms) who first made words as well as actions liable to indictment: Cassius Severus furnished the occasion, through his 'famosi libelli' harrying men and women of high rank.[5] As emerges from a later passage concerning Cassius, he was condemned after trial by the Senate and banished to the island of Crete.[6]

The date of this memorable transaction needs to be looked into. It is generally put in 12 because Dio happens to refer to measures against personal libels in that year.[7] But the record (it will be recalled) is defective, a date about four years earlier is by no means excluded. The *Chronicle* of Jerome registers the decease of Cassius Severus under the year 32, after an exile of twenty-five years. Which would take

---

[1] Seneca, *Controv.* X, praef. 4–10. Apart from Seneca, Labienus is named only in Suetonius, *Cal.* 16. 1 and in three passages of Quintilian.

[2] Quintilian XII. 10. 11, cf. X. 1. 116 f. For the testimonia *PIR*[2], C 522; for his oratory, Brzoska in *RE* III, 1744 ff. Cf. above, p. 142.

[3] Seneca, *Controv.* II. 4. 11; X, praef. 7.

[4] Not among Dio's ten items for that year. Dio, or his source, was not so percipient.

[5] *Ann.* I. 72. 3: 'primus Augustus cognitionem de famosis libellis specie legis eius tractavit, commotus Cassii Severi libidine, qua viros feminasque inlustris procacibus scriptis diffama-verat.'   [6] *Ann.* IV. 21. 3.

[7] Thus *PIR*[2], C 522: 'anno p.C. 12 (cf. Dio 56. 27. 1)'. Also 'A.D. 12?' in *Rom. Rev.* (1939), 487.

one back to the vicinity of A.D. 8.[1] But Jerome's figures (it must be conceded) are notoriously untrustworthy.

In any event, the year 8 may assert no small significance for developments in the law of *maiestas*. A document often neglected falls neatly into place. It is an edict of Caesar Augustus, dated by suffect consuls to the second half of the year. The Princeps declares that the torture of slaves is expedient and necessary for establishing the truth about 'capitalia et atrociora maleficia'.[2] That is, not offences like the mere 'famosi libelli' published by Cassius Severus. The language smacks of high treason. One is impelled towards Paullus and Julia. Prosecution entails witnesses as well as informers.[3] In the torturing of slaves, law and practice were not always concordant.[4] The *Lex Iulia*, it is stated, exempted them in cases of adultery.[5]

Whether the banishment of Cassius Severus belongs to 8 or to 12, freedom of speech was now curbed and subverted under pretext of social harmony. Not only the licence of libel and invective that had exhilarated the closing epoch of the Free State. From protecting persons of high rank from defamation, prosecutions could now be extended to take in personal attacks on the ruler or criticism of the government; and praise of the Republican past was held to reflect ominously on the present dispensation.

Thus historians got into trouble. Of poetry being incriminated as pernicious to order and morality, there is no sign until a quarter of a century had elapsed after the *Leges Iuliae*. The blow fell abruptly, in the late autumn of 8. It was the result of accident, the bad luck of Ovid, and the rancour of the ruler.

[1] Strong arguments for the year 8 are now adduced by R. A. Baumann, *Impietas in Principem* (1974), 28 ff.

[2] *Dig.* XLVIII. 18. 8: 'cum capitalia et atrociora maleficia non aliter explorari et investigari possunt quam per servorum quaestiones, efficacissimas eas esse ad requirendam veritatem existimo et habendas censeo.'

[3] An entertaining parallel is the ferocious legislation against sexual offences decreed by Constantine in 326: the year in which he suppressed his wife Fausta and the young Caesar Crispus. See now F. Paschoud, *Cinq études sur Zosime* (1975), 35 ff.

[4] For a summary statement, A. Ehrhardt, *RE* VIA, 1789.

[5] *Dig.* XLVIII. 18. 4: 'servorum tormenta cessant quia et lex Iulia cessat de adulteriis.' However, in the affair of the elder Julia in 2 B.C. the slave of Demosthenes was put to torture (Macrobius I. 11. 17). Pertinent to what Tacitus says about Augustus in the context of adulterous princesses: 'suasque ipse leges egrediebatur' (*Ann.* III. 24. 2).

XII

THE ERROR OF CAESAR AUGUSTUS

I. THAT Caesar Augustus consigned the foremost of poets to exile on
the far edge of the Roman dominions was an action that ought not to
have escaped the attention of historians, biographers, and moralists.
Apart from Statius (*Silvae* I. 2. 254 f.), the first record comes in the
Chronicle of Jerome, compiled in the year 381. Next, the *Epitome* of
Pseudo-Victor, not long after 395. In comment on the licentious
character of Augustus, the author points out that men are prone
to punish in others the vices they indulge in themselves; and so
'Ovidius qui et Naso' was sent into exile because he had written 'tres
libellos amatoriae artis'.[1]

Occurring in an opuscule of this type and date, the item cannot
fail to arouse surprise—and a curiosity extending to the general
renascence of Latin scholarship and letters in that season. Forgotten
writers were now discovered, notably Juvenal.[2] In their train arrived
scholiasts, with their frequent blunders or inventions—and in due
course erudite fraud, as witness that glorious imposture, the *Historia
Augusta*.[3]

About half a century later Sidonius Apollinaris transmits a prime
piece of misbegotten ingenuity,

> et te carmina per libidinosa
> notum, Naso tener, Tomosque missum,
> quondam Caesareae nimis puellae
> ficto nomine subditum Corinnae.   (*Carm.* XXIII. 158 ff.)

In Sidonius Ovid's Corinna thus comes up as the daughter of Caesar
Augustus, both the mistress of the poet and a cause of his exile.

---

[1] Pseudo-Victor, *Epit.* 1. 24. For another noteworthy statement, above, p. 150.

[2] G. Highet, *Juvenal the Satirist* (1954), 185 ff.; A. D. E. Cameron, *Hermes* XCII (1964),
363 ff.

[3] Various signs show the author of the *HA* in close vicinity to scholiasts, cf. *Ammianus and
the Historia Augusta* (1968), 183 ff. For errors and inventions of scholiasts, ibid. 86.

Confusion between the two Julias, or an amalgamation, may also be surmised in a Juvenalian *scholium* which states that the granddaughter was exiled not once but twice.[1] The item is not merely suspect—it must be dismissed. Ignorance of history, or inadvertence, can lead to similar misconceptions in more recent times.[2]

.   .   .

II. Two charges were brought against Ovid—'duo crimina, carmen et error' (*Tr.* II. 207). The nature of Ovid's mistake has long engaged the attentions of the erudite, the ingenious, the frivolous. Hence a plethora of writing. A book recently published registers the names of some two hundred scholars.[3] The catalogue is useful, and also a warning. It serves to attest a misdirection of the labour force, and other regrettable phenomena. Nor is the exposition exempt.[4] The latest contributions are not always the best. The conspicuous lack is political sense, and common sense.

In these late days no prospect offers of devising a solution both novel and convincing. None the less, a short and sharp treatment may prove salutary (albeit largely negative), in defiance both of wild speculation and bibliographical excesses. Order and formulation are vital. One starts from statements in Ovid, and a brief selection will do.[5]

First, Ovid had not committed any action susceptible of indictment in a court of law. No 'scelus', only an 'error', a 'peccatum'. Ovid had been ingenuous: a silly fellow, guilty of 'simplicitas', of 'stultitia' even.[6]

---

[1] Schol. on Juv. VI. 158 (quoted above, p. 209); cf. R. Syme, o.c. 86.

[2] Thus G. Highet refers to Augustus' 'bad daughter Julia' and 'her accomplice Ovid' (o.c. 30). Observe also, as worthy of a scholiast, B. Otis: 'the Ars (I. 182) refers to the return of C. Julius Agrippa (the son of Julia and Agrippa) from the Orient in 1 B.C.' (*Ovid as an Epic Poet* (1966), 18). Further, Julia, daughter of the elder Julia and Aemilius Paullus, occurs in J. André's edition of the *Tristia* (Budé, 1948), x.

[3] J. C. Thibault, *The Mystery of Ovid's Exile* (1964).

[4] Despite the praises of a reviewer, who states that Thibault and other scholars 'have not been wasting their time', and concludes with 'an admirable book'. Thus E. J. Kenney in *CR* XV (1965), 296 f. Polite and not impressed is the judicious L. P. Wilkinson, *Gnomon* XXXVII (1965), 734 ff.

[5] For register and quotation of all passages, S. G. Owen in his edition of *Tristia* II (1924), 10 ff.

[6] *Tr.* I. 5. 42 ('simplicitas'); III. 6. 35 and *Ex P.* I. 7. 44 ('stultitia').

Second, he had not done anything at all. Not even incautious talk, or a betrayal of state secrets when in his cups,

> non aliquid dixive, elatave lingua loquendo est,
> lapsaque sunt nimio verba profana mero.   (*Tr.* III. 5. 47 f.)

The language recalls what Ovid had previously said about the offence of another poet,

> non fuit opprobrio celebrasse Lycorida Gallo,
> sed linguam nimio non tenuisse mero.   (II. 445 f.)

Third, Ovid had seen something,

> cur aliquid vidi? cur noxia lumina feci?
> cur imprudenti cognita culpa mihi?   (II. 103 f.)

And he goes on to compare himself to the hunter who had surprised a goddess,

> inscius Actaeon vidit sine veste Dianam.   (II. 105)

The latter sentence has excited foolish and depraved fancies. Perhaps Ovid had come upon some disrobed lady of the imperial family at the hour of bathing. Or again, he had intruded on some ceremonies in the cult of Isis that were restricted to women.[1]

More elaborate, and supported by a wealth of erudition (mainly superfluous), Ovid's involvement with a group of sinister Pythagoreans, who went in for sorcery, divination, and astrology.[2] Ovid was a devotee, but innocuous. He had undergone some kind of conversion after abandoning erotic verse: observe his sympathetic portrayal of the sage of Samos and his doctrines in Book XV of the *Metamorphoses*. Ovid's aristocratic friend Fabius Maximus was one of them, and so was the grammarian Julius Hyginus.[3] The imprudent poet happened to be present (it is suggested) at a conventicle held in his own house, he saw forbidden arts applied to elicit occult information about the health and survival of the ruler.

---

[1] A. Deville, *Essai sur l'exil d'Ovide* (1859); R. Ellis in his edition of the *Ibis* (1881), xxviii ff.

[2] J. Carcopino, *Rencontres de l'histoire et de la littérature romaines* (1963), 143 ff.

[3] Carcopino, o.c. 145 ff. He adduces the *De astronomia* (of 'Hyginus', a later author). It is dedicated to M. Fabius: for Carcopino, 'M(aximus) Fabius'. An earlier scholar had surmised 'Fabius Marcellinus', one of the bogus authors cited in the *Historia Augusta*. The authentic Julius Hyginus, custodian of the Palatine Library, was in fact a close friend of Ovid (Suetonius, *De gramm.* 20, cf. above, p. 92).

Better even, why not combine the themes of ritual and nudity? More bold and resourceful than the modern advocate of the Pythagoreans, another ingenious scholar has proffered an explanation, and that more than once.[1] As follows. Ovid saw Livia presiding unclothed at the mysteries of the Bona Dea in early December of the year 8. Not by accident or for an amorous intrigue (like P. Clodius Pulcher in 62 B.C.). The devoted researcher was doing field work, he was after authentic material for Book XII of the *Fasti*. The sacrilege was detected—and that is why Ovid never published the second half of the *Fasti*.

'Ingenio perii qui miser ipse meo' (*Tr*. II. 2). The formula need not be confined to poets. It is strange that fantasies of this order are accorded respectful attention.[2]

To proceed therefore on a straight path of sober discourse. Ovid had been present in some compromising situation. Cotta Maximus was alarmed when told about it (*Ex P*. II. 3. 61 ff.). The poet's offence provoked 'laesi gravis ira dei' (I. 4. 44), it touched Augustus personally: 'tua vulnera, Caesar' (*Tr*. II. 209). The enormity was attended with fear: 'aut timor aut error' (*Tr*. IV. 4. 39), cf. 'timidus' (*Ex P*. II. 2. 17). That is, Ovid neglected to protest at the time, or to reveal and denounce in the sequel.[3]

The nature of Ovid's transgression was generally known,

> causa meae cunctis nimium quoque nota ruinae
> indicio non est testificanda meo.   (*Tr*. IV. 10. 99 f.)

At the same time, not safe or easy to explain,

> nec breve nec tutum peccati quae sit origo
> scribere: tractari vulnera nostra timent.   (*Ex P*. I. 6. 21 f.)

Indeed, these shameful things are best covered up in darkness,

> illa tegi caeca condita nocte decet.   (*Tr*. III. 6. 32)

---

[1] L. Herrmann, *Revue belge* XVII (1938), 695 ff., and in three subsequent and verbose papers, down to *Ant. Cl.* XLIV (1975), 126 ff.

[2] In the opinion of Thibault, 'a serious contribution'. Further, 'his hypothesis . . . is more plausible than most' (o.c. 104). Similarly E. J. Kenney, stating that it 'satisfies the evidence better than most' (o.c. 296).

[3] No doubt others did; and slaves could be put to torture, observe the edict of Augustus issued in the second half of the year 8 (above, p. 214).

Therefore, when Ovid begged Messallinus to intercede on his behalf, he urged discretion and silence on that count,

> vulneris id genus est quod, cum sanabile non sit,
> non contrectari tutius esse puto.   (*Ex P.* II. 2. 57 f.)

Some scandal or other in the dynasty, it is clear. And in the light of the above statements, there is no reason whatsoever to suppose that the action of Augustus was an attempt to protect guilty persons in the imperial family by sending away the eye-witness to a region out of reach.[1]

III. And now to come closer to the known but not to be named transgression. Ovid had been in the vicinity of scandalous behaviour that touched ruler and dynasty: adultery, treason in plan or talk, or perhaps even some gay charade in mockery of Augustus and Livia.

Was it a matter of politics or of morals? The political aspect has been firmly discounted in some standard manuals.[2] A false dichotomy. The two things are not easily disseverd, immoral conduct being normally alleged to disguise a political offence—or to aggravate it.

Most theories adduce and exploit the scandal of Julia. That is natural, and painless.[3] Registering her decease on an island twenty years later, the careful Tacitus fixes the date as well as the charge.[4] Attempts to shift the date from the year 8 and put it either at 7 or at 9 will suitably be deprecated.[5]

There is something else. In the crisis of 2 B.C. preoccupation with the behaviour of Julia's mother tends to obscure the truth and devalue the role of Iullus Antonius.[6] This time L. Aemilius Paullus, the husband of Julia, gets left out or is disjoined. Paullus was guilty of conspiracy, so Suetonius states.[7] The date, nowhere indicated, has

---

[1] As Thibault concludes: 'it is reasonable to suppose,' etc. (o.c. 119).

[2] Schanz–Hosius, *Gesch. der r. Lit.* II¹ (1935), 209: 'also keinen politischen Charakter'.

[3] G. Boissier, *L'Opposition sous les Césars* (1875), 140 ff.; and recently L. P. Wilkinson, *Ovid Recalled* (1955), 299 ff. But, for Thibault, 'the burden of the historical evidence, therefore, weighs, on the whole, against this hypothesis' (o.c. 67).

[4] Tacitus, *Ann.* IV. 71. 4: 'convictam adulterii'.

[5] Thibault tries to discount A.D. 8 (o.c. 56 f.).   [6] Above, p. 193.

[7] Suetonius, *Divus Aug.* 19. 1, cf. the *scholium* on Juvenal VI. 158.

been in dispute. It was commonly believed that the fate of Paullus fell earlier than the banishment of Julia in the year 8; that he was no longer among the living.[1] That notion is false.[2] Therefore, the nexus holds. Theirs was a common catastrophe, albeit on different pretexts.

When Julia's mother came to grief, a single and scandalous episode aroused the wrath of the Princeps, hitherto inadvertent, so the evidence indicates. This time informers or false friends may have reported comparable excesses, which led easily to graver charges: treason or even sacrilege. For example, the staging of a mock funeral for the aged ruler, with suitable recitations in prose or verse, would have appealed to society wits.[3] When in the next reign a poet composed a premature valedictory on the son of Tiberius, he was promptly condemned to death by the Roman Senate.[4]

Paullus and Julia had no place or function subsequent to June of the year 4. Of no utility, and perhaps noxious, they became vulnerable and could be excised without disturbance for the benefit of Tiberius Caesar and the two princes, Germanicus and Drusus: 'firma adiumenta parentis'.[5]

Of the lovers of Julia only one is known, D. Junius Silanus. Caesar Augustus revoked 'amicitia', and Silanus departed from Rome and Italy.[6] Against Ovid, however, an edict was published and he was despatched to Tomis. The contrast is flagrant. Ovid should be the worse offender, if truth and justice were in cause.

They were not. The 'error' of Ovid was known but not to be talked about in public. The edict which the ruler issued, though 'immite minaxque' (*Tr.* II. 135), may have enveloped the offence in vague and ambiguous language—as happens with governmental pronouncements in other ages.

---

[1] Thus, e.g., Thibault, o.c. 81; and for L. P. Wilkinson Julia was 'actually a widow' (o.c. 298). Husband and wife were also disjoined by J. P. V. D. Balsdon, *Roman Women* (1962), 88. Neglect of the precise term 'adulterium' can have alarming consequences for scholars of either sex. Julia was 'convicted of adultery' in 8, as admitted by B. Levick, *Tiberius the Politician* (1976), 55—whereas her husband had perished late in 6 or early in 7 (ibid. 59), and she is a widow and available for marriage to D. Silanus in 8 (ibid. 60).

[2] Above, p. 208.

[3] For municipal derision of a senator through a mock funeral see Tacitus, *Hist.* IV. 45. 1.

[4] *Ann.* III. 49 (Clutorius Priscus). Tacitus signalized this shocking case with a sagacious oration from M. Lepidus.

[5] *Ex P.* IV. 13. 31.

[6] *Ann.* III. 24. 3 (above, p. 207).

If that is so, no actionable charge being specified, and no named crime, Ovid was baffled. The victim could not answer, argue, refute. Instead, only protest his innocence and his folly.

．　　　．　　　．

IV. The Princeps, however, added the *Ars Amatoria*. That, so the argument may now insinuate, was a mistake of the first magnitude. How and why did he fall in?

First, rational calculations. If the ruler was trying to cover up or explain away a crisis in dynastic politics through imputations of immorality, it was helpful to slide in as an accessory the notorious 'praeceptor amoris'. Similarly, and in consequence, if the charge against that person was fragile and flimsy, a guilt by association and not capable of being sustained in any court of law, the *Ars Amatoria* offered, adding patent corroboration of nocivity.

As Ovid states,

> nec mea decreto damnasti facta senatus,
>   nec mea selecto iudice iussa fuga est.   (II. 131 f.)

The language is precise. Compare Tiberius Caesar in explanation to the Senate: Silanus may come back to Rome 'quia non senatus consulto non lege pulsus foret'.[1]

Second, the anger and resentment of the septuagenarian despot. Augustus can never have liked a man who spurned the career of honours and continued to be proud of his secession. Ovid should have entered the Senate as quaestor in the salubrious season of the *Leges Iuliae*, perhaps to rise high as a loyal representative of old Italy. Instead, something noxious and odious: a declared and defiant 'praeceptor amoris'.[2] The parent of Julia did not forget the *Ars Amatoria*, published soon after the calamity of 2 B.C. He had given vent to anger against Julia, 'parum potens irae', though he came to repent of it.[3]

If Augustus, learning a lesson of restraint, had been content to allege a personal affront in a delicate and painful matter, keeping it studiously vague, he could have said 'hoc rei publicae causa facio';

---

[1] *Ann.* III. 24. 4.

[2] For justification of Augustus' action on grounds of public morality, see M. Hammond, *Harvard Studies* LXIX (1965), 139 ff.

[3] Seneca, *De ben.* VI. 32. 2 (above, p. 193).

and he might have persuaded the poet to go away quietly. But Caesar was vindictive, ordering relegation to the ends of the world.

'Carmen et error'. The question is sometimes asked, which was the cause, which the pretext. The antithesis might be scouted, the answer being 'both'. Still, there is something to be said for the view that the *Ars* was more potent, the root and cause of enduring resentment.[1] Furthermore, emphasis on that misdemeanour would serve to demonstrate that injured morality was in cause, not high politics.[2] To sum up: the 'carmen' and the 'error' are in a tight nexus. Neither charge was good enough without the other.

.   .   .

V. Impelled by anger to incriminate the *Ars Amatoria*, and needing that adjunct, the ruler gave Ovid a plea in defence and a weapon for attack. He responded with alacrity in spring or summer of the next year with Book II of the *Tristia*: a fine piece of work, lucid, coherent, and forceful, worthy of a great orator or a good historian. The structure repays analysis.[3]

As a general theme, Ovid insists that his own life was blameless, that erotic verse had never been impugned. Further, three lines, not of defence but of attack, are also developed in other poems.

First, Augustus has been unjust. He chooses to incriminate a 'vetus libellus', the product of the poet's youth and therefore comparable to the *Eclogues* of Virgil.[4] Though Ovid in this apologia, as elsewhere, exploits a poet's licence, and invents boldly, the plea cannot be ignored or dismissed. A first edition of the *AA*, in two books, had appeared long ago, perhaps about 8 B.C., so it may be conjectured.[5] What posterity knows is the second edition, published in 1 B.C. or A.D. 1.

Second, the action of the Princeps is treated as an exercise of power; and in fact no law laid down the place of residence when an offender was banished by 'relegatio'. Ovid makes emphatic use of the verb 'iubeo'.[6] At the outset he states that his destination was under

[1] Boissier, o.c. 144.   [2] As assumed in *Rom. Rev.* (1939), 468.
[3] Owen, o.c. 48 ff.
[4] *Tr.* II. 539 ff.; I. 9. 61; III. 1. 7 f.; V. 1. 7 f. See further above, p. 15.
[5] Ch. I.
[6] A powerful word: compare the jurist's retort to the 'Prisce, iubes' of a poet (Pliny, *Epp.* VI. 15. 2).

command.[1] Further, he confesses 'et iubet, et merui' (I. 2. 95). Then, in the next poem,

> discedere Caesar
> finibus extremae iusserat Ausoniae.   (3. 5 f.)

And again,

> te iubet e patria discedere Caesaris ira.   (3. 85)

Third, and most important, the frequency of the word 'ira'. The first of the poems from exile introduces 'principis ira' (*Tr.* I. 1. 33), and before long a single piece has 'numinis ira', 'Iovis ira', 'ira dei' (I. 5). In a later poem (III. 11) 'Caesaris ira' appears three times. Variants occur such as 'vindicis ira', 'ira deorum', 'iratum numen'.

Some frequencies are remarkable. Thus 'ira dei' and 'numinis ira' (five times each). Above all, 'principis ira' (seven) and 'Caesaris ira' (nineteen).

The iteration is deliberate and ominous. Whereas 'iracundia' denotes the manifestation of bad temper, or the propensity to it, 'ira' is choice and concentrated: anger excited by resentment at an affront or an injustice, and often infused with the spirit of revenge.[2] 'Ira' is appropriate to signal the wrath of deities unrelenting. Thus in the exordium of the *Aeneid*, with 'saevae memorem Iunonis ob iram' and 'tantaene animis caelestibus irae?' Or, for that matter, in another author,

> Hellespontiaci sequitur gravis ira Priapi.[3]

Ovid's iterations carry a double edge. First, if Caesar is a 'caelestis vir', nay, a divinity in person, he ought not to display anger, since he is omnipotent. Rather mildness and mercy. The word is 'clementia' (which occurs ten times in these poems), now becoming reputable: it was dubious and equivocal in the previous age, when 'clementia' connoted the power of a master who may forgive but need not. The much advertised 'Clementia Caesaris' was not liked by men of his own class. Ovid does not venture on 'inclementia', which occurred in

---

[1] *Tr.* I. 2. 62; 89; 102.

[2] The definition of Seneca is not very good (*De ira* I. 4. 1). Statistics in Tacitus are instructive. For 'ira', nearly three columns in the lexicon of Gerber–Greef; for 'iracundia', *Agr.* (1); *Hist.* (8); *Ann.* (2).

[3] Petronius, *Sat.* 139.

Virgil, 'divum inclementia, divum'—and is applied by Tacitus to the grim demeanour of Tiberius Caesar.[1]

Second, a 'princeps' should not give way to anger, neither should a Caesar. Ovid makes 'ira' adhere to both impressive names, repeatedly. Therefore, at the lowest, the comportment of this Caesar is shown discrepant with the dignity of his station.

One may usefully adduce Sallust's version of the oration of Julius Caesar, the praetor designate, deprecating anger and hasty decisions: if small men surrender to passion, who knows, who cares? It is otherwise with governments or with persons of rank and power and prestige, who 'magno imperio praediti in excelso aetatem agunt'.[2] The orator quietly concludes, 'minume irasci decet.'

The use of 'ira' and 'iracundia' in political contexts affords instruction and entertainment—and deserves a disquisition. The latter word conveys strong disparagement. Thus bad temper in Caesar's enemies: Ariovistus the German king and Calpurnius Bibulus, his erstwhile colleague in the consulship.[3] At the same time, Caesar allows an envoy, on mission from Pompeius Magnus, both to appeal to Caesar's 'dignitas' and deprecate 'iracundia'.[4] In his last months, however, the Dictator found it hard to keep his composure and curb his temper.

Claudius Caesar knew that he was prone to both 'ira' and 'iracundia'. He confessed it in an edict; and an imperial letter conveys a solemn admonition to the people of Alexandria, who run a risk of learning what a benevolent prince is like when moved to righteous anger.[5]

On Ovid's showing, Caesar Augustus is unjust: no true 'princeps', and no gentleman. Anger impaired the 'dignitas' of an aristocrat and degraded the eminent station of the Princeps. A treatise much admired by the Romans taught that a 'iustum imperium' blended 'gravitas' with 'comitas'.[6]

The error of Caesar Augustus played into Ovid's hands. It gave him something to write about and a reason for waging defensive warfare over long years, although he abated one theme towards the

---

[1] *Aen.* II. 602; *Ann.* IV. 42. 3.   [2] Sallust, *Cat.* 51. 12.
[3] Caesar, *BG* I. 31. 13; *BC* III. 16. 3.   [4] Caesar, *BC* I. 8. 3.
[5] Suetonius, *Divus Claudius* 38. 1; *P. Lond.* 1912, col. 4, 79 ff. Claudius is called 'irae properus' in *Ann.* XI. 26. 2.
[6] Cicero, *Ad Q. fr.* I. 1. 23, referring to the *Cyropaedia*.

end: the last book has only 'principis ira' (IV. 9. 52) and 'sacrae mitior ira domus' (6. 20). Ovid had been aggressive (it is claimed), showing up illegality and rancour in the ruler; and the excess of Ovid's laudations can be interpreted as crafty and insidious.[1]

. . .

VI. The poetry of Ovid has incurred censure on various grounds. Thus the *Ars Amatoria* is 'a shameless compendium of profligacy', his salacity is repulsive.[2] Nor should his frivolous operations with the Roman calendar be condoned.[3] As for the last poems, 'a devious and tawdry compromise between conformity and rebellion'.[4]

The time has come to put in a word for those poems. Let a footnote of Edward Gibbon be quoted.[5]

The nine books of Poetical Epistles. . . possess, besides the merit of elegance, a double value. They exhibit a picture of the human mind under very singular circumstances; and they contain many curious observations, which no Roman, except Ovid, could have an opportunity of making.

Gibbon was dealing with the 'manners of the Sarmatians', enchanted no doubt by the wealth of information about native tribes, by the geography of plains and rivers, by operations of warfare and by the exotic names (some, such as the Iazyges, here on record for the first time in Latin). The alert historian would also observe the pageantry of a Roman triumph, the ceremonial induction of a consul, the literary or aristocratic friends of a poet, the forms of elegant address obtaining in polished society.

In fact, Book IV of the *Epistulae Ex Ponto* acquires clear and various merit.[6] Late products may happen to be among the best. Such is the verdict on Cicero's eloquence pronounced in the *Dialogus*

---

[1] R. Marache in *Ovidiana* (ed. N. I. Herescu, 1958), 412 ff.; W. Marg in *Ovid* (ed. E. Zinn and M. v. Albrecht, Darmstadt, 1968), 502 ff. There is some exaggeration in both papers, or needless subtlety. Thus Marg adduces *Met.* XV. 871: 'nec Iovis ira nec ignis' (o.c. 511).

[2] S. G. Owen, o.c. 6; F. Jacoby, *Rh. Mus.* LX (1905), 98: 'jene Lüsternheit . . . die bei Ovid oft widerwärtig wirkt.' The erotism is condoned, as not 'tense and sultry', by H. Fränkel, *Ovid, a Poet between Two Worlds* (1945), 170. The non-frivolous Macaulay admired the *Ars*.

[3] U. v. Wilamowitz-Moellendorff, *Der Glaube der Hellenen* II (1932), 434: 'das geht bis zu frivolem Spiele'.

[4] B. Otis, *Ovid as an Epic Poet* (1966), 339.

[5] E. Gibbon, *Decline and Fall*, Ch. XVIII, n. 40.   [6] Above, p. 163.

by Marcus Aper, himself the advocate of progress and the modern style. The author had the *Philippics* in mind.[1] He was right.[2]

The poems from exile are commonly held monotonous and tedious. The title *Tristia* contributes, hence the use of the word 'mournful'.[3] Better might be a stronger word, such as 'baneful'. However that be, Ovid's technical skill betrays no signs of deterioration; and his performance is now in course of being vindicated. Able revaluations are to hand.[4] The poems exhibit force and clarity of language, ingenuity in variation and fantasy, a subtle sense of structure. Especial commendation should go to the *Epistulae Ex Ponto*. At one stage Ovid was composing with speed and confidence. On *Tristia* V, published in 12, follow quickly three books of the new series before the end of 13.[5]

·   ·   ·

VII. Ovid's efforts were all in vain. The formal apologia (*Tristia* II) addresses the Princeps in person. Yet here, so it may be suggested, he saw no chance of persuading the ruler. The audience he desired to reach and influence was the educated class—and notably old friends in high places.[6]

In one sense his writing was effective. Too much so perhaps. In oratory it was Ovid's habit to insist and persist. He did not know when to stop: 'nescit quod bene cessit relinquere.' Thus the elder Seneca; and Quintilian styles him in his verse 'nimium amator ingenii sui'.[7] From clever, Ovid easily becomes tactless. For example, Livia is invoked by name six times, apart from the references to the consort of a divinity and the mother of Tiberius; and he obtruded

---

[1] Tacitus, *Dial*. 22. 2: 'utique in iis orationibus quas senior iam et iuxta finem vitae composuit'.

[2] One could also invoke the style, energy, and humour in some of the last letters of Seneca (e.g. 114; 122).

[3] As by H. J. Rose, *A Handbook of Latin Literature* (1936), 333.

[4] E. J. Kenney, *Proc. Camb. Phil. Soc.* XI (1965), 37 ff.; G. Luck in his edition of the *Tristia*, vol. II (1968), 4 f.; R. J. Dickinson in the volume *Ovid* (ed. J. W. Binns, 1973), 154 ff., especially 186 f. (arguing against L. P. Wilkinson on the theme 'monotony'). Nor should one omit J.-M. Frécaut, *L'Esprit et l'humour chez Ovide* (1971). For an early and general rehabilitation of the poet, T. F. Higham, *CR* XLVIII (1934), 105 ff.

[5] Above, p. 42.

[6] Cf. now T. Wiedemann, *CQ* XXV (1975), 271.

[7] *Controv*. IX. 5. 17; Quintilian X. 1. 88.

Germanicus on the triumphal pageantry of Tiberius, with untimely zeal.

Yet Ovid was saved and preserved by his 'ingenium'. The head and the heart, nothing else matters, so he reminds the poetess Perilla, his former disciple,

> nil non mortale tenemus
> pectoris exceptis ingeniique bonis.   (*Tr.* III. 7. 43 f.)

Caesar can take all away, life, home, and happiness, but there is a limit to his authority,

> ingenio tamen ipse meo comitorque fruorque:
> Caesar in hoc potuit iuris habere nihil.   (7. 47 f.)

Ovid therefore kept going, tenacious, though aged fifty when sent away, never strong in body, and subject to maladies.[1] Like Edward Gibbon, banished for imprudence by an angry parent and turning to scholarship for mental sustenance, Ovid put exile to good employ, disdaining sloth or idle recreation—though hardly going so far as to experiment with native languages. Nor will he with safety be given credit for exacting researches into the nomenclature and habits of the Black Sea fish.[2]

Many years before, in protest against detractors, he asserted that he had not wasted his talents; and he now says,

> non sum, qui segnia ducam
> otia: mors nobis tempus habetur iners.   (*Ex P.* I. 5. 43 f.)

The maxim recalls the robust and Roman gospel of action, as asserted by Sallust in the prologue of the *Bellum Iugurthinum*, with insistence on 'ingenium' and the energetic pursuit of 'bonae artes'— and also by Seneca and by the elder Pliny.[3] This feature deserves strong emphasis.[4]

---

[1] As an exile he makes a better showing than did Cicero.

[2] The *Halieutica* come in for firm condemnation: J. Richmond, *Philol.* CXX (1976), 92 ff.; A. La Penna, *Gnomon* XLVIII (1976), 359 ff. (in review of the edition of F. Capponi).

[3] Seneca, *Epp.* 82. 3: 'otium sine litteris mors est et hominis vivi sepultura'; 96. 5: 'atqui vivere, Lucili, militare est'; Pliny, *NH*, praef. 18: 'profecto enim vita vigilia est.'

[4] Rather than fantasies about theosophy and Pythagoreanism (as Carcopino, above, p. 217), or the notion that 'without knowing his own mission, Ovid was one of those to help prepare the passage from Antiquity to Christianity' (H. Fränkel, o.c. 5).

Already, when proclaiming the primacy of personal achievement, Ovid discounted birth and ancestry,

> nam genus et proavos et quae non fecimus ipsi,
> vix ea nostra voco. (*Met.* XIII. 140 f.)

He now imparts advice to an unnamed friend. Shun the eminent—'longe nomina magna fuge' (*Tr.* III. 4. 4). Only the 'potentes' can help, but they can also harm (4. 61). Friendship should be confined to equals—'amicitias et tibi iunge pares' (4. 44).

Again, consoling Cotta Maximus on the death of a certain Celsus, faithful in friendship to both, Ovid indicates clearly that Celsus was not of high rank, yet inferior to none on the true criterion:

> si modo non census nec clarum nomen avorum
> sed probitas magnos ingeniumque facit. (*Ex P.* I. 9. 39 f.)

Ovid exploits in his fashion the memory of loyal integrity. Celsus had lent him welcome encouragement, along with the assurance that Cotta and his brother would exert their good offices (9. 25 ff.).[1]

Ovid did not take for himself the warning he transmitted to the unnamed friend in the year 10. He went on to solicit the eminent: Fabius Maximus and the sons of Messalla. As Ovid might have known, these noblemen, high in favour with Caesar, were anxiously subservient to power. They failed him, and after a time he gave up.[2]

Nor could he now make a direct approach to Tiberius, although the new ruler, keen for style and words, liked poetry (some types at least), set an aristocratic value on personal independence, and was hostile to the state-enforced betterment of morals. Despite some mutual friends, there is no sign that Tiberius had found Ovid congenial;[3] and in most matters he was constrained to profess himself bound by the actions and policy of his predecessor, even to the revocation of 'amicitia'.[4] And the poetical young prince, who seemed accessible, could not respond.

·   ·   ·

[1] For the identity of Celsus, above, p. 90.

[2] Above, p. 149.

[3] Velleius, however, is instructive: Ovid but not Horace on his select list (II. 36. 3).

[4] *Ann.* III. 24. 4: 'sibi tamen adversus eum integras parentis sui offensiones neque reditu Silani dissoluta quae Augustus voluisset.'

Enemies of Caesar were debarred from public honour, their images absent from funeral processions of the *nobilitas*, but their writings remained in the libraries,

Antoni scripta leguntur,
doctus et in promptu scrinia Brutus habet.   (*Ex P.* I. 1. 23 f.)

By contrast, the *Ars Amatoria* was banned, or withdrawn by the discreet custodians. The rest of Ovid's poems were also removed, so it appears (*Tr.* III. 1. 65 ff.).

Burned the *Ars* could not be, since the author had not been condemned by decree of the Roman Senate. That fate befell other books when the law of treason was extended to take in words and writings.[1]

The signal attack on a historian came in the next reign with the prosecution of Cremutius Cordus, who praised Cassius and Brutus. Tacitus did not miss the occasion. He produced, or rather invented, a splendid and vigorous oration, ostensibly delivered before the Senate.[2] And he subjoins acrid comment on the incineration of books: to punish literature is only to enhance its potency, foreign tyrants and their cruel emulators only bring eternal infamy on themselves, renown to authors.[3]

'Nam contra punitis ingeniis gliscit auctoritas.' In short and to conclude, the poet won his war with Caesar. Industry, tenacity, and style prevailed. As the historian proclaims in another context, 'meditatio et labor in posterum valescit.'[4]

---

[1] Above, p. 213.

[2] *Ann.* IV. 34 f. Certainly not to be found in the *Acta Senatus*. But perhaps in the papers of the deceased historian. His writings were kept and later published by his daughter (Seneca, *Ad Marciam* 1. 3).

[3] Ibid. 35. 5.

[4] Ibid. 61 (in the condemnatory notice on the style of Q. Haterius, the facile and fluent Augustan orator).

BIBLIOGRAPHY

The following list is intended to serve as an index and guide to articles in periodicals, collections or the like that are cited in the footnotes. It does not include books on Ovid, on Latin literature, or on Roman history. They are there registered as they occur, by title and date.

ADAMASTEANU, D. 'Sopra il "Geticum Libellum" '. *Ovidiana*, ed. N. I. Herescu (1958), 391

ALLEN, K. 'The Fasti of Ovid and the Augustan Propaganda'. *AJP* XLIII (1922), 250

ATKINSON, K. M. T. 'The governors of the province Asia in the reign of Augustus'. *Historia* VII (1958), 300

BALL, R. J. 'The structure of Tibullus 1.7'. *Latomus* XXXIV (1975), 729

BARBIERI, G. Review of A. Degrassi, *I Fasti consolari* (1952). *Riv. stor. it.* LXVI (1954), 416

—— 'Pompeo Macrino, Asinio Marcello, Bebio Macro e i Fasti Ostiensi del 115'. *MEFR* LXXXII (1970), 263

BARNES, T. D. 'The victories of Augustus'. *JRS* LXIV (1974), 21

BAYER, E. 'Die Ehen der jüngeren Claudia Marcella'. *Historia* XVII (1968), 118

BERCHEM, D. VAN. 'La conquête de la Rhétie'. *Mus. Helv.* XXV (1968), 1

BICKEL, E. 'Die Lygdamus-Elegien'. *Rh. Mus.* CIII (1960), 97

BOUCHER, J.-P. 'A propos de Cérinthus et de quelques autres pseudonymes dans la poésie augustéenne'. *Latomus* XXXV (1976), 504

BOWERSOCK, G. W. 'Eurycles of Sparta'. *JRS* LI (1961), 112

—— 'A report on Arabia Provincia'. *JRS* LXI (1971), 219

—— 'A date in the *Eighth Eclogue*'. *Harvard Studies* LXXV (1971), 73

BRADSHAW, A. T. VON S. 'Horace, Odes 4.1'. *CQ* N.S. XX (1970), 142

BRUNT, P. A. Review of H. D. Meyer, *Die Aussenpolitik des Augustus und die augusteische Dichtung* (1961). *JRS* LIII (1963), 170

—— 'C. Fabricius Tuscus and an Augustan dilectus'. *ZPE* XIII (1974), 161

BUCHHEIT, V. 'Tibull II.5 und die Aeneis'. *Philol.* CIX (1965), 104

CALDER, W. M. 'Irony in Horace *Carm.* 2.2: *nullus argento color est avaris*'. *CP* LVI (1961), 175

CAMERON, A. D. E. 'Literary allusions in the Historia Augusta', *Hermes* XCII (1964), 363

—— 'The first edition of Ovid's *Amores*'. *CQ* N.S. XVIII (1968), 320

CARCOPINO, J. 'Notes biographiques sur M. Valerius Messala Corvinus'. *Rev. Phil.* LXXII (1946), 96

DAHLMANN, H. 'Cornelius Severus'. *Mainzer Abh.* 1975, no. 6

DAVIS, G. 'The persona of Licymnia: a revaluation of Horace, *Carm.* 2.12'. *Philol.* CXIX (1975), 70

DEGRASSI, A. 'Osservazioni su alcuni consoli suffetti dell'età di Augusto e Tiberio'. *Epigraphica* VIII (1946), 34

DICKINSON, R. J. 'The *Tristia*: poetry in exile'. *Ovid*, ed. J. W. Binns (1973), 154

EADIE, J. W. 'The development of Roman mailed cavalry'. *JRS* LVII (1967), 161

ECK, W. 'Ergänzungen zu den Fasti Consulares des 1. und 2. Jh. n. Chr'. *Historia* XXIV (1975), 324

D'ELIA, S. 'Il problema cronologico degli Amores'. *Ovidiana*, ed. N. I. Herescu (1958), 210

FISCHER, F. 'P. Silius Nerva. Zur Vorgeschichte des Alpenfeldzugs 15 v. Chr.' *Germania* LIV (1976), 147

FISHWICK, D. 'Genius and Numen'. *Harvard Theol. Review* LXII (1969), 356

FISKE, G. C. 'The politics of the patrician Claudii'. *Harvard Studies* XIII (1902), 1

GALINSKY, K. 'The triumph theme in the Augustan elegy'. *Wiener Studien* LXXXII (1969), 75

GESCHE, H. 'Die Datierung der 8. imperatorischen Akklamation des Tiberius'. *Chiron* II (1972), 339

GOAR, R. J. 'Horace, Velleius Paterculus and Tiberius Caesar'. *Latomus* XXXV (1976), 43

GOOLD, G. P. 'Amatoria critica'. *Harvard Studies* LXIX (1965), 1

GRAY, E. W. 'The Imperium of M. Agrippa'. *ZPE* VI (1970), 227

—— Review of D. Timpe, *Der Triumph des Germanicus* (1968). *CR* XX (1970), 347

GRIFFIN, J. 'Augustan poetry and the life of luxury'. *JRS* LXVI (1976), 87

—— 'Propertius and Antony'. *JRS* LXVII (1977), 17

GRIFFIN, M. T. 'The Elder Seneca and Spain'. *JRS* LXII (1972), 1

GRIMAL, P. 'Les conséquences d'un '*cursus*': Tibulle, Properce et Messalla'. *Mélanges Carcopino* (1966), 433

—— 'Les *Odes romaines* d'Horace et les causes de la guerre civile'. *Rev. ét. lat.* LIII (1975), 135

GROAG, E. Studien zur Kaisergeschichte III. Der Sturz der Julia'. *Wiener Studien* XLI (1919), 74

HAMMER, J. *Prolegomena to an edition of the Panegyricus Messallae* (New York, 1925)

HAMMOND, M. 'The sincerity of Augustus'. *Harvard Studies* LXIX (1965), 139

HERESCU, N. I. 'Poeta Getes'. *Ovidiana*, ed. N. I. Herescu (1958), 404

HERRMANN, L. 'La faute secrète d'Ovide'. *Revue belge* XVII (1938), 695

—— 'Ovide, la *Bona Dea* et Livie'. *Ant. Cl.* XLIV (1975), 126

HIGHAM, T. F. 'Ovid: some aspects of his character and aims'. *CR* XLVIII (1934), 105

HOHL, E. 'Zu den Testamenten des Augustus'. *Klio* XXX (1937), 323

HOLLIS, A. S. 'The *Ars Amatoria* and *Remedia Amoris*'. *Ovid*, ed. J. W. Binns (1973), 84

JACOBY, F. 'Zur Entstehung der römischen Elegie'. *Rh. Mus.* LX (1905), 38

JOHNSTON, W. R. 'The emotions of patriotism: Propertius'. *Calif. Studies in Class. Ant.* VI (1973), 151

KENNEY, E. J. 'The poetry of Ovid's exile'. *Proc. Camb. Phil. Soc.* XI (1965), 37

—— Review of J. C. Thibault, *The Mystery of Ovid's Exile* (1964). *CR* XV (1965), 299

KOENEN, L. 'Die "Laudatio Funebris" des Augustus für Agrippa'. *ZPE* V (1970), 217

KOESTERMANN, E. 'Tacitus und die Transpadana'. *Athenaeum* XLIII (1965), 167

LAFFI, U. 'Le iscrizioni relative all'introduzione nel 9 A. C. del nuovo calendario della provincia d'Asia'. Repr. from *Studi classici ed orientali* XVI (1967), 5

232 BIBLIOGRAPHY

LAMBRINO, S. 'Tomes, cité gréco-gète, chez Ovide'. *Ovidiana*, ed. N. I. Herescu (1958), 379

LA PENNA, A. Review of F. Capponi's edition of the *Halieutica* (Leiden, 1972). *Gnomon* XLVIII (1976), 359

LASCU, N. 'Notizie di Ovidio sui Geto-Daci'. *Maia* X (1958), 307

LETTA, C. 'La dinastia dei Cozii e la romanizzazione delle Alpi Occidentali'. *Athenaeum* LIV (1976), 37

LEVICK, B. M. 'The fall of Julia the Younger'. *Latomus* XXXV (1976), 301

LOZOVAN, E. 'Ovide et le bilinguisme'. *Ovidiana*, ed. N. I. Herescu (1958), 396

LUCE, T. J. 'The dating of Livy's first decade'. *TAPA* XCVI (1965), 209

MARACHE, R. 'La révolte d'Ovide exilé contre Auguste'. *Ovidiana*, ed. N. I. Herescu (1958), 412

MARG, W. 'Zur Behandlung des Augustus in den "Tristien" Ovids'. *Ovid*, ed. E. Zinn and M. v. Albrecht (1968), 502

MARX, F. 'Das Todesjahr des Redners Messalla'. *Wiener Studien* XIX (1897), 150

MEYER, H. D. *Die Aussenpolitik des Augustus und die augusteische Dichtung* (Kölner hist. Abh. 5, 1961)

MOMIGLIANO, A. '*Panegyricus Messallae* and '*Panegyricus Vespasiani*'. Two references to Britain'. *JRS* XL (1950), 39

MORRIS, J. 'Leges Annales under the Principate'. *Listy Filologické* LXXXVII (1964), 316

—— 'Munatius Plancus Paulinus'. *Bonner Jahrbücher* CLXV (1965), 88

MÜNZER, F. 'Die Todesstrafe politischer Verbrecher in der späteren römischen Republik'. *Hermes* XLVII (1912), 161

NORDEN, E. 'Ein Panegyricus auf Augustus in Vergils Aeneis'. *Rh. Mus.* LIV (1899), 466 = *Kleine Schriften* (1966), 422

NORWOOD, F. 'The riddle of Ovid's *relegatio*'. *CP* LVIII (1963), 150

OLIVER, R. P. 'The first edition of the *Amores*'. *TAPA* LXXVI (1945), 191

OTIS, B. 'Horace and the Elegists'. *TAPA* LXXVI (1945), 177

PANCIERA, S. 'Ancora sui consoli dell'anno 13 D.C.'. *Bull. Com.* LXXIX (1963–4), 94

PETRIKOVITS, H. v. Review of C. M. Wells, *The German Policy of Augustus* (1972). *Göttingsche gel. Anz.* 1976, 163

PIPPIDI, D. M. 'Tomis, cité géto-grecque à l'époque d'Ovide'. *Athenaeum* LV (1977), 250

POHLENZ, M. 'Die Abfassungszeit von Ovids Metamorphosen'. *Hermes* XLVIII (1913), 1

QUINN, K. Review of D. O. Ross, *Backgrounds to Augustan Poetry: Gallus, Elegy and Rome* (1975). *Phoenix* XXX (1976), 293

REED, N. 'Three fragments of Livy concerning Britain'. *Latomus* XXXII (1973), 766

RICHARDSON, L. 'Hercules Musarum and the Porticus Philippi in Rome'. *AJA* LXXXI (1977), 355

RICHMOND, J. 'The authorship of the Halieutica ascribed to Ovid'. *Philol.* CXX (1976), 92

ROBERT, L. 'Rapport sommaire sur un second voyage en Carie'. *Rev. arch.* 1935, 152

RYBERG, I. S. 'The procession of the Ara Pacis'. *Mem. Am. Ac. Rome* XIX (1949), 79

SATTLER, P. 'Julia und Tiberius. Beiträge zur römischen Innenpolitik zwischen den jahren 12 v. und 2 n. Chr.'. *Augustus* (*Wege der Forschung* CXXVIII, 1969), 486

SCHILLING, R. 'Ovide, poète des Fastes'. *Mélanges Carcopino* (1966), 863

—— '*Dea Dia* dans la liturgie des frères Arvales'. *Hommages à Marcel Renard* II (1969), 675

SCHMITTHENNER, W. Review of H. D. Meyer, *Die Aussenpolitik des Augustus und die augusteische Dichtung* (1961). *Gnomon* XXXVII (1965), 152

SCOTT, K. 'Emperor worship in Ovid'. *TAPA* LXI (1930), 43

SEGAL, C. 'Myth and philosophy in the *Metamorphoses*: Ovid's Augustanism and the Augustan conclusion of Book XV'. *AJP* XC (1969), 257

STEWART, A. F. 'To entertain an emperor: Sperlonga, Laokoon, and Tiberius at the dinner-table'. *JRS* LXVII (1977), 76

SUMNER, G. V. 'The family connections of L. Aelius Seianus'. *Phoenix* XIX (1965), 134

—— 'Germanicus and Drusus Caesar'. *Latomus* XXVI (1967), 413

—— 'The truth about Velleius Paterculus: prolegomena'. *Harvard Studies* LXXIV (1970), 257

—— 'The Lex Annalis under Caesar'. *Phoenix* XXV (1971), 246

SYME, R. 'The *Argonautica* of Valerius Flaccus'. *CQ* XXIII (1929), 129

—— 'Some notes on the legions under Augustus'. *JRS* XXIII (1933), 14

—— 'The Spanish War of Augustus (26–5 B.C.)'. *AJP* LV (1934), 293

—— 'Galatia and Pamphylia under Augustus: the governorships of Piso, Quirinius and Silvanus'. *Klio* XXVII (1934), 122

—— 'The origin of Cornelius Gallus'. *CQ* XXXII (1938), 39 = *Roman Papers* (1978), 40

—— *JRS* XXXV (1945), 108. Review of A. Stein, *Die Legaten von Moesien* (1940)

—— 'Personal Names in Annals I–VI'. *JRS* XXXIX (1949), 6 = *Ten Studies in Tacitus* (1970), 58

—— 'Marcus Lepidus, *capax imperii*'. *JRS* XLV (1955), 22 = *Ten Studies in Tacitus* (1970), 30

—— *CP* L (1955), 127. Review of T. R. S. Broughton, *The Magistrates of the Roman Republic*

—— 'Some Pisones in Tacitus'. *JRS* XLVI (1956), 17 = *Ten Studies in Tacitus* (1970), 50

—— 'Obituaries in Tacitus'. *AJP* LXXIX (1958), 18 = *Ten Studies in Tacitus* (1970), 79

—— 'Imperator Caesar, a study in nomenclature'. *Historia* VII (1958), 172 = *RP*, 361

—— 'Livy and Augustus'. *Harvard Studies* LXIV (1959), 27 = *RP*, 415

—— 'Piso Frugi and Crassus Frugi'. *JRS* L (1960), 12 = *RP*, 503

—— 'Who was Vedius Pollio?' *JRS* LI (1961), 23 = *RP*, 518

—— 'Ten Tribunes'. *JRS* LIII (1963), 55 = *RP*, 565

—— 'Pliny and the Dacian Wars'. *Latomus* XXIII (1964), 750 = *Danubian Papers* (1971), 245

—— 'Governors of Pannonia Inferior'. *Historia* XIV (1965), 342 = *Danubian Papers*, 231

—— 'The consuls of A.D. 13'. *JRS* LVI (1966), 63

—— 'A governor of Tarraconensis'. *Epigraphischer Studien* VIII (1969), 125 = *RP*, 732

—— 'Domitius Corbulo'. *JRS* LX (1970), 27 = *RP*, 805

—— 'The conquest of north-west Spain'. *Legio VII Gemina* (León, 1970) = *RP*, 825

—— 'The Titulus Tiburtinus'. *Akten des VI. Internat. Cong. für gr. u. lat. Epigraphik* (1973), 585

—— 'The crisis of 2 B.C.'. *Bayerische S.-B.*, 1974, Heft. 7

—— 'History or biography: the case of Tiberius Caesar'. *Historia* XXIII (1974), 481

—— 'How Tacitus wrote Annals I–III'. *Historiographia Antiqua* (Louvain, 1977), 231

TIMPE, D. *Der Triumph des Germanicus* (1968).
—— 'Der römische Verzicht auf die Okkupation Germaniens'. *Chiron* I (1971), 267

DE LA VILLE DE MIRMONT, H. 'Les déclamateurs espagnols au temps d'Auguste'. *Bulletin Hispanique* XII (1910), 1
VULPE, R. 'Ovidio nella città dell'esilio'. *Studi Ovidiani* (1959), 39

WEINSTOCK, S. 'Pax and the 'Ara Pacis' '. *JRS* L (1960), 44
WEISS, P. 'Die "Säkularspiele" der Republik—eine annalistische Fiktion?'. *R. Mitt.* LXXX (1973), 205
WELLESLEY, K. Review of D. Timpe, *Der Triumph des Germanicus* (1968). *JRS* LIX (1969), 277
WHITE, P. 'The friends of Martial, Statius and Pliny, and the dispersal of patronage'. *Harvard Studies* LXXIX (1975), 265
WIEDEMANN, T. 'The political background to Ovid's *Tristia* 2'. *CQ* N.S. XXV (1975), 264
WILKINSON, L. P. Review of J. C. Thibault, *The Mystery of Ovid's Exile* (1964). *Gnomon* XXXVII (1965), 734
WILLIAMS, G. 'Poetry in the moral climate of Augustan Rome'. *JRS* LII (1962), 28
—— *Horace. Greece & Rome*, New Surveys in the Classics, No. 6 (1972)
WISSOWA, G. 'Neue Bruchstücke des römischen Festkalenders'. *Hermes* LVIII (1923), 369
WOODMAN, A. J. 'Questions of date, genre, and style in Velleius: some literary answers'. *CQ* N.S., XXV (1975), 272

ZETZEL, J. E. G. 'New light on Gaius Caesar's eastern campaign'. *Greek, Roman and Byzantine Studies* XI (1970), 259

INDEX OF PROPER NAMES

Emperors, members of their families, and Latin authors are registered by their normal or conventional names.

Date Due

DEC 0 2 1992		
OCT 3 1 1995		
MAR 1 9 2001		
OCT 1 6 2002		
OCT 2 0 2002		
MAR 2 2 2004		

BRODART, INC.   Cat. No. 23 233   Printed in U.S.A.